MURPHY'S CHEAP EDITION.

THE

Catholic Christian

INSTRUCTED

IN THE

Sacraments, Sacrifice, Ceremonies,

AND

OBSERVANCES OF THE CHURCH.

BY WAY OF QUESTION AND ANSWER.

BY THE MOST REV. DR. CHALLONER.

BALTIMORE:
PUBLISHED BY JOHN MURPHY & Co.
PUBLISHERS, BOOKSELLERS AND PRINTERS,
182 BALTIMORE STREET.
1878.

PREFACE.

THE design of the following sheets being to explain the doctrine and ceremonies of the Catholic Church, and to vindicate the same from the misrepresentations of our adversaries, the reader, whether Catholic or Protestant, may reasonably expect that I should not send them abroad into the world without taking some notice of a late performance of Dr. Conyers Middleton's, entitled, "A letter from Rome, showing an exact Conformity between Popery and Paganism; or the Religion of the present Romans derived from that of their heathen Ancestors." This being a work directly levelled against some part of the ceremonies of the Church, and having been received with great applause by many in England, so as to have passed through three editions in the space of a few years; it is to comply with so reasonable an expectation that I have determined to employ my preface in making some animadversions upon this letter of the Doctor; to which, though consisting of seventy pages in quarto, I hope, with the help of God, in one short sheet to give a full and satisfactory answer.

The chief particulars which the Doctor objects against in the religion of modern Rome, and upon which he grounds the parallel which he pretends to make between popery and paganism, are these: 1st, The use of incense and perfume in churches: 2dly, The use of holy water: 3dly, The burning of lamps and candles: 4thly, Offerings or votive gifts: 5thly, Images, which he jumbles together with the veneration of the saints: 6thly, Chapels on the way-side for the devotion of travellers, crosses and sometimes chapels upon hills; 7thly, Processions: 8thly, Miracles, with which, it seems, he is very much offended wherever he meets them, and therefore he dwells longer upon that subject than any other. All these things he pretends to discover in the religion

3

of the old pagans; and therefore imagines he has a right to conclude, that the modern Romans have derived their whole religion from them.

Before I proceed to examine these particulars, and to answer the Doctor's objections against them, I cannot but take notice of a piece of foul play in him, unworthy of that candour of which he makes profession, and which he acknowledges he met with in all those whom he had the honour to converse with at Rome, which is, that having undertaken in his title-page to show an exact conformity between the religion of the present Romans and that of their pagan ancestors; and in the body of his book having more than once given the preference to the latter, yet in drawing his parallel he has been so disingenuous as to dissemble, on the one side, all the grosser superstitions of the Pagans, and for the most part only to take notice of certain observances, which were in no otherwise criminal than in being applied to the worship of false gods. and on the other side he has quite passed over in silence the most substantial parts of the religion of the present Romans, and only cavilled at some ceremonies or matters of less importance. For, can the Doctor really think, that the belief of the Scripture, and of the creeds, is no part of the religion of Rome? Is not the one, true, and living God worshipped there in three persons, the Father, and the Son, and the Holy Ghost? Do not the people universally believe in Jesus Christ? Is not the eucharistic sacrifice offered in all their churches, in memory of his death and passion? Is not the word of God preached amongst them; the divine office, consisting of psalms, Scripture lessons, &c. daily sung; the sacraments frequented, &c.? And which of all these things has been derived to the modern Romans from their heathen ancestors? But it was not for the Doctor's purpose to take any notice of any of these things, not so much as even of the articles of the profession of faith, published by Pope Pius IV., which he very well knows to be the standard of what he calls popery, and yet has not so much as offered to show any conformity in any one of them (except ing the articles of saints and their images, which he grossly misrepresents) with the doctrine or practice of the pagans. To such shifts as these are persons unhappily driven, who are resolved to maintain a bad cause.

But let us see what these gross superstitions are, upon which the Doctor grounds his charges against the modern Romans, and would have his readers believe they are no better than Pagans. In the first place, he instances the use of incense in churches; and we may presume he is too well acquainted with the rules of rhetoric not to rank in the front some of those which he esteems the strongest arguments; so that he looks upon this as one of the most notorious instances of heathenish superstition. But has he any thing to urge against it from Scripture, the only rule of a Protestant's faith? Not one single word. On the contrary, if he had been as well read in the Scriptures, as he would seem to be in the heathen poets, he would have found the use of incense in the temple of God, and that by God's own ordinance,* in records of a far more ancient date than any he can produce for the use of it among the heathens, who in this, as in many other things, did but mimic the sacred ceremonies prescribed in the law of God. And certainly a person who has been but moderately versed in the sacred writings, will be surprised to find the use of incense ranked by the Doctor amongst heathenish rites, since it is so frequently mentioned with honour in God's holy word; as when the psalmist desires that his prayer may ascend as incense in the sight of God, Psalm cxli. 2; as the prophet Malachy (as his words are rendered in the Protestant Bible) foretells, chap. i. 11, that in the church of Christ, incense shall be offered in every place to God's holy name; as when St. John in the Revelation, chap. v. 8, and chap. viii. 4, &c., represents to us odours and incense burning before God in the heavenly Jerusalem. For, allowing these texts to be figurative, yet we are not to suppose that the sacred

* See Exod. xxx. 7, 8; xl. 27. Lev. xvi. 12, &c

1*

penmen would describe to us the service either of the militant or triumphant church, by figures borrowed from heathenish superstition. As for what the Doctor has alleged against the use of incense out of the Acts of the Martyrs, who chose rather to die than offer incense to false gods, and out of the law of Theodosius, which confiscates the places in which the pagans had offered incense to their deities, he could not but know, that all this was utterly foreign to his purpose: but if he had a mind to be informed of the antiquity of the ceremonial use of incense amongst the Christians, he might have found it in the most ancient liturgies, and even in the very canons attributed to the apostles, can. 3.

The next thing the Doctor objects against as heathenish, is the use of holy water, which he pretends to derive from the heathens, because he finds in his poets that the pagans of old, in entering into their temples, used to be sprinkled with water; and he thinks he has discovered in some scraps of old Greek verses, that there was salt mingled with this water; and, which is still a more wonderful discovery, in poring upon old medals, he imagines he has found out something not unlike a sprinkling-brush among the things used by the pagan priests. But what a pity it is that amongst all these great discoveries he has not met with any account of the heathens ever making use of water sanctified by the word of God and prayer, in the name, and by the virtue of Jesus Christ: for this is what we call holy water, and this the pagans never used. As for the rest, we find mention of holy water, that is, water sanctified for religious uses, in the most sacred records of the divine law, long before the heathens abused it to their superstition: See Numb. xix. And the Doctor might with full as good a grace have proved the sacrament of baptism to be a heathenish practice, from the pagans' use of water in their temples, as to have alleged it against holy water, which is with us a memorial of our baptism, as that in the old law was a figure of it. As for the yearly festival which the Doctor says is celebrated with great solemnity in the month of January, and is called the Benediction of Horses, I never yet met with it in the Roman Calendar; and though I have spent the greatest part of my life abroad, never saw nor heard of any such ceremony as that which he pretends is practised upon that day by the monks of St. Antony, near St. Mary Major, in Rome. But however this be, we may hope there is nothing heathenish in this ceremony, since the Doctor, who is so good a Christian, procured, though it was as he says, at the expense of eighteen pence, his own horses to be blessed by these good monks, p. 20.

The third thing which the Doctor quarrels with, as derived from the heathens, is the burning of lamps before the altars, and setting up wax candles to burn in the time of divine service. This, he says, was first introduced by the Egyptians; for which he quotes in the margin, Clement of Alexandria Stromat, l, 1. c. 16. But this author says no such thing, and the true original of setting up lights or burning lamps in temples, s to be found in the law of God, Exod. xxv. and xxxvii. And as the devil affected to have his temples, altars priests, sacrifices, and all other things which were used in the worship of the true God, so no wonder that he procured also to have lamps set up in his temples in imitation of those which by the law of God were appointed to burn before the sanctuary. The Doctor therefore is very much mistaken, when he too hastily concludes that every ceremony used by the heathens in the worship of their false gods is consequently heathenish, and as such ought to be banished from the worship of the true God, since the greatest part of these ceremonies were indeed borrowed by the heathens from the worship of the true God.

Next to the lamps or wax-lights burning before the altars, he falls upon the number of offerings or votive gifts hung up, in testimony of cures or deliverances, around the altars, or the shrines of the saints: all which he takes for downright heathenism, because he finds the footsteps of the like offerings hung up in the temples of the heathens. But here let him take notice once for all that practices in themselves innocent, are not rendered unlawful by having been abused by the heathens to their superstition; that all that was heathenish in this case was the referring and dedicating these things to the honour of their false deities; and that it cannot be disagreeable to the true and living God that such as believe they have received favours from him, by the prayers of his saints, should make a public acknowledgment of it.

The Doctor could not but be sensible, that the things which he has hitherto objected against had nothing heathenish in their nature, and that not one of them was ever condemned or prohibited by the law of God; and, therefore, since truth would furnish him with no arms in order to make out his charge of idolatry and heathenish superstition, in which he pretends that modern Rome equals or exceeds her pagan ancestors, he is forced to call in to his assistance misrepresentation and slander. For what is it else but the grossest misrepresentation and downright slander to charge the Church of Rome, as he does, p. 29, of *the finishing act and last scene of genuine idolatry, in crowds of bigot votaries prostrating themselves before some image of wood or stone, and paying divine honours to an idol of their own erecting?* The Doctor should have remembered here what he promised in his preface, viz. to produce, for what he should charge upon us, such vouchers as we ourselves would allow to be authentic. Instead of which we are, it seems, upon his bare word, without either proof or witness, to believe a charge which in itself is highly improbable, and which every one, that is acquainted with the doctrine and practice of the Catholic Church, knows to be absolutely false. The second Council of Nice, to which the Council of Trent refers in the decree concerning images, declares that divine honour (Latria) is not to be given them, Acts vii., and the Council of Trent, sess. 25, declares, that we are not to believe there is any divinity or virtue in them, for which they are to be worshipped; that we are not to pray to them, nor put our trust in them. And every child among us knows, that if we keep with respect the images or pictures of Christ and his saints,

it is not to make them our gods, as the heathens did
their idols, nor to give them the honour that belongs to
God; but, by the honour we show to the memorials, to
express our esteem, love, and veneration for the persons
represented by them, and to use them as helps to raise
our thoughts and affections to heavenly things.

But the easier to make out this charge of idolatry
against us, the Doctor has made an important discovery,
which he fathers upon St. Jerome, though indeed it is
an invention of his own; which is, that all images of the
dead are idols, and consequently are liable to all those
censures which in the Scripture, in the fathers, and in
the laws of Christian emperors, are pronounced against
idols.   An important discovery, indeed! by which it appears, that, after all the pretences of his own church to
a thorough reformation, she has not yet got rid of idols,
but has them everywhere standing, and new ones daily
erected, in spite of the law of God; and that not only in
every private house, inhabited by her children, (scarce
one of which is found without some image or picture of
the dead,) but also in her very churches, out of which
though she has generally removed the images of Christ,
(which it is hoped the Doctor will not look upon to be
idols, if he believes the resurrection of his Redeemer,)
yet she has brought in, in their stead, the images of
Moses and Aaron, who are certainly dead; and, what is
worse still, has introduced dead lions and unicorns into
the sanctuary, in place of the cross of Christ; though
this also of late has been erected upon the top of the
chief church of the kingdom, surrounded with many
other of the Doctor's idols, to the great offence of the
Puritans, who are the only people that will thank the
Doctor for the pains he has been at to furnish them with
arms against the Established Church.   Though it is to
be feared, if they take for good the Doctor's definition of
an idol, their zeal against idolatry may raise some scruple in them, with relation to the images of kings
deceased, which they carry in their pockets, or hoard
up their in bags, and which, it is thought, they worship
more than either their living king or any deity what
soever.

What then is the real difference between idola (Lat Simulacra) and those images or pictures which we have in our churches? It is this, that idols, according to the ecclesiastical use of the word, adopted by the holy fathers and all antiquity, are only such images as are set up for gods, and honoured as such; or in which some divinity or power is believed to reside by their worshippers, who accordingly offer prayers and sacrifice to them, and put their trust in them. Such were the idols of the Gentiles, and such were those images of the dead, of which St. Jerome speaks, (in chap. 37. Isaiæ;) viz. the gods of those nations which Senacherib and his predecessors the Asyrian kings had destroyed; which, having been no better than the images of men doubly dead, were by Senacherib and his servants foolishly and impiously compared to the true and living God. So that it is true enough that these idols were images of the dead, which is all that St. Jerome asserts;* but it is not true, that all images of the dead are idols, which is what Dr. Middleton would infer. I shall only add, with relation to St. Jerome, that he expressly affirms that the saints are not to be called dead, but living; and therefore their images are out of the question, *E contra Vigilant. Sancti non appellantur mortui sed viventes.*

"But our notion of the idolatry of modern Rome (says the Doctor, p. 31) will be much heightened still, and confirmed, as oft as we follow them into those temples, and to those very altars which were built originally and dedicated by their heathen ancestors, the old Romans, to the honour of their pagan deities; where we shall hardly see any other alteration than the shrine of some old hero filled now by the meaner statue of som modern saint." There is another trifling difference, which he does not think worth while to take notice of; which is, that all these temples are now dedicated to the service of the true and living God; that the word of God is there preached, the divine praises sung, and the great

* Quæ idola intelligimus imagines mortuorum. In cap. 37, Isaiæ

eucharistic sacrifice, the memorial of the passion of
Jesus Christ, daily celebrated; whereas before they
were dedicated to the worship of the devil.

But, besides this, the Doctor cannot be ignorant that
the modern Roman altars are not the same as those the
heathens made use of for their sacrifices; that the
image of Christ crucified is placed upon all our altars,
not to be worshipped as a god, like those idols which he
calls the shrines of his old heroes, but as a memorial of
Christ's passion; that the churches, though called by
the names of the saints whose relics are there reposited,
or memory celebrated, are not erected to the saints, much
less to their images, but the God of the saints; that
our devotion to the saints goes no farther than the desiring their prayers; and that their pictures or images
are no more with us than their memorials, which we respect for their sakes.

But the Doctor, it seems, is offended that the Pantheon
and other temples of the pagans have been changed into
churches of the blessed Virgin and the saints, and thinks
that the old possessors (the heathen deities) had a better
title to them than the Mother of Christ or his martyrs;
and declares, that he should be much more inclined to
pay his devotion to a Romulus or Antonine, than to (the
illustrious martyrs) Laurence or Damian, p. 33, 34. I
suppose, by the same rule, he must take it very ill to
find so many popish churches, nigher home, changed
into Protestant temples, without so much as taking the
pains to christen them anew: so that, without going to
Rome, we may find a Laurence, an Albian, and a great
number of other Romish saints in the very heart of London. For since he openly declares, that the pagan deities
had a juster title to religious veneration than any of these
saints, consequently a church of St. Laurence must
needs give more offence than a temple of Bacchus.

But some may possibly apprehend, from the way that
the Doctor speaks of the martyrs of Christ, that he is no
greater friend to Christianity in general than he is to
popery: for though some ancient heretics have objected
of old to the Catholic church, as he now does, that we

had but changed our idols in worshipping the saints instead of the pagan deities, (which was the objection of
Vigilantius and of Faustus the Manichæn, as we learn
from the writings of St. Jerome against Vigilantius,
and of St. Augustine against Faustus, l. 20, c. 21,) yet
no one, that pretended to the name of Christian, ever
ventured to prefer the pagan deities before the martyrs
of Christ. This was an extravagance that none but
Julian the Apostate was capable of, from whom the
Doctor has copied it. See St. Cyril of Alexandria, l. 6
contra Julianum.

As to what he tells us upon hearsay, that some of the
images of the saints were originally statues of the pagan
deities, and others designed by the sculptors or painters
for the representation of their own mistresses; till he
brings some better authority for it, than *it is said*, we
shall not think it worth while to take any notice of it.
For if, in things that he positively asserts, he makes no
scruple of advancing notorious untruths, as when he tells
us, p. 33, that many of the Romish saints were never
heard of but in our legends; and that many more have
no other merit but that of raising rebellions in defence of
their idols and throwing whole kingdoms into convulsions
for the sake of some gainful imposture: if, I say, in
such things as these, which he affirms to be certain, he
advances such falsehoods, who will venture to believe
what he tells only upon hearsay?

His pretending to derive the name of St. Orestes from
Mount Soracte is ridiculous beyond measure: and his
suspecting that some who are honoured as martyrs were
originally no other than the heathen deities, by reason
of some affinity which he decovers in their names, is a
groundless suspicion, as any one will be convinced, that
is not entirely a stranger to ancient church history;
in which we find, by innumerable instances, that as a
great part of the primitive saints and martyrs had been
converts from paganism, so a great many of their names
had no small affinity with those of the heathenish deities; and sometimes were the very same, as in the New
Testament itself we find a Dionysius, Acts xvii. 34,

which is the Greek name of Bacchus, and Hermes, Rom. xvi. 14, which is the Greek name of Mercury.

As to what he writes of Julia Evodia, no such saint was ever honoured in our church, much less any saint Viar, so that these petty stories, like the inscriptions which he alleges, which are the works of private persons without any authority, are not worth our notice, no more than Usher's conjecture concerning St. Amphibalus, or Mabillon's concerning St. Veronica: for allowing them both to be as well grounded as the Doctor can desire, it will only follow that there has been a mistake in the name of the ecclesiastic harboured by St. Alban, and that of the pious woman, on whose handkerchief our Saviour imprinted the image of his face. But after all, neither the one nor the other was ever canonized by the church, nor are their names found in the Roman martyrology.

I cannot comprehend why the Doctor, p. 44, should bring in the adoration of the hosts, which he calls the principal part of worship, and the distinguishing article of faith in the creed of modern Rome; of which he confesses he cannot find the least resemblance or similitude in any part of the pagan worship; unless it were to disprove that exact conformity, which in his title-page he had promised to prove betwixt popery and paganism or rather to make way for alleging against us the authority of Tully, which he prefers before that of the apostles and evangelists, of the absurdity of believing that to be God which we receive under the sacramental veils: an absurdity, which the Doctor could have had no room to have objected to us, had he not forgotten his own catechism, which informed him, that the body and blood of Christ are verily and indeed taken and received by the faithful in the Lord's Supper. For if the faithful in this system may not be said to feed upon their God, neither can they in the system of transubstantiation.

But now the Doctor is pleased to leave the churches, and make an excursion into the country, the whole face

2

of which, as he is pleased to tell us, p. 44, has the visible characters of paganism upon it; because of the little chapels which frequently occur upon the way, where tra-vellers often kneel down to say a prayer; and because of the many crosses everywhere erected. And who will dare presume after this to open his mouth in favour of popery, when he understands that the Doctor has de-monstrated, by what he has discovered in his travels, that all Papists are pagans; because their very travel-lers are so superstitious as sometimes to kneel down and say a prayer before a country chapel, where they find some memorial of Christ's passion; and because they have everywhere erected that antichristian standard, the cross of Christ? But what is still more heathenish in the Doctor's eyes, is that these little oratories or crosses are sometimes under trees, and sometimes upon the tops of hills, which he ingeniously interprets to be the high-places condemned in the Old Testament. But the truth is, and all Papists are convinced of it, that a place is neither better nor worse for divine worship, be-cause it is on a high place or low; near trees or at a distance from them: and what was condemned of old in the high-places mentioned in the Scripture, was not their being upon hills, for God is no less the God of the mountains than of the valleys; and his temple in Je-rusalem was built upon a hill, viz. on Mount Moria, 2 Paral. iii. 1; but they were condemned because the worship there exhibited was either heathenish or schis-matical, that it was either given to strange gods, or, if to the God of Israel, was given contrary to his appoint-ment, who had forbidden sacrifice to be offered in any other places but in his temple at Jerusalem; see Deut xii. 5, 11, 13, 14.

From the country the Doctor returns again to the owns, and there quarrels with the images and altars which he pretends to meet with everywhere, and which he takes to be visible marks of paganism: but were the old pagans to come to life again, and to understand whose images these are, viz. of Jesus Christ, of his bless-ed Mother, of his apostles and martyrs, by whose preaching, labours, and blood, paganish superstition was banished out of the world, and who, upon that account, are now honoured, they would be far from being of the Doctor's mind, and would look upon these images as evident proofs of these people being Christians, who show so much regard for Christ and his saints.

But in the towns the Doctor is also offended with processions, which, as he is pleased to say, are seen on every festival of the Virgin, or rather Romish saint, which he supposes to be the sacrifices, pomps, and dances, mentioned by Plutarch in Numa, p. 16, and concludes that these processions must needs be heathenish, the more because he finds in Apuleius, an account of something like a procession performed by the heathens in honour of their gods. But the Doctor might have found an account of a religous procession in an author much more ancient than Apuleius, amongst the worshippers of the true God, if he would have consulted 2 Kings vi. I fear the Doctor has no great opinion of this kind of monuments of antiquity: the less, because he finds therein frequent mention of miracles, which are things he never can digest, wherever he meets them.

But the pagans, it seems, pretended to miracles, and therefore the Romish religion which pretends to miracles must needs be paganish. It is a pity the Doctor did not here speak out in favour of his friends the freethinkers, and argue thus: the pagans pretended to build their religion upon miracles; therefore the Jewish religion of old, and the Christian now, both which appeal to miracles as their first and chief foundation, are no better grounded than paganism. But, even in the instances which the Doctor alleges, (and we may be sure he has picked out such as he thought most for his purpose,) it is easy to take notice that the miracles pretended to by the pagans had no probable grounds to support them, no number of witnesses to attest them, no contemporary writers to vouch from them, but, as in the case of the victory supposed to have been gained over the Latins by the assistance of Castor and Pollux, all was built upon a popular

opinion, or the testimony of one or two that pretended
to have seen those deities; which was greedily swal
lowed by the general and the senate as a token of the
divine favour, who thereupon erected a temple to them.
Whereas, in the case which the Doctor supposes to be
parallel to this, of the victories gained against the in
fidels in the holy wars by the assistance of the martyrs
these saints, as appears by what he has in the margin
were seen by both the Christian and infidel army ; and
the history of it was written, as we learn from the Doc
tor himself, by an eyewitness.

But whether the miracles which he has pitched upon
for the subject of his ridicule be true or false, there is
nothing at least heathenish in them, and consequently
nothing that can be of any service to him to make out
the exact conformity, which he pretends to demonstrate,
between popery and paganism. In the mean time, the
Doctor is not ignorant, that it is not upon such things as
most of those are which he alleges, that we lay any
stress ; neither have we any need to appeal to them ; for
God has been pleased in every age to work far more
evident miracles in his church, by the ministry of his
saints : in raising the dead to life, in curing the blind
and the lame, in casting out devils, in healing in a mo
ment inveterate diseases, and the like stupendous works
of his power, attested by the most authentic monuments,
and very frequently (as may be seen in the acts the
canonizations of the saints) by the depositions of in
numerable eyewitnesses, examined upon oath ; and by
the public notoriety of the facts ; which kind of mi
racles, so authentically attested, will be to all ages a
standing evidence, that the church, in whose communion they have all been wrought, is not that idolatrous
pagan church which the Doctor pretends, but the true
Spouse of Christ, which alone has inherited in all ages
that promise which the Lord made at his departure, St.
John xiv. 12, 13. ' Amen, amen, I say unto you he that
believeth in me, the works that I do, he also shall do,
and greater than these shall he do. Because I go to
the Father. And whatsoever ye shall ask the Father in
my name, that will I do '

And here I might take my leave f the 'Joctor, for
what he adds, p. 65, &c., to derive the church sanctua-
ries from the asylum opened by, Romulus to receive
fugitives, the authority of the pope from the pagan pon-
tiff, and the religious orders from the colleges of the
Augurs, Falii, &c., is so very weak, that it would be trifling away my time to take any notice of it. But, before
we part, I must put the Doctor and his friends in mind
that some people will naturally infer, from what he imagines he has so fully proved, viz. that popery and paganism stand upon the same bottom, and that one is
no better than the other; they will infer, I say, that
the orders which his church pretends to have by succession from the Church of Rome are no more valid than
if they proceeded from an Indian Brachman or a Ma-
hometan dervise. (Chandler's Sermon, p. 36.) And by
the selfsame way of arguing, by which he pretends to
demonstrate an exact conformity between the religion
of the present Romans and that of their heathen ancestors, these same gentlemen will, with a much fairer show
of probability, prove an exact conformity between the
religion by law established, and popery. The consequence of which will be, if the Doctor be not mistaken
in his parallel. that English protestancy is no better than
heathenish idolatry.

But that I may not seem to say this without reason,
let us suppose that Chandler, or some other of the same
stamp, should take into his head to charge the church
by law established, with popery: and to this purpose,
should heap together all that he could of ceremonies,
observances, &c., which Protestants have retained from
the old religion, and in one of his learned declamations deliver himself as follows to his dissenting audi-
tory :

"Beware, my dearly beloved, of these people who call
themselves the Church of England; for their religion is
wholly derived from that of their Romish ancestors, and
has an exact conformity or uniformity rather with popery, and consequently with paganism, from which, as
Dr. Middleton has lately demonstrated, the Papists have

borrowed the r whole religion. Now mark ye, my beloved, how plainly I shall prove that these people who call themselves Protestants have taken their whole reli gion from the Papists.

"1st, Their churches are the very same which were originally built by their popish ancestors, and are still dedicated to the same popish saints, as formerly they were, though one of their own divines plainly tells them they had better have dedicated them to Bacchus or Venus. Now, of all the honours that the Papists have ever given to their saints, this of dedicating temples to them was certainly the greatest, far greater then t..at of kissing their relics or desiring their prayers; and, consequently, if the Church of Rome were ever guilty of idolatry in relation to the saints, her daughter, the Church of England, stands guilty of the same, which has ten churches dedicated to Mary for one dedicated to Christ.

"2dly, In their churches they have altars too, like the Papists; and what should altars do there, if they did not offer sacrifice like the Papists? To these altars they cringe and bow; which is giving religious honour, which God has appropriated to himself, to insensible creatures, and therefore is no better than downright idolatry. In many places they have over these altars images and pictures, like the Papists, in spite of the second commandment. And though they are pleased to tell us that they worship them not, yet what can we think when we see them perpetually bowing down to that which is indeed no more than an image, viz. the name of Jesus, which of all images of Christ has the least of solid substance in it, as being only formed in the air by the empty sound of the two syllables of his name. But what respect they have for images we may judge by that which they show to the cross, which they have lately erected in the highest place of the capital city of the kingdom; and so much are they bewitched with. the notion of this standard of popery, that they look upon none rightly baptized without being signed with the sign of the cross.

" 3dly, Their liturgy or common prayer-book is wholly popish, and at the best but a bungling imitation of the Romish Mass: from this they have borrowed their collects, lessons, &c., and a great part of what they call their communion service. Their orders of bishops, priests, and deacons, both as to the name and thing, were taken from Rome; and from thence they all pretend to derive their succession. Their way of ordaining ministers resembles that of the Papists; and is equally blasphemous, in their bishops pretending to give the Holy Ghost, with the power of forgiving and retaining sins. Their surplices are but the rags of the whore of Babylon. Their organs and music in their churches, their singing boys, their anthems and Te Deums are all popish invention.

" 4thly, Their church government by archbishops, and bishops, their spiritual courts, their dignities of deans, archdeacons, prebendaries, &c., are all visibly derived from the Papists; and like the Papists, their bishops pretend to give confirmation; in which they are the less excusable, because in their very articles of religion, art. 25, they declare that confirmation comes of a corrupt following of the apostles. The same thing they declare with regard to the popish sacrament of penance or priestly absolution, and yet have retained it in their order for the visitation of the sick; where they prescribe auricular confession and a form of absolution the same in substance as that used in the Church of Rome.

" 5thly, Like the Papists they pay an idolatrous worship to the elements of bread and wine, to which they kneel at the time of communion: and their declaring (contrary to the express words of their catechism) that they do not believe the body and blood of Christ to be there, does but aggravate their guilt beyond that of the Papists, because these believe that in the sacrament they worship Christ, whereas our pretended Protestants believe they have nothing there but bread and wine.

" 6thly, They observe days like the Papists in honour

of the saints and angels; which, if it be not religious worship, I know not what it is. They pray to be defended by the angels in their collect for Michaelmas-day, which is rank popery. Their calendar is full of popish saints. They prescribe fasts and abstinence like the Papists; and from them have taken into their books the fasts of Lent, Vigils, Ember-days, and Fridays: though, to give them their due, this part of popery, for a long time, has been found nowhere but in their books.

"In fine, their godfathers and godmothers in baptism, their churching of women after child-bearing, their whole order of matrimony, their consecration of churches, their anointing of kings, and such like observances, are no better than popery; and, in a word, the whole face of their religion, both in town and country, is an exact resemblance of that of their popish forefathers. And, consequently, since popery and paganism stand upon a level, I cannot but conclude, that English protestancy is nearly allied to paganism. For whilst we see these pretended Protestants worshipping at this day in the same temples, at the same altars, sometimes before the same images, and always with the same liturgy, and many of the same ceremonies, as the Papists did, they must have more charity, as well as skill in distinguishing, than I pretend to, who can absolve them from the same crime of superstition and idolatry with their popish ancestors." Dr. Middleton, p. 70, 71.

So far the nonconformist, agreeably to the copy which the Doctor has set him in his parallel between popery and paganism. Now, this kind of rhetoric, I am persuaded, whatever effect it might have with regard to Dissenters, would excite no other emotions in the minds of Church-Protestants than those of indignation or contempt; and the same would be their dispositions with regard to Dr. Middleton's performance, if they would make use of the same weights and measures in our own case as in their own.

I shall add no more, but that I cannot but apprehend that the Doctor, in pretending to impeach us of paganism, has impugned the known truth; a truth so evident,

tha⸱ notwithstanding the violent humour of Luther, and
all his bitter declamations against us, yet he could not
help acknowledging, in his book against the Anabaptists, "That under the papacy are many good Christian
things, yea, all that is good in Christianity; and that
Protestants had it from thence. I say, moreover," says
he, "that under the papacy is true Christianity, even
the very kernel of Christianity." So far the father and
apostle of the Reformation, who, whilst he is forced to
grant that we have the very kernel of Christianity, I
fear has kept nothing for himself but the shell. If the
Doctor, in quality of one of his children, has inherited any part of his treasure, I do not envy him the
inheritance, but shall leave him in the quiet possession
of it.

CATHOLIC CHRISTIAN

INSTRUCTED

IN THE

SACRIFICE, SACRAMENTS, CEREMONIES,

AND

OBSERVANCES OF THE CHURCH.

CHAPTER I.

ON THE SIGN OF THE CROSS.

Q. WHY do you treat of the sign of the cross before you begin to speak of the sacraments?

A. Because this holy sign is made use of in all the sacraments, to give us to understand that they all have their whole force and efficacy from the cross, that is, from the death and passion of Jesus Christ. What is the sign of Christ, says St. Augustine,* which all know, but the cross of Christ, which sign, if it be not applied to the foreheads of the believers, to the water with which they are baptized, to the chrism with which they are anointed, to the sacrifice with which they are fed, none of these things is duly performed.

Q. But did the primitive Christians make use of the sign of the cross only in the administration of the sacraments?

A. Not only then, but also upon all other occasions; at every step, says the ancient and learned Tertullian,† at every coming in and going out, when we put on our clothes or shoes, when we wash, when we sit down to table, when we light a candle, when we go to bed; whatsoever conversation employs us, we imprint on our foreheads the sign of the cross.

* Tract 119 in Joan.   † L. de Corona Milit. c. 3.

Q. What is the meaning of this frequent use of the sign of the cross?

A. It is to show that we are not ashamed of the cross of Christ ; it is to make an open profession of our believing in a crucified God ; it is to help us to bear always in mind his death and pasion; and to nourish thereby in our souls the three divine virtues of faith, hope, and charity.

Q. How are these three divine virtues exercised in the frequent use of the cross?

A. 1st, Faith is exercised, because the sign of the cross brings to our remembrance the chief article of the Christian belief, viz., The son of God dying for us upon the cross. 2dly, our hope is thereby daily nourished and increased; because this holy sign continually reminds us of the passion of Christ, on which is grounded all our hope for mercy, grace, and salvation. 3dly, Charity, or the love of God, is excited in us by that sacred sign, by representing to us the love which God has showed us in dying upon the cross for us.

Q. In what manner do you make the sign of the cross?

A. In blessing ourselves, we form the sign of the cross, by putting our right hand to the forehead, and so drawing, as it were, a line down to the breast or stomach, and then another line crossing the former, from the left shoulder to the right ; and the words that we pronounce at the same time are these : 'In the name of the Father, and of the Son, and of the Holy Ghost;' by which we make a solemn profession of our faith in the blessed Trinity. But, in blessing other persons or things, we form the cross in the air, with the right hand extended towards the thing we bless.

Q. Have you any thing more to add in favour of the cross, and the use of signing ourselves with the sign of the cross ?

A. Yes, the cross is the standard of Christ, and is called by our Lord himself, St. Matt. xxiv. 30, the sign of the Son of Man. It is the badge of all good Christians, represented by the letter Tau,* ordered to be set as a mark upon the forehead of those that were to escape

* St. Hierom. upon Ezek. ix.

the wrath of God. Ezekiel ix. 4. It was given by our Lord to Constantine, the first Christian emperor, as a token and assurance of victory, when he and his whole army, in their march against the tyrant Maxentius, saw a cross formed of pure light above the sun, with this inscription: 'By this conquer;' which account the historian Eusebius, in his first book of the life of Constantine, declares he had from that emperor's own mouth. To which we may add that the sign of the cross was used of old by the holy fathers as an invincible buckler against the devil, and a powerful means to dissipate his illusions; and that God has often made it an instrument in their hands of great and illustrious miracles, of which there are innumerable instances in ancient church history, and in the writings of the fathers, which it would be too tedious here to recount.

CHAPTER II.

OF THE SACRAMENT OF BAPTISM.

Q. What do you mean by a sacrament?

A. An outward sign or ceremony of Christ's institution, by which grace is given to the soul of the worthy receiver.

Q. What are the necessary conditions for a thing to be a sacrament?

A. These three. 1st, It must be a sacred sign, and, consequently, as to the outward performance, it must be visible or sensible. 2dly, This sacred sign must have annexed unto it a power of communicating grace to the soul. 3dly, This must be by virtue of the ordinance or institution of Christ.

Q. How then do you prove that baptism is a sacrament, since the Scripture nowhere calls it so?

A. Because it has these three conditions. 1st, It is an outward visible sign, consisting in the washing with water, with the form of words prescribed by Christ. 2dly, It has a power of communicating grace to our souls in the way of a new birth; whence it is called by

the apostle, Tit. iii. 5, 'the laver of regeneration and renovation of the Holy Ghost.' 3dly, We have the ordinance and institution of Christ, St. Matt. xxviii. 19: 'Go teach all nations, baptizing them in the name of the Father, and of the Son, and of the Holy Ghost.' And St. John iii. 5: 'Except a man be born again of water and the Holy Ghost, he cannot enter into the kingdom of God.'

Q. In what manner must baptism be administered so as to be valid!

A. It must be administered in true natural water, with this or the like form of words: 'I baptize thee in the name of the Father, and of the Son, and of the Holy Ghost;' which words ought to be pronounced at the same time the water is applied to the person that is baptized, and by the same minister, who ought to have the intention of doing what the church does.

Q. What if these words, 'I baptize thee,' or any one of the names of the Three Persons, should be left out?

A. In that case it would be no baptism.

Q. What if the baptism should be administered in rose-water, or any of the like artificial waters?

A. It would be no baptism.

Q. Ought baptism to be administered by dipping or by pouring of the water; or by sprinkling of the water?

A. It may be administered validly any of these ways; but the custom of the church is to administer this sacrament either by dipping in the water, which is used in the East, or by pouring of the water upon the person baptized, which is more customary in these parts of Christendom. Moreover, it is the custom in all parts of the Catholic church, and has been so from the apostles' days, to dip or pour three times, at the names of the three divine Persons; though we do not look upon this so essential, that the doing otherwise would render the baptism invalid.

Q. What think you of those who administer baptism so slightly, that it is doubtful whether it may in any sense be called an ablution or washing; as for instance those that administer it only with the filip of a wet finger?

A. Such as these expose themselves to the danger of administering no baptism.

Q. What do you think of baptism administered by heretics, or schismatics ?

A. The church receives their baptism, if they observe the Catholic matter and form ; that is, if they baptize with true natural water, and have the intention of doing what the church does ; pronouncing at the same time these words : 'I baptize thee in the name of the Father, and of the Son, and of the Holy Ghost.'

Q. What think you of baptism administered with the due forms of words, but without the sign of the cross ?

A. The omission of this ceremony does not render the baptism invalid.

Q. What is your judgment of the baptism said to be administered by some modern Arians, 'In the name of the Father, through the Son, in the Holy Ghost ?'

A. Such a corruption of the form makes the baptism null and invalid.

Q. What is the doctrine of the church as to baptism administered by a layman or woman ?

A. If it be attempted without necessity, it is a criminal presumption; though even then the baptism is valid, and is not to be reiterated ; but, in a case of necessity, when a priest cannot be had, and a child is in immediate danger of death, baptism may not only validly, but also lawfully be administered by any person whatsoever. In which case a cleric, though only in lesser orders, is to be admitted preferably to a layman, and a man preferably to a woman, and a Catholic preferably to a heretic.

Q. How do you prove that infants may be baptized who are not capable of being taught or instructed in the faith ?

A. I prove it, 1st, By a tradition which the church has received from the apostles,* and practised in all ages ever since. Now, as none were more likely or

* St. Irenæus, i. 2, c.39. Origen, l. 5, in c. 6, ad Rom. St. Cyprian Ep. ad Fidum. St. Chrysostom, Hom. ad Neophves St. Augustine, l. 10 de Gen. c. 23, &c.

better qualified than the apostles, to understand the true meaning of the commission given them by their Master to baptize all nations, so none were more diligent than they to execute faithfully this commission according to his meaning, and to teach their disciples to do the same. St. Matt. xxviii. 20. So that what the church has received by tradition from the apostles and their disciples was undoubtedly agreeable to the commission of Christ.

Secondly, I prove it by comparing together two texts of Scripture, one of which declares that without baptism no one can enter into the kingdom of Heaven; St. John iii. 5: ' Except a man be born again of water and the Holy Ghost, he cannot enter into the kingdom of God.' The other text declares that infants are capable of this kingdom; St. Luke xviii. 16: ' Suffer little children to come to me, and forbid them not; for of such is the kingdom of God :' and consequently they must be capable of baptism.

Thirdly, Circumcision in the old law corresponded with baptism in the new law, and was a figure of it: Coloss. ii. 11, 12. But circumcision was administered to infants, Gen. xvii. Therefore baptism in like manner is to be administered to infants.

Fourthly, We read in scripture of whole families baptized by St. Paul, Acts xvi. 15 and 33. 1 Cor. i. 16. Now, it is probable that in so many whole families there were some infants.

Fifthly, As infants are not capable of helping themselves by faith and repentance, were they not capable of being helped by the sacrament of baptism, they could have no share in Christ, and no means to be delivered from original sin; and, consequently, almost one-half of mankind, dying before the use of reason, must inevitably perish, if infants were not to be baptized.

Sixthly, If infants' baptism were invalid, the gates of hell would have long since prevailed against the church, yea, for many ages there would have been no such thing as Christians upon earth; since for many ages before the Anabaptists arose, all persons had been baptized in their infancy; which baptism, if it were null, they were no Christians, and consequently there was no chuich. Where then was that promise of Christ, St. Matt. xvi. 19 : ' Upon this rock I will build my church, and the gates of hell shall not prevail against it?'   And St. Matt. xxviii. 20: ' Lo, I am with you always, even to the end of the world ?'

Besides, if infants' baptism be null, the first preachers of the Anabaptists had never received baptism, or had received it from those who never had been baptized.   A likely set of men for bringing back God's truth banished from the world, who had not so much as received the first badge or character of the Christian ; and who, so far from having any orders or mission, had not so much as been baptized.

Q. How do .you prove against the Quakers that all persons ought to be baptized.

A. From the commission of Christ, St. Matt. xxviii. 19 : ' Go teach all nations, baptizing them in the name of the Father, and of the Son, and of the Holy Ghost.' From that general sentence of our Lord, St. John iii. 5 : ' Except a man be born again of water and the Holy Ghost, he cannot enter into the kingdom of God.'   From the practice of the apostles, and of the first Christians, who were all baptized. Thus we read, Acts ii. 38, with relation to the first converts to Christianity at Jerusalem, when they asked of the apostle what they should do, that Peter said unto them, ' Do penance and be baptized, every one of you, in the name of Jesus Christ.'   And ver. 41 : ' They therefore that received his word were baptized,' &c.   Thus we read of the Samaritans converted by Philip, Acts viii. 12, 13, that ' They were baptized, *both* men and women.   Then Simon himself also be lieved, and being baptized,' stuck close to Philip; as was also the eunuch of Queen Candace, ver. 36, 38. Thus we find Paul baptized by Ananias, Acts ix. 18. Cornelius and his friends by order of St. Peter, Acts x. 47, 48.   Lydia and her household, by St. Paul, Acts xvi. 15, &c.   In fine, from the perpetual belief and practice of the whole church, ever since the apostles' days, which in all ages and all nations has ever admit nistered baptism in water to all her children, and never looked upon any as Christians until they were baptized. Now, ' if a person will not hear the church, let him be to thee as a heathen and a publican.' St. Matt. xviii. 17.

Q. How do you prove from Scripture that the apostles gave baptism in water ?

A. From Acts viii. 36, 38. ' See, here is water,' said the eunuch to St. Philip, ' what doth hinder me from being baptized ?—and they went down into the water, both Philip and the eunuch, and he baptized him.' And Acts x. 47, 48 : ' Can any man forbid water,' said St. Peter, ' that these should not be baptized, who have received the Holy Ghost as well as we ? and he commanded them to be baptized in the name of the Lord Jesus Christ.' Where we see that even they who received the Holy Ghost, and consequently had been baptized by the Spirit, were nevertheless commanded to be baptized in water. Hence St. Paul, Ephes. v. 25, 26, tells us that ' Christ loved the church, and delivered himself for it, that he might sanctify it, cleansing it by the laver of water, in the word of life.' And Heb. x. 22: ' Let us draw near with a true heart, in fulness of faith, having our hearts sprinkled from an evil conscience, and our bodies washed with clean water.'

Q. What are the effects of the sacrament of baptism ?

A. 1st, It washes away original sin, in which we are all born, by reason of the sin of our first father, Adam. 2dly, It remits all actual sin, which we ourselves have committed, (in case we have committed any before baptism,) both as to the guilt and pain. 3dly, It infuses the habit of divine grace into our souls, and makes us the adopted children of God. 4thly, It gives us a right and title to the kingdom of heaven. 5thly, It imprints a character or spiritual mark in the soul. 6thly, In fine, it lets us into the church of God, and makes us children and members of the church.

Q. How do you prove that all sins are remitted in baptism ?

A. From Acts ii. 38. Do penance and be baptized, every

one of you, in the name of Jesus Christ, for the remission of sins:' Acts xxii. 16. 'Arise and be baptized,' says Ananias to Paul, and wash away thy sins, (in the Greek, be washed from thy sins,) calling upon the name of the Lord.' Ezekiel xxxvi. 25. 'I will pour clean water upon you, and you shall be cleansed from all your filthiness.' Hence, in the Nicene creed, we confess one baptism unto the remission of sins.

Q. May not a person obtain the remission of his sins, and eternal salvation, without being actually baptized?

A. In two cases he may. The first is, when a person not yet baptized, but heartily desiring baptism, is put to death for the faith of Christ, before he can have that sacrament administered to him; for such a one is baptized in his own blood. The second case is, when a person that can by no means procure the actual administration of baptism, has an earnest desire of it, joined with a perfect love of God, and repentance of his sins, and dies in the disposition: for this is called the baptism of the Holy Ghost: Baptismus Flaminis.

Q. From whence has baptism the power of conferring grace, and washing away our sins?

A. From the institution of Christ, and in virtue of his blood, passion, and death. From whence also all the other sacraments have their efficacy. For there is no obtaining mercy, grace, or salvation, but through the passion of Jesus Christ.

Q. In what manner must a person, that is come to years of discretion, prepare himself for the sacrament of baptism?

A. By faith and repentance: and therefore it is necessary that he be first well instructed in the Christian doctrine, and that he firmly believe all the articles of the Catholic faith. 2dly, That he be heartily sorry for all his sins, firmly resolving to lead a good Christian life, to renounce all sinful habits, and to make full satisfaction to all whom he has any ways injured.

Q. But what if a person should be baptized without being in these dispositions?

A. In that case he would receive the sacrament and character of baptism, but not the grace of the sacrament nor the remission of his sins, which he cannot obtain until by a sincere repentance he detests and renounces all his sins.

Q. Is it necessary for a person to go to confession before he receives the sacrament of baptism !

A. No, it is not: because the sins committed before baptism are washed away by baptism, and not by the sacrament of penance; and therefore there is no need of confessing them.

Q. What think you of those that put off for a long time their children's baptism ?

A. I think they are guilty of a sin, in exposing them to the danger of dying without baptism : since, as daily experience ought to convince them, young children are so quickly and so easily snatched away by death.

CHAPTER III.

OF THE CEREMONIES OF BAPTISM ; AND OF THE MANNER OF ADMINISTERING THE SACRAMENT IN THE CATHOLIC CHURCH.

Q. Why does the church make use of so many ceremonies in baptism?

A. 1st, To render thereby this mystery more venerable to the people. 2dly, To make them understand the effects of this sacrament, and what the obligations are which they contract in the sacrament.

Q. Are the ceremonies of baptism very ancient?

A. They are all of them very ancient, as may be demonstrated from the writings of the Holy Fathers; and as we know no beginning of them, we have reason to conclude that they come from apostolic tradition.

Q. In what places does the church administer the sacrament of baptism?

A. Regularly speaking, and excepting the case of necessity, she does not allow baptism to be administered anywhere else but in the churches which have fonts, the water of which by apostolical traditions is solemnly blessed every year on the vigils of Easter and Whit-Sunday.

Q. What is the meaning of having godfathers and godmothers in baptism?

A. 1st, That they may present to the church the person that is to be baptized, and may be witnesses of his baptism. 2dly, That they may answer in his name, and be sureties for his performance of the promises which they make for him.

Q. What is the duty of godfathers and godmothers?

A. To see, as much as lies in them, that their godchildren be brought up in the true faith, and in the fear of God; that they be timely instructed in the whole Christian doctrine, and that they make good those engagements which they have made in their name.

Q. May all sorts of persons be admitted for godfathers and godmothers?

A. No: but only such as are duly qualified for discharging the obligations of a godfather or godmother. Upon which account none are to be admitted that are not members of the Catholic church; none whose lives are publicly scandalous; none who are ignorant of the Christian doctrine, &c. Rit. Rom.

Q. How many godfathers and godmothers may a person have in the Catholic church?

A. The Council of Trent, sess. 24, chap. 2, orders, That no one should have any more than one godfather and one godmother: That the spiritual kindred, which the child and its parents contract with the godfathers and godmothers, and which is an impediment of marriage, may not be extended to too many persons.

Q. In what order or manner does the Catholic church proceed in the administration of baptism?

A. 1st, The priest having asked the name of the person that is to be baptized, (which ought not to be any profane or heathenish name, but the name of some saint,

by whose example he may be excited to a holy life, and
by whose prayers he may be protected) inquires of him :
'*N*, what dost thou demand of the church of God ?
To which the person himself, if at age, or the godfather
and godmother for him, answer, Faith : by which is meant
not the bare virtue, by which we believe what God
teaches, but the whole body of Christianity, as compre-
hending both belief and practice; into which the faithful enter by the gate of baptism. The priest goes on
and asks; 'What does faith give thee ?' Answ. Life
everlasting.

Priest. 'If then thou wilt enter into life, keep the commandments, thou shalt love the Lord thy God with thy
whole heart, and with thy whole soul, and with thy
whole mind ; and thy neighbour as thyself.'

After this, the priest blows three times upon the face
of the person that is to be baptized, saying, ' Depart out
of him or her, O unclean spirit, and give place to the
Holy Ghost, the Comforter.' This ceremony was practised by the universal church long before St. Augustine's
days, who calls it* a most ancient tradition ; and it is
used in contempt of Satan, and to drive him away by the
Holy Ghost, who is called the Spirit or breath of God.

Then the priest makes the sign of the cross on the
forehead and on the breast of the person that is to be
baptized, saying, ' Receive the sign of the cross upon
thy forehead, and in thy heart; receive the faith of the
heavenly commandments, and let thy manners be such
that thou mayest now be the temple of God.' This sign
of the cross upon the forehead, is to give us to understand, that we are to make open profession of the faith
of a crucified God, and never to be ashamed of his cross ;
and the sign of the cross upon the breast is to teach
us that we are always to have Christ crucified in our
hearts.

After this, there follow some prayers, for the person
that is to be baptized, to beg of God to dispose his sou.
for the grace of baptism. Then the priest blesses
some sal , and puts a grain of it in the mouth of the

* L. de Nuptis, c. 18 and 29.

person that is to be baptized. By which ancient ceremony we are admonished to procure and maintain in our souls true wisdom and prudence; of which salt is an emblem or figure, inasmuch as it seasons and gives a relish to all things. Upon which account it was commanded in the law, Lev. ii. 23, that salt should be used in every sacrifice or oblation made to God; to whom no offering can be pleasing where the salt of discretion is wanting. We are also admonished by this ceremony so to season our souls with the grace of God as to keep them from the corruption of sin, as we make use of salt to keep things from corrupting.

Then the priest proceeds to the solemn prayers and exorcisms, used of old by the Catholic church in the administration of baptism, to cast out the devil from the soul under whose power we are born by original sin. 'I exorcise thee,' says he, 'O unclean spirit, in the name of the Father, + and of the Son, + and of the Holy Ghost, + that thou mayest go out, and depart from this servant of God, N. For he commands thee, O thou accursed and condemned wretch, who with his feet walked upon the sea, and stretched forth his right hand to Peter that was sinking. Therefore, O accursed devil, remember thy sentence, and give honour to the living and true God. Give honour to Jesus Christ, his Son, and to the Holy Ghost, and depart from this servant of God, N. For our God and Lord Jesus Christ has vouchsafed to call him to his holy grace and blessing and to the font of baptism.' Then he signs the forehead with the sign of the cross, saying, 'And this sign of the holy cross, which we imprint on his forehead, mayest thou, O cursed devil, never dare to violate, through the same Christ our Lord. Amen.'

All that has been hitherto set down of the prayers and ceremonies of baptism, is usually performed in the porch or entry of the church, to signify that the catechumen or person that is to be baptized, is not worthy to enter into the church, until the devil first be cast out of his soul. But after these prayers and exorcisms the priest reaches forth the extremity of his stole to the catechumen; or, if it be an infant, lays it upon him, and so introduces him into the church, saying, ' *N*, come into the temple of God, that thou mayest have part with Christ, unto everlasting life. Amen.'

Being come into the church, the priest, jointly with the party that is to be baptized, or, if it be an infant, with the godfather and godmother, recites aloud the apostles' creed and the Lord's prayer. Then reads another exorcism over the catechumen, commanding the devil to depart in the name, and by the power of the most blessed Trinity. After which, in imitation of Christ, who cured with his spittle the man that was deaf and dumb, St. Mark vii. 32, &c., he wets his finger with his spittle, and touches first the ears of the catechumen, saying, ' Ephphetha,' that is, be thou opened : then his nostrils, adding these words, ' unto the odour of sweetness.' ' But be thou put to flight, O devil, for the judgment of God will be at nand ;' by which ceremony the church instructs her catechumens to have their ears open to God's truth, and to smell its sweetness ; and begs this grace for them. .

Then the priest asks the person that is to be baptized, ' *N*, Dost thou renounce Satan ?' To which the person himself, if at age, otherwise the godfather and godmother in his name, answer, I renounce him. The priest goes on, ' And all his works ?' Answ. I renounce them. Priest. ' And all his pomps ?' Answ. I renounce them.

This solemn renouncing of Satan, and his works, and his pomps, in the receiving of baptism, is a practice as ancient as the church itself, and in a particular manner requires our attention : because it is a promise and vow that we make to God, by which we engage ourselves to abandon the party of the devil, to have nothing to do with his works, that is, with the works of darkness and sin ; and to cast away from us his pomps, that is, the maxims and vanities of the world. It is a covenant we make with God, by which we, on our parts, promise him our alle giance, and to fight against his enemies: and he, on his part, promises us life everlasting, if we are faithful to our engagements.   But in the moment we break this solemn covenant by wilful sin, we lose both the grace of baptism, and all that title to an eternal inheritance which we received in baptism, together with the dignity of children of God ; and become immediately slaves to the devil, and children of hell.

After this renouncing Satan, and declaring war against him, to give us to understand what kind of arms we are to procure in this spiritual conflict, the priest anoints the catechumen upon the breast, and between the shoulders, with holy oil, which is solemnly blessed by the bishop every year on Maunday-Thursday ; which outward unction is to represent the inward anointing of the soul by divine grace, which, like a sacred oil, penetrates our hearts, heals the wounds of our souls, and fortifies them against our passions and concupiscences.   Where note, that the anointing of the breast is to signify the necessity of fortifying the heart with heavenly courage, to act manfully, and to do our duty in all things ; and the anointing between the shoulders is to signify the necessity of the like grace to bear and support all the adversities and crosses of this moral life.   The words which the priests uses at this conjuncture are, ' I anoint thee with the oil of salvation in Christ Jesus our Lord, that thou mayest have eternal life, Amen.'

Then the priest asks the catechumen, 'N, Dost thou believe in God the Father Almighty, Creator of heaven and earth ?'   Answ. I believe.   Priest. 'Dost thou believe in Jesus Christ, his only Son, our Lord, who was born, and who suffered for us ?'   Answ. I believe. Priest. ' Dost thou believe in the Holy Ghost, the holy Catholic Church, the Communion of Saints, the Forgiveness of Sins, the Resurrection of the Body, and Life everlasting ?' Answ. I believe. Which answers are made either by the catechumen himself, if able, or by the godfather and godmother, and imply another part of the covenant of baptism, viz. the covenant of faith; by which we oblige ourselves to a steady and sincere o >

4

fession of the great truths of Christianity, and that not by words alone, but by the constant practice of our lives.

After this the priest asks : '*N*, wilt thou be baptized ? Answ. I will. Then the godfather and godmother both holding or touching their godchild, the priest pours the water upon his head three times, in the form of a cross; or, where the custom is to dip, dips him three times, saying at the same time these words: '*N*, I baptize thee in the name of the Father, and of the Son, and of the Holy Ghost.' Which words are pronounced in such manner, that the three pourings of the water concur with the pronouncing of the three names of the divine Persons. For the form is to be pronounced out once.

But if there be a doubt whether the person has been baptized before or not, then the priest makes use of this form : '*N*, If thou art not already baptized, I baptize thee in the name of the Father, and of the Son, and of the Holy Ghost.'

Then the priest anoints the person baptized on the top of the head in the form of a cross with holy chrism, which is a compound of oil and balm, solemnly consecrated by the bishop. Which ceremony comes from apostolical tradition, and gives us to understand, 1st, That in baptism we are made partakers with Christ, (whose name signifies anointed,) and have a share in his unction and grace. 2dly, That we partake also in some manner in his dignity of king and priest, as all Christians are called by St. Peter, 1 Pet. ii. 9, a royal or kingly priesthood, and therefore we are anointed, in this quality, as kings and priests are anointed. 3dly, That we are consecrated to God by baptism, and therefore are anointed with holy chrism, which the church is accustomed to make use of in anointing all those things which she so solemnly consecrates to the service of God.

The prayer which the priest recites on this occasion is as follows : 'May the Almighty God, the Father of our Lord Jesus Christ +. anoint thee with the chrism

THE CATHOLIC CHRISTIAN INSTRUCTED.

of salvation, in the same Christ Jesus our Lord, unto life everlasting, Amen.' Then the priest says, 'Peace be to thee.' Answ. And with thy spirit.

After which the priest puts upon the head of the person that has been baptized, a white linen cloth, commonly called the chrism, in place of the white garment with which the new Christians used formerly to be clothed in baptism, to signify the purity and innocence which we receive in baptism, and which we must take care to preserve until death. In putting on this white linen, the priest says, 'Receive this white garment, which thou mayest carry unstained before the judgment seat of our Lord Jesus Christ, that thou mayest have eternal life, Amen.'

Then he puts a lighted candle into the hand of the person baptized, or of the godfather, saying, 'Receive this burning light and keep thy baptism without reproof; observe the commandments of God, that when our Lord shall come to his nuptials, thou mayest meet him together with all the saints in the heavenly court, and mayest have life eternal, and mayest live forever and ever, Amen.' Which ceremony alludes to the parable of the ten virgins, St. Matt. xxv., who took their lamps and went forth to meet the bridegroom, and admonishes us to keep the light of faith ever burning by the oil of good works; that whensoever our Lord shall come, we may be found with our lamps burning, and may go in with him into the eternal life of his heavenly kingdom.

Lastly. The priest, addressing himself to the person baptized, says, ' *N,* Go in peace, and the Lord be with thee, Amen.' Then he admonishes as well the parents, as the godfather and godmother, of their respective duty, with regard to the education and instruction of their child; and of the care which the church requires of the parents not to let the child lie in the same bed with them or with the nurse, for fear of its being overlaid. And, lastly, informs them of the spiritual kindred which is contracted between the gossips and the child, as also between the gossips and the parents of the child:

which makes it unlawful for them afterwards to marry with those with whom they are thus spiritually allied

---

CHAPTER IV.

OF THE SACRAMENT OF CONFIRMATION, AND OF THE MANNER OF ADMINISTERING IT.

Q. What do you mean by confirmation?

A. A sacrament by which the faithful after baptism receive the Holy Ghost, by the imposition of the hands of the bishop and prayer, accompanied with the unction or anointing of their foreheads with holy chrism.

Q. Why do you call it confirmation?

A. From its effect, which is to confirm or strengthen those that receive it in the profession of the true faith, to make them soldiers of Christ, and perfect Christians, and to arm them against their spiritual enemies.

Q. How do you prove from Scripture, that the apostles practised confirmation?

A. I prove it from Acts viii. 14, 15, 16, 17, 18, where we read of St. Peter and St. John confirming the Samaritans. They 'prayed for them that they might receive the Holy Ghost, ... then they laid their hands upon them, and they received the Holy Ghost,' &c., item. Acts xix. 5, 6: 'They were baptized in the name of the Lord Jesus. And when Paul had imposed his hands on them, the Holy Ghost came upon them.' It is of confirmation also that St. Paul speaks, Heb. vi. 1, 2: 'Not laying again the foundation, &c., of the doctrine of baptism and imposition of hands,' &c. And 2 Cor. i. 21, 22: 'Now he that confirmeth us with you in Christ, and that hath anointed us, is God: who also hath sealed us, and given the pledge of the Spirit in our hearts.'

Q. How do you prove that confirmation is a sacrament?

A. 1st, Because it is plain from Acts viii. that the visible sign of the imposition of hands has annexed to it an invisible grace, viz. the imparting of the Holy Ghost: consequently confirmation is a visible sign of invisible grace, and therefore is a sacrament. 2dly, because the church of God, from the apostles' days, has always believed it to be a sacrament, and administered it as such. See St. *Dionysius, L. de Eccles. Heriarch, c. 4. Tertullian L. de Baptismo, c. 7. L. de Resurrectione carnis, c. 8. L. Præscrip adversus Hæresus, c. 4. St. Cornelius Epist. ad Fabium Antioch. apud Eusebium, L. 6. Histor. c. 43. St. Cyprian, Epist. 70, ad Januarium, Epist. 72, ad Stephanum Papam, Epist. 73, aa Jubaianum, Epist. 74, ad Pompeium. Firmilian, Epist. ad St. Cyprianum. The Council of Illiberis, Can. 38. The Council of Laodicea, Can. 48. St. Cyril of Jerusalem, Catech. 3. Mystag. St. Pacian, Epist. 1 & 3, ad Symnon. & in Sermone de Baptismo St. Ambrose, L. de iis qui mysteriis initiantur, c. 7. The Author of the Books of the Sacraments attributed to St. Ambrose, L. 3, c. 2. St. Optat. of Milevis. L. 7 contra Parmenianum. St. Hierome in Dialogo contra Luciferianos. St. Innocentius, Epist. 9, ad Dicentium. St. Augustine, Tract. 6, in Epist. 1. Joannis, L. 2, contra Literas Petilani, c. 104, &c. St. Cyril of Alexandria, ad Joelis, 2, v. 24 St. Leo Pope, Serm. 4. de native. Theodoret in comment. ad Cantic. 1, v. 3. St. Gregory the great, Homil. 17, in Evangelia, &c.*

Q. Who is the minister of this sacrament?

A. The ordinary minister of this sacrament is a bishop only.

Q. Can this sacrament be received any more than once?

A. No, because, like baptism, it imprints a character or spiritual mark in the soul, which always remains. Hence, those that are to be confirmed are obliged to be so much the more careful to come to this sacrament worthily, because it can be received but once; and if they then receive it unworthily, they have no share in the grace which is thereby communicated to the soul; instead of which, they incur the guilt of a grievous sacrilege.

Q. In what disposition is a person to be, in order to approach worthily to the sacrament of confirmation?

4*

A. He must be free from mortal sin, and in the state of grace; for the Holy Ghost will never come into a soul which Satan possesses by mortal sin.

Q. In what manner then must a person prepare himself for the sacrament of confirmation?

A. 1st, he must examine his conscience, and if he finds it charged with wilful sin, he must take care to purge it by a good confession. 2dly, He must frequently and fervently call upon God to dispose his soul for receiving the Holy Ghost.

Q. What kind of grace does this sacrament communicate to the soul?

A. It communicates to the soul the fountain of all grace, the Holy Ghost, with all its gifts; but more in particular a fortifying grace to strengthen the soul against all visible and invisible enemies of the faith.

Q. Is then this sacrament absolutely necessary to salvation?

A. It is not so necessary, but that a person may be saved without it: yet, it would be a sin to neglect it, when a person might conveniently have it; and a crime to contemn or despise it.

Q. What kind of persons stand most in need of the grace of this sacrament?

A. Those that are the most exposed to persecutions upon account of their religion, or to temptations against faith.

Q. At what age may a person be confirmed?

A. Ordinarily speaking, the church does not give confirmation until a person is come to the use of reason, though sometimes she confirms infants; in which case great care must be taken, that they be put in mind, when they come to the use of reason, that they have received this sacrament.

Q. What is the obligation that a Christian takes upon himself in confirmation?

A. He lists himself there for a soldier of Christ; and consequently is obliged, after having received this sacrament, to fight manfully the battles of his Lord.

Q. May a person have a godfather or godmother in confirmation?

A. He may by way of an instructer and an encourager in the spiritual warfare; and this godfather or godmother contracts the like obligations as in the sacrament of baptism, and the same spiritual kindred.

Q. May a person that is confirmed take a new name?

A. It is usual to do so, not by way of changing one's name of baptism, but by way of adding to it another name of some saint, to whom one has a particular devotion, and by whose prayers he hopes to acquit himself more faithfully of the obligations of a soldier of Christ.

Q. Is a person obliged to receive this sacrament fasting?

A. No, he is not, though it is advisable so to receive it.

Q. In what manner is the sacrament of confirmation administered?

A. First: The bishop turning towards those who are to be confirmed, with his hands joined before his breast, says, ' May the Holy Ghost come down upon us, and the power of the Most High keep you from sin.'

A. Amen.

Then signing himself with the sign of the cross, he says, ' Our help is in the name of the Lord.'

Ans. Who made heaven and earth, &c.

Then extending his hands towards those that are to be confirmed, (which is what the ancients call the imposition of hands,) he prays that they may receive the Holy Ghost.

Bishop. *Let us pray.*

O Almighty, everlasting God, who hast vouchsafed to regenerate these thy servants by water and the Holy Ghost, and who hast given them the remission of all their sins; send forth upon them thy sevenfold Holy Spirit, the Comforter, from heaven.

Answ. Amen.

Bish. The spirit of wisdom and of understanding.

Answ. Amen.

Bish. The spirit of council and of fortitude.

Answ. Amen.

Bish. The spirit of knowledge and of piety.

Answ. Amen.

Bish. Replenish them with the spirit of thy fear, and sign them with the sign of the + cross of Christ, in thy mercy, unto life everlasting. Through the same Jesus Christ, thy Son, our Lord, who liveth and reigneth with thee in the unity of the same Holy Spirit, one God, for ever and ever. Amen.'

Then the bishop makes the sign of the cross with holy chrism, upon the forehead of each one of those that are to be confirmed, saying, '*N,* I sign thee with the sign of the cross. I confirm thee with the chrism of salvation, in the name of the Father, and of the Son, and of the Holy Ghost. Amen.

After which he gives the person confirmed a little blow on the cheek, saying, *Pax tecum,* that is, Peace be with thee.

Then the bishop, standing with his face towards the altar, prays for those that have been confirmed, that the Holy Ghost may ever dwell in their hearts, and make them the temple of his glory. And then dismisses them with this blessing; 'Behold, thus shall every man be blessed, who feareth the Lord. May the Lord bless you from Sion, that you may see the good things of Jerusalem all the days of your life; and may have life everlasting. Amen.

Q. I would willingly be instructed in the meaning of these ceremonies: therefore pray tell me first why the church makes use of chrism in confirmation, and what this chrism is?

A. Chrism is a compound of oil of olives and balm of Gilead, solemnly consecrated by the bishop on Maunday-Thursday: and the unction, or outward anointing of the forehead with chrism, is to represent the inward anointing of the soul in this sacrament with the Holy Ghost. The oil, whose properties are to fortify the limbs, and to give a certain vigour to the body, to assuage our pains, &c., represent the like spiritual effects of the grace of this sacrament in the soul. And the balm, which is of a sweet smell, represents the good odour or sweet savour of Christian virtues, and an innocent life, with which we are to edify our neighbours after having received this sacrament.

Q. Why is this unction made on the forehead, and in form of the cross?

A. To give us to understand that the effect of this sacrament is to arm us against worldly fear and shame: and therefore we receive the standard of the cross of Christ upon our foreheads, to teach us to make an open profession of his doctrine and maxims; and not to flinch from this profession, for fear of any thing that the world can either say or do.

Q. What is the meaning of the bishop's giving a little blow on the cheek to the person that is confirmed?

A. It is to imprint in his mind, that from this time forward he is to be ready, like a true soldier of Jesus Christ, to suffer patiently all kinds of affronts and injuries for his faith.

Q. And why does the bishop, at the same time that he gives the blow, say, Peace be with thee?

A. To signify that the true peace of God, which, as St. Paul says,* exceeds all understanding, is chiefly to be found in patient suffering for God and his truths.

CHAPTER V.

OF THE SACRAMENT OF THE EUCHARIST.

Q. WHAT do you mean by the sacrament of the Eucharist?

A. The sacrament which our Lord Jesus Christ instituted at his last supper, in which he gives us his body and blood under the forms or appearance of bread and wine.

Q. Why do you call this sacrament the Eucharist?

A. Because the primitive church and the holy Fathers† have usually called it so: for the word Eucharist

* Philip. iv. 7.
† St. Iustin, in Apolog 2. St. Irenæus, l. 4, c. 34. Tertullian L. de Cor militis, c. 3. St. Cyprian Epist. 54. First Council of Nice, Can. 18

in the Greek signifies thanksgiving, and is applied to this sacrament, because of the thanksgiving which our Lord offered in the first institution of it, St. Matt. xxvi. 27 St. Mark xiv. 23. St. Luke xxii. 19. 1 Cor. xi. 24. And because of the thanksgiving with which we are obliged to offer and receive this great sacrament and sacrifice, which contains the abridgment of all God's wonders, the fountain of all grace, the standing memorial of our redemption, and the pledge of a happy eternity. This blessed sacrament is also called the holy communion, because it unites the faithful with one another, and with their head, Christ Jesus. 1 Cor. x. 16, 17. And it is called the supper of the Lord, because it was first instituted by Christ at his last supper.

Q. What is the faith of the Catholic Church concerning this sacrament ?

A. That the bread and wine are changed by the consecration into the body and blood of Christ.

Q. Is it then the belief of the church that Jesus Christ himself, true God and man, is truly, really, and substantially present in the blessed sacrament ?

A. It is ; for where the body and blood of Christ are, there his soul also, and his divinity must needs be. And, consequently, there must be whole Christ, God and man: there is no taking him in pieces.

Q. Is that which they receive in this sacrament the same body as that which was born of the Blessed Virgin, and which suffered for us upon the cross.

A. It is the same body: for Christ never had but one body: the only difference is, that then this body was mortal and passible; it is now immortal and impassible.

Q. Then the body of Christ in the sacrament cannot be hurt or divided, neither is it capable of being digested or corrupted ?

A. No, certainly, for though the sacramental species, or the outward forms of bread and wine, are liable to these changes, the body of Christ is not.

Q. Is it then a spiritual body ?

A. It may be called a spiritual body, in the same sense

as St. Paul, 1 Cor. xv. 44, speaking of the resurrection of the body, says, 'It is sown an animal body, it shall rise a spiritual body :' not but that it still remains a true body, as to all that is essential to a body ; but that it partakes in some measure of the qualities and properties of a spirit.

SECTION I.

THE FIRST PROOF OF THE REAL PRESENCE, FROM THE WORDS OF CHRIST AT THE FIRST INSTITUTION OF THIS BLESSED SACRAMENT.

Q. How do you prove the real presence of the body and blood of Christ in this sacrament?

A. I prove it first from the express and plain words of Christ himself, the eternal truth, delivered at the time of the first institution of this blessed sacrament, and recorded in no less than four different places in the New Testament ; viz., St. Matt. xxvi. 26, 27. St. Mark xiv. 22, 24. St. Luke xxii. 19. 1 Cor. xi. 24, 25. In all these places Christ himself assures us what he gives us in the blessed sacrament is his own body and blood. St. Matt. xxvi. : ' Take ye, and eat: this is my BODY— This is my BLOOD of the new testament, which shall be shed for many unto remission of sins.' St. Mark xiv. : ' Take ye, This is my body—This is my blood of the new testament, which shall be shed for many.' St. Luke xxii. : ' This is my body which is given for you —This is the chalice, the new testament in my blood, which shall be shed for you.' 1 Cor. xi. : ' This is my body which shall be delivered for you—This chalice is the new testament in my blood.' Now, the body, which was given and sacrificed for us, the blood of the new testament, which was shed for us, is verily and indeed the real body and blood of Christ. Therefore, what Christ gives us in this blessed sacrament is his real body and blood : nothing can be more plain.

Q. Why do you take these words of Christ at his

last supper according to the letter, rather than in the figurative sense?

A. You might as well ask a traveller why he chooses the high-road rather than to go by-paths, with evident danger of losing his way. We take the words of Christ according to their plain, obvious, and natural meaning, agreeably to that general rule acknowledged by our adversaries,* that in interpreting Scripture, the literal sense of the words is not to be forsaken, and a figurative one followed, without necessity; and that the natural and proper sense is always to be preferred, where the case will admit it. It is not therefore incumbent upon us to give a reason why we take these words of Christ according to their natural and proper sense; but it is our adversaries' business to show a necessity of taking them otherwise. The words themselves plainly speak for us; for Christ did not say, This is a figure of my body; and, This is a figure of my blood; but he said, This is my body, and, This is my blood. It is their duty, as they tender the salvation of their souls, to beware of offering violence to texts so plain, and of wresting them from their evident meaning.

However, we have many reasons to offer, why we take the words of Christ (which he spoke at his last supper in the institution of the blessed sacrament) in their most plain, natural, and obvious meaning. *First,* Because he was then all alone with his twelve apostles, his bosom friends and confidants, to whom he was always accustomed to explain in clear terms whatever was obscure in his parables or other discourses to the people. St. Mark iv. 21: 'To you,' says he to his disciples, 'it is given to know the mystery (the secrets) of the kingdom of God; but to them that are without, all things are done in parables.' And ver. 34: 'Without parable he did not speak unto them; but apart, he explained all things to his disciples.' St. John xv. 15: 'I will not now call you servants: for the servant knoweth not what his lord doth. But I have called you friends: because all things what-

* Dr Harris's Sermon on Transubstantiation, p. 7, 8.

soever I have heard of my Father, I have made known to you.' How then is it likely that on this most important occasion of all, when, the very night before his death, he was taking his last leave and farewell of these his dear friends, he should deliver himself to them in terms which (if they are not to be taken according to the letter) are obscure beyond all example, and not anywhere to be paralleled?

Secondly, He was at that time making a covenant, which was to last as long as time itself should last; he was enacting a law, which was to be forever observed in his church; he was instituting a sacrament, which was to be frequented by all the faithful until he should come; he was, in fine, making his last will and testament, and therein bequeathing to his disciples, and to us all, an admirable legacy and pledge of his love Now, such is the nature of all these things, viz., of a covenant, of a law, of a sacrament, of a last will and testament, that, as he that makes a covenant, a law, &c., always designs, that what he covenants, appoints, or ordains, should be rightly observed and fulfilled; so, of consequence, he always designs that it should be rightly understood; and therefore always expresses himself in plain and clear terms in his covenants, laws, &c. This is what all wise men ever observe in their covenants, laws, and last wills, industriously avoiding all obscure expressions, which may give occasion to their being misunderstood; or to contentions and lawsuits about their meaning. This is what God himself observed in the old covenant; in all the ceremonial and moral precepts of the law; in all the commandments, in the institution of the legal sacraments, &c. All are expressed in most clear and plain terms. It can then be nothing less than impeaching the wisdom of the Son of God, to imagine that he should make his new law and everlasting covenant in figurative and obscure terms, which he knew would be misunderstood by the greatest part of Christendom; or to suppose that he should institute the chief of all his sacraments, under such a form of words, which, in their plain, natural, and obvious meaning, imply a thing so widely different from what he gives us therein, as his own body is from a bit of bread ; or, in fine, to believe that he would make his last will and testament in words affectedly ambiguous and obscure; which, if taken according to that sense which they seem evidently to express, must lead his children into a pernicious error concerning the legacy that he bequeaths them.

In effect, our Lord certainly foresaw that his words would be taken according to the letter by the bulk of all Christendom; hat innumerable of the most learned and most holy would understand them so, that the church even in her general councils would interpret his words in this sense. It must be then contrary to all probability that he who foresaw all this would affect to express himself in this manner in his last will and testament, had he not meant what he said, or that he should not have somewhere explained himself in a more clear way, to prevent the dreadful consequence of his whole church's authorizing an error in a matter of so great importance.

Q. Have you any other reason to offer for taking the words of the institution according to the letter, rather than in a figurative sense?

A. Yes, we have for so doing, as I have just now hinted, the authority of the best and most authentic interpreter of God's word, viz. his holy church ; which has always understood these words of Christ in their plain, literal sense, and condemned all those that have presumed to wrest them to a figure. Witness the many synods held against Berengarius; and the decrees of the general councils of Lateran, Constance, and Trent Now, against this authority, hell's gates shall never prevail ; St. Matt. xvi. 18. And with this interpreter Christ has promised, that both he himself and the Holy Ghost, the Spirit of Truth, should abide forever : St. Matt. xxviii. 20, and St. John xiv. 16, 17.

Q. But are not many of Christ's sayings to be understood figuratively, as when he says, that he is a door, a vine, &c.? And why then may not also the words of the institution of the blessed sacrament be understood figuratively?

A. It is a very bad argument to pretend to infer that because some of Christ's words are to be taken figuratively, therefore all are to be taken so: that because in his parables or similitudes his words are not to be taken according to the letter, therefore we are to wrest to a figurative sense the words of the institution of his solemn covenant, law, sacrament, and testament at his last supper: that because he has called himself a door, or a vine, in circumstances in which he neither was, nor ever could be misunderstood by any one, (he having taken so much care in the same places to explain his own meaning,) therefore he would call bread and wine his body and blood, in circumstances in which it was natural to understand his words according to the letter, as he foresaw all Christendom would understand them, and yet has taken no care to prevent this interpretation of them.

There is therefore a manifold disparity between the case of the expression you mention, viz., I am the door, the vine, &c., and the words of the last supper, 'this is my body, this is my blood.' 1st, Because the former are delivered as parables and similitudes, and consequently as figures; the latter are the words of a covenant, sacrament, and testament, and therefore are to be understood according to their most plain and obvious meaning. 2dly, Because the former are explained by Christ himself in the same places in a figurative sense, the latter are not. 3dly, Because the former are worded in such a manner as to carry with them the evidence of a figure, so that no man alive can possibly misunderstand them, or take them in any other than a figurative meaning; the latter are so expressed, and so evidently imply the literal sense, that they that have been the most desirous to find a figure in them have been puzzled to do it :* and all Christendom has for many ages judged with-

---

* It was the case of Luther himself, as we learn from his epistle to his friends at Strasburg, tom. 5, fol. 502, and of Zuinglius, as we learn from his epistle to Pomeranus, f. 256.

out the least scruple that they ought to be taken according to the letter. 4thly, Because the church of God
has authorized the literal interpretation of the words of
the institution of the blessed sacrament; not so of those
other expressions.   In fine, because, according to the
common laws and customs of speech, a thing may indeed,
by an elegant figure, be called by the name of that
thing of which it has the qualities' or properties; and
thus Christ, by having in himself the property of a door,
inasmuch as it is by him that we must enter into his
sheepfold, St. John x. 9 ; and the property of the vine,
in giving life and fruit to its branches, St. John xv. 1 ;
might, according to the usual laws of speech, elegantly
call himself a door and a vine; but it would be no elegant metaphor to call bread and wine, without making
any change in them, his body and blood ; because bread
and wine have in themselves neither any similitude, nor
quality, nor property of Christ's body and blood ; as it
would be absurd, for the same reason, to point at
any particular door or vine, and say, this is Jesus
Christ.

Q. But may not the sign or figure, according to the
common laws of speech, be called by the name of the
thing signified ?   And have we not instances of this
nature in Scripture; as when Joseph, interpreting the
dream of Pharaoh, Gen. xli. 26, says, ' the seven good
kine are seven years ;' and our Lord, interpreting the
parable of the sower, St. Luke viii. 11, says, ' the seed
is the word of God ;' and St. Paul, 1 Cor. x 4, says,
'the rock was Christ ?'

A. In certain cases, when a thing is already known
to be a sign or figure of something else, which it signifies or represents, it may, indeed, according to the common laws of speech and the use of the Scripture, be said
to be such or such a thing, as in the interpretation of
dreams, parables, ancient figures, and upon such like
occasions ; where, when a thing is said to be this or that,
the meaning is evident ; viz. that it signifies or represents this or that.   But it is not the same in the first
institution of a sign or figure ; because, when a thing

is not known beforehand to be a sign or representation of some other thing, to call it abruptly by a foreign name would be contrary to all laws of speech, and both absurd and unintelligible. As, for instance, if a person by an art of memory had appointed within himself, that an oak tree should be a sign or memorandum of Alexander the Great, and, pointing to the tree, should gravely tell his friends, (who were not acquainted with his design,) This is that hero that overcame Darius, such a proposition as this would justly be censured as nonsensical and unworthy of a wise man; because such a figure of speech would be contrary to all laws of speech, and unintelligible. Just so would it have been, if our Saviour at his last supper, without giving his disciples any warning beforehand, any meaning to speak figuratively, and without their considering beforehand the bread and wine as signs and representations of any thing else, should have abruptly told them, 'This is my body, this is my blood,' had he not meant that they were so indeed. For, abstracting from the change which Christ was pleased to make in the elements by his almighty word, a bit of bread has no more similitude to the body of Christ, than an oak tree has to Alexander the Great. So that nothing but the real presence of Christ's body and blood could verify his words at his last supper, or vindicate them from being highly absurd and unworthy the Son of God.

Q. But do not those words which our Lord spoke, St. Luke xxii. 19, 'Do this for a commemoration of me,' sufficiently clear up the difficulty, and determine his other words to a figurative sense.

A. These words, 'Do this for a commemoration of me,' inform us indeed of the end for which we are to offer up, and to receive the body and blood of Christ, viz., for a perpetual commemoration of his death, 1 Cor. xi. 26, but they no way interfere with those other words, 'This is my body, and this is my blood,' so as to explain away the real presence of Christ's body and blood. For why should Christ's body and blood be less present in the sacrament, because we are commanded in the receiving

5*

of them to remember his death? Certainly St. Matthew and St. Mark, who in their gospels have quite omitted these words, 'Do this in remembrance of me,' never looked upon them as a necessary explication of the words of the institution, or as any ways altering or qualifying the natural and obvious meaning of these words, This is my body, this is my blood.

Q. But does not the remembrance of a thing suppose it to be absent? for, otherwise, why should we be com manded to remember it?

A. Whatsoever things we may be liable to forget, whether really present or really absent, may be the object of our remembrance; and thus we are commanded in Scripture to remember God, Deut. viii. 18. Eccles. xii 1, though in him we live, move, and have our being, Acts xvii. 28. So that this command of remembering Christ is no ways opposite to his real presence: but the most that can be inferred from it is, that he is not visibly present; which is very true; and, therefore, lest we should forget him, this remembrance is enjoined. Besides, if we hearken to the apostle, 1 Cor. xi. 26, he will inform us that what we are commanded to remember is the death of Christ; now, the death of Christ is not a thing really present, but really past, and therefore a most proper subject for our remembrance.

SECTION II.

THE SECOND PROOF OF THE REAL PRESENCE, FROM ST. JOHN, VI. 51, &c.

Q. WHAT other proof have you for the real presence of Christ's body and blood in the sacrament of the Eucharist, besides the words of the institution, This is my body, and this is my blood.

A. We have a very strong proof in the words of Christ, spoken to the Jews in the 6th chapter of St. John, where, upon occasion of the miracle of feeding the multitude with five loaves, having spoken of the necessity of believing in him who is the living bread that came down from heaven, he passes from this discourse concerning faith, to speak of this sacrament, ver. 51, &c. 'I am the living bread, which came down from heaven. If any man eat of this bread, he shall live forever: and the bread that I will give, is my flesh for the life of the world. The Jews therefore strove among themselves, saying: How can this man give us his flesh to eat? Then Jesus said to them: Amen, amen, I say unto you: Except you eat the flesh of the Son of man, and drink his blood, you shall not have life in you. He that eateth my flesh, and drinketh my blood, hath everlasting life: and I will raise him up in the last day. For my flesh is meat indeed: and my blood is drink indeed: He that eateth my flesh, and drinketh my blood, abideth in me, and I in him. As the living Father hath sent me, and I live by the Father: so he that eateth me, the same also shall live by me. This is the bread that came down from heaven. Not as your fathers did eat manna, and are dead. He that eateth this bread shall live forever.' In which words the eating of Christ's flesh, and the drinking his blood, is so strongly, so clearly, and so frequently inculcated, and we are so plainly told, that the bread which Christ was to give, is that very flesh which he gave for the life of the world, that one must be resolved to keep one's eyes shut against the light, if one will not see so plain a truth.

Q. How do you prove that Christ in this place is speaking of the blessed sacrament?

A. By comparing the words which he spoke upon this occasion with those which he delivered at his last supper in the institution of the blessed sacrament. In the one place he says, ' the bread that I will give is my flesh, which I will give for the life of the world;' in the other, taking bread and distributing it, he says, ' this is my body which is given for you.' Where it is visible that the one is a promise which the other fulfils, and consequently that both the one and the other have relation to the same sacrament. Hence we find, that the current sense of the holy fathers has always explained these of the sixth chapter of St. John, as spoken of the sacrament.

See St. Irenæus, L. 4, c. 34. Origin Hom. 16, upon Numbers. St. Cyprian upon the Lord's Prayer. St. Hilary, in his eighth Book of the Trinity. St. Basil, in his Moral Rules, Reg. 1, c. 1. St. Cyril, of Jerusalem, Catech. Mystag. 4. St. Ambrose, of the mysteries, c 8. St. John, Chrysostom, St. Augustine, and St. Cyril, of Alexandria, writing upon the sixth chapter of St. John. St. Epiphanius Hæresi 55, Theodoret L. 4. Hist. Eccles. c. xi., &c.

Q. But does not Christ promise eternal life, St. John vi. 51, 54, and 58, to every one that eateth of that bread of which he is there speaking; which promise cannot be understood with relation to the sacrament, which many receive to their own damnation, 1 Cor. xi. 29 ?

A. He promises eternal life to every one that eateth of that bread; but this is to be understood, provided that he eat it worthily, and that he persevere in the grace which he thereby receives. And in this sense it is certain that this sacrament gives eternal life: whereas the manna of old had no such power, ver. 54. In like manner our Lord promises, St. Matt. vii. 7, 8, that every one that asketh shall receive:' and yet many ask and receive not, because they ask not as they ought. St. James iv. 3. Thus St. Paul tells us, Rom. x. 13, that 'whosoever shall call upon the name of the Lord, shall be saved;' which also certainly must be understood, provided they do it worthily and perseverantly; lest this text contradict that other, St. Matt. vii. 21. 'Not every one that saith to me, Lord, Lord, shall enter into the kingdom of heaven; but he that doeth the will of my Father who is in heaven.' Thus, in fine, Christ tells us, St. Mark xvi. 16, 'He that believeth and is baptized shall be saved.' And yet many believe and are baptized, like Simon Magus, Acts viii. 13, who, for want of a true change of heart, or of perseverance in good, are never saved.

Q. But if those words of Christ, St. John vi. 52, 53, &c., be understood of the sacrament, will it not follow that no one can be saved without receiving this sacrament, and that also in both kinds; contrary to the belief and practice of the Catholic church, since our Lord tells us, verse 54, ' Amen, amen, I say unto you : Except you eat the flesh of the Son of man, and drink his blood, you shall not have life in you.'

A. It follows from those words that there is a divine precept for the receiving this blessed sacrament, which if persons wilfully neglect, they cannot be saved. So that the receiving this sacrament either actually, or in desire, is necessary for all those that are come to the years of discretion; (not for infants, who are not capable of discerning the body of the Lord : 1 Cor. xi. 29.) But that this sacrament should be received by all in both kinds, is not a divine precept, nor ever was understood to be such by the church of God, which always believed that under either kind Christ is received whole and entire, and, consequently, that under either kind we sufficiently comply with the precept of receiving his flesh and blood.

Q. Why may not these words of Christ, St. John vi. 51, 52, 53, &c., be taken figuratively, so as to mean no more than the believing in his incarnation and death ?

A. Because it would be too harsh a figure of speech, and unbecoming the wisdom of the Son of God, to express the believing in him by such strange metaphors as eating his flesh, and drinking his blood, such as no man ever used before or since. And to repeat and inculcate these expressions so often, to the great offence both of the Jews, and even of his own disciples, who upon this account went back and walked no more with him, ver. 60, and 66 ; when he might so easily have satisfied both the one and the other, by telling them that he meant no more by all that discourse, than that they should believe in him.

Q. Did then the Jews and those disciples who cried out, ver. 60, ' This is a hard saying, and who can hear it ?' understand our Saviour right, or did they mistake his meaning ?

A. They understood him right, so far as relates to the real receiving his flesh and blood ; but as to the manner of receiving they understood him not; since they had no thoughts of his giving himself whole and entire, veiled in a sacrament, but apprehended the eating of his flesh, cut off from his bones, and drinking of his blood, according to the vulgar manner of other meat and drink, which we digest and consume. However, their not understanding him seems not to have been so faulty as their refusing to believe him: hence our Lord reprehends not their want of understanding, but their not believing, ver. 64. And Peter, in the name of the apostles, ver. 68, 69, in opposition to those disciples that had fallen off, says, 'Lord, to whom shall we go? thou hast the words of eternal life. And we believe and are sure that thou art Christ, the Son of the living God.' So that these people ought, like the apostles, to have submitted themselves to believe what they as yet understood not; and not to have run away from him, who by his evident miracles proved himself to be the Son of God, and consequently incapable of an untruth. By which example, we may see how much more wisely Catholics act (who in this mystery, like the apostles, submit themselves to believe what they cannot comprehend, because they know that Christ has the words of eternal life) than those who, like the apostate disciples, cry out, 'This is a hard saying, and who can hear it?' and thereupon will walk no more with Christ and his church.

Q. What did our Lord say to his disciples, who were offended with his discourse concerning the eating of his flesh?

A. He said unto them, ver. 61, 62, 'Doth this offend you? what, and if ye shall see the Son of Man ascend up where he was before?' which words are variously interpreted, and may either be understood to signify that they who made a difficulty of believing that he could give them his flesh to eat then, whilst he was visible amongst them, would have much more difficulty of believing it after he was gone from them by his ascension: or else Christ, by mentioning his ascension, would correct their mistaken notion of giving them his flesh and blood, in that gross manner which they apprehended: or, in fine, he mentioned his ascension into heaven, to convince their incredulity, by the evidence of so great a miracle, which at once was to demonstrate both his almighty power and the truth of his words.

Q. What is the meaning of the following words, ver. 64: 'It is the spirit that quickeneth, the flesh profiteth nothing: the words that I have spoken to you, are spirit and life.'

A. The meaning is, that the flesh separated from the spirit, in the manner which the Jews and incredulous disciples apprehended, would profit nothing: for what would it avail us to feed upon dead flesh, separated from the soul and divinity, and consequently from the life-giving spirit? But then it would be blasphemy to say that the flesh of Christ, united to his spirit, (in that manner in which the Catholic church believes his flesh to be in the blessed sacrament, accompanied with his soul and divinity,) profits nothing: for if the flesh of Christ were of no profit, he would never have taken flesh for us, and his incarnation and death would be unprofitable to us; which is the height of blasphemy to affirm.

What means, the flesh profits nothing? says St. Augustine, writing upon this text. Tract 27, in Joan. It profits nothing, as they understood it; for they understood flesh as it is torn in pieces in a dead body, or sold in the shambles; and not as it is animated by the spirit. Wherefore it is said, the flesh profits nothing, in the same manner as it is said, knowledge puffeth up: 1 Cor. viii. 1. Must we then fly from knowledge? God forbid: what then means, knowledge puffeth up? That is, if it be alone without charity; therefore the apostle added, but charity edifieth. Join therefore charity to knowledge, and knowledge will be profitable, not by itself, but through charity: so here also the flesh profiteth nothing, viz. the flesh alone; let the spirit be joined with the flesh, as charity is to be joined with knowledge, and then it profits much. For if the flesh profiteth nothing, the Word would not have been made flesh, that he might dwell in us. So far St. Augustine.

Besides, according to the usual phrase of Scripture flesh and blood are often taken for the corruption of our nature, as for man's natural sense and apprehension, &c. As when it is said, 1 Cor. xv. 50, ' that flesh and blood cannot inherit the kingdom of God.' And St. Matt. xvi. 17: ' Flesh and blood hath not revealed it unto thee,' &c. And in this sense the flesh profiteth nothing, but it is the spirit and grace of God that quickeneth and giveth life to our souls. And as the words which our Lord had spoken to them tended to insinuate to them so great a sacrament, in which they should receive this spirit, grace, and life in its very fountain, therefore he tells them, ' the words that I speak to you, are spirit and life.'

SECTION III.

OTHER PROOFS OF THE REAL PRESENCE OF CHRIST'S BODY
AND BLOOD IN THE BLESSED SACRAMENT.

Q. HAVE you any other proofs from Scripture of the real presence of the body and blood of Christ in the blessed sacrament?

A. Yes, 1 Cor. x., where the apostle, to discourage Christians from having any thing to do with the sacrifices offered to idols, says, ver. 16, ' The chalice of benediction, which we bless, is it not the communion of the blood of Christ? And the bread, which we break, is it not the partaking of the body of the Lord.'

Secondly, 1 Cor. xi. 27. ' Therefore, whosoever shall eat this bread, or drink the chalice of the Lord unworthily, shall be guilty of the body and of the blood of the Lord.' How so, if what the unworthy receiver takes be no more than bread and wine ?

Thirdly, 1 Cor. xi. 29: ' For he that eateth and drinketh unworthily, eateth and drinketh judgment to himself, not discerning the body of the Lord.' How shall he discern it, if it be not there really present?

Q. Have you any thing more to add, by way of proof out of Scripture?

A. Yes, from the ancient figures of the eucharist, which demonstrate that there is something more noble in it than bread and wine, taken only in remembrance of Christ.

Q. What are those ancient figures?

A. There are many; but I shall take notice chiefly of three, viz. the paschal lamb, the blood of the testament, and the manna from heaven.

Q. How do you prove that these three were figures of the eucharist?

A. I prove it with regard to the paschal lamb, (which is acknowledged at all hands to have been a type of Christ,) because it is visible, that the rites and ceremonies of it prescribed, Exodus xii., had chiefly relation to eating of it; and consequently to this typical lamb in the Old Testament, corresponds in the New Testament the Lamb of God, as eaten by his people in this sacrament: which for this reason was instituted immediately after our Lord had eat the passover with his disciples, that the figure might be both explained and accomplished, and might make way for the truth. See concerning this figure the current sense of the fathers in Tertullian, L. 4, in Marcionem; St. Cyprian, L. de unitate Ecclesiæ; St. Hierome in c. 26, St. Matthæi; Chrysostom, Homil. de Proditione Judæ; St. Augustine, L. 2, contra Literas Petiliani, c. 37; St. Gaudentius Tract. 2, in Exod.; St. Cyril, of Alexandria, contra Nestor, p. 112; Theodoret in 1 Cor. xi.; St. Leo Serm. 7. de Passione Domini; Hesychius in c. 23, Levit.; St. Gregory Hom. 22, in Evang.

Secondly, That the blood of the testament with which Moses sprinkled the people, Exod. xxiv. and Heb. ix. saying, ' This is the blood of the testament which God hath enjoined to you,' was a figure of the blood of Christ in this sacrament, our Lord himself sufficiently declared by evidently alluding to this figure, when he gave the cup to his disciples, saying, ' This is my blood of the new testament,' St. Matt. xxvi. 28. St. Mark xiv. 24, or, ' This cup is the new testament in my blood,' St. Luke xxii. 20. 1 Cor. xi. 25.

6

Thirdly, That the manna was a figure of this sacrament, appears from St. John vi. 58. 'Not as your fathers did eat manna, and are dead. He that eateth this bread shall live forever.' And from 1 Cor. x. where the apostle, speaking of the figures of our sacrament in the old law, and taking notice of the cloud, and the passage of the Red Sea, as figures of baptism, ver. 1 and 2; in the third and fourth verses, gives the manna and the water from the rock as figures of the eucharist. The same is the current doctrine of the holy fathers, and is sufficiently demonstrated from the analogy which is found between the manna and this blessed sacrament. For which see the annotations, in the Doway Bible,, upon the XVI. chapter of Exodus.

Q. How do you prove from these ancient figures the real presence of Christ's body and blood in this sacrament?

A. Because, if in this sacrament there were nothing more than bread and wine, taken in remembrance of Christ, and as types and figures of his body and blood, then would the figures of the old law equal the sacraments of the new law, yea, far excel them. For who does not see that the paschal lamb was a more noble type and far better representing Christ than bread and wine? Who does not perceive that the blood of victims solemnly sacrificed to God was a better figure of Christ's blood than the juice of the grape? Who can question but the heavenly manna, which is called the bread of angels, and was so many ways miraculous, was far beyond the bread of men? Who will not acknowledge that it is something more excellent and divine to foretell things to come, than only to commemorate things past? It must therefore be visible to every Christian, that if the paschal lamb, the blood of the testament, and the manna were types of Christ, given to us in this sacrament; that this sacrament itself must be something more than a type, figure or remembrance of Christ; and consequently must contain and exhibit him really to us

Q. But why may not a person suppose that the figures of the Old Testament might equal or excel the sacrament of the New?

A. No one that pretends to the name of Christian can suppose this, since the apostle assures us that the old law had nothing but 'a shadow of the good things to come.' Heb. x. 1. That all its sacrifices and sacraments were but 'weak and needy elements,' Gal. iv. 9, and that it was annulled by reason of 'the weakness and the unprofitableness thereof.' Heb. vii. 18. And does not the very nature of the things assure us, that the figure must be inferior to the things prefigured.

Q. Have you any other argument from Scripture in favour of the real presence of our Lord's body in the blessed sacrament?

A. Yes. Those innumerable texts of Scripture which prove the unerring authority of the church of Christ, and the indispensable obligation of the faithful to follow the judgment of the church, and to rest in her decisions, plainly demonstrate that to be truth which the church has so long ago declared with relation to this controversy; and that all Christians are obliged to yield to this decision.

Q. When did the church decide this matter?

A. As soon as ever it was called in question, that is, about seven hundred years ago, in the days of Berengarius, who was the first that openly attacked the doctrine of the real presence, and was thereupon condemned by the whole church in no less than fourteen councils held during his lifetime in divers parts of Christendom; and the determination of these councils was afterwards confirmed by the general councils of Lateran, Constance, and Trent.

Q. What Scripture do you bring to show that all Christians are obliged to submit to these decisions of the councils and pastors of the church?

A. St. Matt. xviii. 17: 'If he neglect to hear the church, let him be to thee as a heathen and a publican. St. Luke x. 16: 'He that heareth you, heareth me, and he that despiseth you, despiseth me, and he that despiseth me, despiseth him that sent me.' St. John xx. 21: 'As my Father hath sent me, even so I send you.' Heb. xii.

7: 'Remember your prelates who have spoken the word of God to you: whose faith follow.' Ver. 17: 'Obey your prelates, and be subject to them.' 1 John iv. 6: 'He that knoweth God, heareth us; (the pastors of the Church) he that is not of God heareth us not: by this we know the spirit of truth and the spirit of error.' And what wonder that Christ should require this submission to his Church, and her pastors, and teachers, whom he has given for the perfecting of the saints, &c., that we henceforth be no more children tossed to and fro, and carried about with every wind of doctrine: since even in the old law he required, under pain of death, a submission to the synagogue and her ministers in their decision relating to the controversies of the law; as may be seen, Deut. xvii. 8, 9, &c.

Q. What Scripture do you bring to show that the Church is not liable to be mistaken in these decisions?

A. This is evidently proved from a great many texts both of the Old and New Testaments: in which we are assured, 1st, ' That the church is the pillar and ground of the truth,' 1 Tim. iii. 15. and consequently not liable to error. 2dly, 'That Christ has built his church upon a rock, and that the gates of hell (the powers of darkness and error) shall not prevail against her,' St. Matt. xvi. 18. 3dly, that Christ (who is the 'way, the truth and the life,' St. John xvi. 6,) 'will always be with the teachers of his church, even to the end of the world,' St. Matt. xxviii. 20. 4thly, That the Holy Ghost, the Spirit of truth, shall abide forever with these same teachers of the church, St. John xvi. 16, 17, 'and guide them unto all truth,' c. xvi. 13. 5thly, That God has made a covenant with the church, that his Spirit, and his words, which he has put in her mouth at the time when our Redeemer came, should not depart out of her mouth, nor out of the mouth of her seed, nor out of the mouth of her seed's seed, from henceforth and forever,' Isaiah lix. 20, 21. 6thly, 'That God has made a solemn oath to his church, like that which he made to Noah, that he would not be wroth with her, nor rebuke her. Isaiah iv 9, 10; 'that he has promised to be her everlasting light,' Isaiah lx. 18, 19, &c., 'and to set his sanctuary in the midst of her for evermore,' Ezek. xxxvii. 6; all which is inconsistent with her being led astray by damnable errors; and thus the Scripture, by plainly giving testimony to the church and church authority, plainly also gives testimony to the truth of Christ's real presence in the eucharist, which has been so often declared by that authority.

Q. Besides these arguments from Scripture and church authority, have you any thing else to allege in proof of the real presence?

A. First, The authority of all the ancient fathers, whose plain testimonies may be seen in an appendix to a book entitled 'A Specimen of the Spirit of the Dissenting Teachers, &c.; anno 1736.'*

Secondly, The perpetual consent of the Greeks, and all the oriental Christians, demonstrated by Monsieur Arnauld and the Abbe Renaudoit in their books bearing title, La perpetuite de La Foy, &c. confirmed by the authentic testimonies† of their patriarchs, archbishops,

---

* See also The Faith of Catholics, ed. 1836.

† See the testimony of seven archbishops of the Greek church, *Perpetuité*, iii. p. 569, the testimonies of the archbishops and clergy of the isles of the Archipelago, &c. p. 572, &c.; of divers abbots and religious, chap. iv. and v.; of four patriarchs of Constantinople; of the patriarchs of Alexandria, and of thirty-five metropolitans or archbishops, anno 1762, chap. vi. p. 623; of the churches of Georgia and Mingrelia, chap. vii. p. 634; of the patriarch of Jerusalem, and of several other archbishops, abbots, &c., p. 703. Of Macarious and Neophyrus, patriarchs of Antioch, p. 723, &c., of Mocroditus, patriarch of Constantinople, *Response Generale*, p. 151. See also the orthodox confession of the oriental church, signed by the four patriarchs and many other bishops, ibidem, p. 138. That the same is the faith of the Armenians, is proved by the testimonies of Haviadour, an Armenian prelate, of Uscanus, Bishop of St. Sergius; also of David, the patriarch, and other bishops and priests of the Armenians given at Aleppo, anno 1668

6*

bishops, abbots, &c., by the decrees of their synods[*] against Cyril Lucar, by the writings of their ancient[†] and modern divines ; and by all their liturgies : and ac-

In the appendix to the first volume of the *Perpetuité*, p. 78, 81, 82. Of James, patriarch of the greater Armenia, and many other bishops and priests. Responge Generale, L. 1, chap. xviii. Of the archbishops of the Armenians in Constantinople, Adrianople, and Amassæa, ibid. Of Cruciadorus, patriarch of the lesser Armenia, with other bishops and priests, anno 672, tom. 3. Perpetuite, p. 774. Of the Armenians, of Grand Cairo, anno 1671. And of several bishops, at Ispahan, the same year, ibid. p. 775 and 778. See also in the first and third volume of the Perpetuite, and in the Response Generale, many other attestations of the belief of the Moscovites, Jacobites, or Surians Cophts, Maronites, and Nestorians, touching the real presence and transubstantiation.

[*] See the acts of the synods of Constantinople, under the patriarch Cyril, of Beræa, anno 1639. And of the synod under the patriarch Parthenius, anno 1642. And of the synod of Cyprus, anno 1668.

[†] See (besides the testimonies of the Greek fathers of the first six centuries) Anastasius of Sina, in his Odegos ; Germanus, patriarch of Constantinople, in his Theoria ; St. John Damascene. Orat. 3 de Imaginibus, Lib. 2. Parallel. c. 5, L. 4. Fidei Orthodoxæ, c. 13. The second Council of Nice, of 350 bishops, Act 6. Elias Cret. Comment. in Orat. 1. St. Greg. Naz. Nicephorus, Patriarch of Constantinople, Antirhetico 2. Theodorius Studites, Antirhetico 1, Num. 10. Theophylactus ad Cap. 26. Samonus, Bishop of Gaza, in Discep. contra Achmet Saracenum. Nicholas, of Methone, de Corp. et Sang. Christ. Nicholas Cabefilas, Mark, of Ephesus and Bessarion ; *qui omnes in suis opusculis*, says Bishop Forbes de Euch. L. 1, c. 3, *apertissime Transubstantiationem confitentur.* Jeremias, Patriarcho in Resp. 1 and 2 ad Lutheranos. Gabriel Philadelph. de Sacrament. The Greeks, of Venice, in Resp. ad Cardinal. Guis. Agapius, &c. See also in the two additional volumes of Renaudoit to the Perpetuite de La Foy &c., the concurrent testimonies of the divines of the other oriental sects, and of all heir liturgies.

knowledged by many* Protestant witnesses. Now, what can be a more convincing evidence of this doctrine having been handed down by tradition from the apostles, than to see all sorts of Christians, which have any pretensions to antiquity, all agreeing in it?

Thirdly, Both ancient and modern church history furnish us with many instances of miracles the best attested, which from time to time have been wrought in testimony of this same truth: of which in divers parts of Christendom there are standing monuments to this day. It would be too tedious to descend to particulars, and so much the less necessary, because all the miracles of Jesus Christ himself, as they prove that he could not be a liar, so they demonstrate that what he gives us in this sacrament is verily and indeed his body and blood, as he has so clearly told us.

SECTION IV.

TRANSUBSTANTIATION PROVED.   OBJECTIONS ANSWERED.

Q. WHAT do you understand by transubstantiation?

A. That the bread and wine in the blessed sacrament are truly, really, and substantially changed by consecration into the body and blood of Christ.

Q. In what then does the Catholic doctrine of transubstantiation differ from the consubstantiation maintained by the Lutherans?

* Sir Edwin Sandy's relation of the Religions of the West, p. 233. Dr. Potter's Answer to Charity mistaken, p. 225. Bishop Forbes de Euch. L. 1, c. 3, p. 412. Crutius in Germanio-græcia, L. 5, p. 226. Danawerus L. de Eccles. Græc. hodierna, p. 46, &c. Hence Dr. Philip Nicholai, a Protestant, in his first book of the Kingdom of Christ, p. 22, writeth thus: "Let my Christian readers be assured, that not only the churches of the Greeks, but also the Russians, and the Georgians, and the Armenians, and the Indians, and the Ethiopians, as many of them as believe in Christ, hold the true and real presence of the body and blood of the Lord," &c.

A. It differs in this, that Luther and his followers maintain the real presence of the body and blood of Christ in the bread and wine, or with the bread and wine; whereas the Catholic church believes that the bread and wine are converted into the body and blood of Christ, so that there remains nothing of the inward substance of the bread and wine after consecration, but only the outward appearances or accidents.

Q. How do you prove this transubstantiation?

A. First, From the texts of Scripture above quoted, especially from the words of the institution, St. Matt. xxvi. 26, &c., and from the words of Christ, St. John vi. 52, &c., for our Lord, when he first gave the blessed sacrament, did not say, ' In this, or with this, is my body and blood:' but he said, ' this is my body and this is my blood.' Neither did he say, St. John vi. 52. ' In the bread that I will give, will I give you my flesh,' &c. ; but he said, 'The bread that I will give is my flesh for the life of the world.'

Secondly, From the tradition of the ancient fathers, whose doctrine may be seen in the book above quoted.

Thirdly, From the authority and decision of the church of God in her general councils of *Lateran, Constance,* and *Trent.*

And, indeed, supposing that the words of Christ, in the institution of the blessed sacrament, are to be taken according to the letter, as both Catholics and Lutherans agree, the most learned Protestants have often urged against Luther and his followers, that the Catholic transubstantiation is more agreeable to the letter of Christ's words than the Lutheran consubstantiation. See the Bishop of Meaux's Historie des Variations, L. 2, Num. 31, 32, 33.

Q. But does not St. Paul, 1 Corinth. x. and xi. speaking of the sacrament after consecration, call it bread?

A. He does, and so do we; 1st, Because it is the bread of life, the food and nourishment of the soul : 2dly Because it still retains the qualities and accidents of bread, and has the whole outward appearance of bread; and, therefore, according to the Scripture phrase, is called bread, as angels appearing in the shape of men, are oftentimes in Scripture called men.   See St. Luke xxvi. 4. Acts i. 10, &c.   3dly, Because it was consecrated from bread, and, therefore, according to the usual method of speaking in Scripture, is called bread, because it was made from bread; as man is called dust. Gen. iii. 19, because made out of dust: and the serpent is called a rod, Exod. vii. 12, because made from a rod, &c.

Besides, we have two very good interpreters, that inform us what this bread is, of which St. Paul is there speaking, viz. the same apostle, when he tells us, 1 Cor. x. 16, that ' the bread which we break is the communion of the body of Christ;' and our Saviour himself, when he tells us, St. John vi. 52, ' The bread that I will give is my flesh, which I will give for the life of the world.'

Q. But what will you say to our Saviour's calling the sacrament the fruit of the vine, St. Matt. xxxvi. 29 !

A. If it were certain our Saviour had so called the consecrated wine of the blessed sacrament, it would prove no more than St. Paul's calling the other kind bread ; that is, it would only show that the name of wine, or the fruit of the vine, might be given to it from having the accidents and appearance of wine, and having been consecrated from wine.   But there is all the reason in the world to think, that this appellation of the fruit of the vine was given by our Saviour, not to the consecrated cup or chalice, but to the wine of the paschal supper, which they drank before the institution of the sacrament: this appears evident from St. Luke, who thus relates the whole manner, chap. xxii.

Ver. 14, ' When the hour was come, he sat down, and the twelve apostles with him.

15 ' And he said to them, With desire I have desired to eat this pasch with you before I suffer.

16 ' For I say to you, that from this time I will not eat it, till it be fulfilled in the kingdom of God.

17 ' And having taken the chalice he gave thanks and said: Take, and divide it among you.

18 ' For I say to you, that I will not drink of the fruit of the vine. till the kingdom of God come.

19 'And taking bread, he gave thanks, and brake, and gave to them, saying: This is my body which is given for you. Do this for a commemoration of me.

20 'In like manner the chalice also, after he had supped, saying: This is the chalice the new testament in my blood which shall be shed for you.

21 'But yet behold, the hand of him that betrayeth me is with me on the table,' &c.

Where it is visible, that it was not the sacramental cup, but that which was drunk with the passover, to which our Saviour gives the name of the fruit of the vine.

Q. But if the bread and wine do not remain after consecration, what then becomes of them?

A. They are changed by the consecration into the body and blood of Christ.

Q. How can bread and wine be changed into the body and blood of Christ?

A. By the almighty power of God, to whom nothing is hard or impossible, who formerly changed water into blood, and a rod into a serpent, Ex. vii., and water into wine, St. John ii.; and who daily changes bread and wine by digestion into our body and blood.

Q. But do not all our senses bear testimony, that the bread and wine still remain?

A. No, they only bear testimony that there remains the colour and taste of bread and wine, as indeed there does: but as to the inward substance, this is not the object of any of the senses, nor can be perceived by any of them.

Q. Are not our senses then deceived in this case?

A. Properly speaking they are not, because they truly represent what is truly there, viz. the colour, shape, taste, &c. of bread and wine. But it is the judgment that is deceived, when, upon account of this colour, shape, taste, &c., it too hastily pronounces that this is bread and wine.

Q But are we not sufficiently authorized, by the testimony of the senses, to make a judgment of a thing's being in effect, that which it has all the appearance of?

A. Regularly speaking we are, when neither reason nor divine authority interpose itself, to oblige us to make another judgment. And thus the miracles and the resurrection of Christ were demonstrated to the apostles by the testimony of their senses. But the case would have been altered had God himself assured them that what appeared to be flesh and bones, was indeed another thing: for in such a case they ought certainly to have believed the testimony of God, rather than their own senses.

Q. Can you give me any instances in which the testimony of man's senses has represented one thing, and the divine authority of God's word has assured us, that it was not indeed what it appeared to be, but quite another thing?

A. Yes, we have many such instances in Scripture; as when angels have appeared in the shape of men, Gen. xix. St. Matt. xxviii. St. Mark xvi. &c.; and the Holy Ghost, in the shape of a dove, St. Luke iii. 22, &c.

Q. Is there not then any of our senses that we may trust to, in relation to the judgment that we are to make concerning the inward part of the sacrament of the eucharist?

A. Yes, we may safely trust to the sense of hearing, which informs us by the word of God, and the authority of the church of God, that what appears to be bread and wine in this sacrament, is indeed the body and blood of Christ; now, faith comes by hearing, saith St. Paul, Rom. x. 17, and hearing by the word of God.

Q. But if the substance of the bread and wine be not there, what is it then that gives nourishment to our bodies when we receive this sacrament?

A. This sacrament was not ordained for the nourishment of the body, but of the soul; though I do not deny but the body also is nourished, when we receive the blessed eucharist, not by the substance of bread and wine, which is not there, nor by the body and blood of Christ, which is incorruptible, and therefore cannot be digested for our corporal nourishment; but by the quantity and other accidents of the bread and wine, (if, with the Aristotelian philosophers, you suppose them really distinguish ed from matter and substance,) or by another substance, which the Almighty substitutes, when, by the ordinary course of digestion, the sacramental species are changed, and the body and blood of Christ cease to be there.

Q. But how can the accidents of bread and wine remain, without the substance?

A. By the Almighty power of God: which answer, if it satisfy you not, I remit you to the Cartesian philosophers, who will tell you, that as the body and blood of Christ, in the sacrament, are contained precisely in the same circumscription and dimensions as the bread and wine were before the consecration, it follows of course that they must affect our senses in the same manner: now, colour, taste, &c., according to modern philosophy are nothing but the affections of our senses. See Purchot, Part 1, Phys. 2, Sect. 5, cap. 1.

Q. How can the whole body and blood of Christ be contained in so small a space as that of the host; nay, even in the smallest sensible particle of it?

A. By the same Almighty power by which a camel can pass through the eye of a needle: with men this is impossible, says our Saviour, St. Matt. xix. 26, and St. Mark x. 27, 'but not with God, for with God all things are possible.'

Q. How can the body of Christ be both in heaven, and at the same time in so many places upon earth?

A. By the same Almighty power of God, which we profess in the very first article of our creed, when we say, 'I believe in God the Father Almighty.' So that it is a question better becoming an infidel than a Christian to ask, How this can be? when we are speaking of a God to whom nothing is impossible; and who would not be God indeed, if he could not do infinitely more than we can conceive. It is like the Jewish question, St. John vi. 53, 'How can this man give us his flesh to eat?' As if the power of God were not as incomprehensible as himself; and as if it were not worse than madness for weak mortals to pretend to fathom this immense depth of the power of the Almighty by the short line and plummet of human reason.

Q. But is it not an evident contradiction for the same body to be at once in two places?

A. Not at all; no more than for one God to subsist in three distinct persons; or one person in two natures; or one soul to be at once both in the head and in the heart, or two bodies to be at once in the self-same place, as when Christ's body came in to the disciples, the doors being shut, St. John xx. 26, or the same body, after having returned to dust, to be many ages after restored at the resurrection.

Q. How do you prove there is no evident contradiction in any of all these things?

A. Because thousands of as good philosophers and divines as any are, cannot see any such contradiction: which is a plain demonstration there is no evidence in the case; and consequently, it would be the highest rashness to deny the possibility of these things to the power of the Almighty.

Q. But what need was there that Christ should leave us his real body and blood in this sacrament; since without this real presence he might have bequeathed the self-same graces to our souls?

A. He might. indeed, if so he had pleased; as he might also have brought about the salvation of mankind, if he had so pleased, without becoming man himself, and dying upon a cross for us: but he chose these wondrous ways as most suitable to his love, and most proper to excite us to love him. And who shall presume to call him to an account why he has condescended so far?

Q. But are not the body and blood of Christ liable to be hurt and abused in the sacrament?

A. The body and blood of Christ is now immortal, impassible, and incorruptible, and consequently not liable to be hurt, nor divided, nor corrupted; though it may be said, indeed, to be abused by the unworthy communicant; and upon that account, St. Paul, 1 Cor. xi. 27, says, that such a one is 'guilty of the body and blood of Christ:' but this abuse no more hurts the immortal body of Christ, than this or any other crime can hurt or violate his divinity.

7

SECTION V.

Of the Bread and Wine made use of in this Sacrament

Q. WHAT kind of bread does the Church make use of for the sacrament of the eucharist?

A. The Church of Rome makes use of wafers of unleavened bread ; that is, of bread made of fine wheaten flour with no other mixture but pure water.

Q. Why does not the Church make use of common bread for this sacrament?

A. Because she follows the example of Christ, who at his last supper, when he first instituted and gave the blessed sacrament to his disciples, made use of unleavened bread.

Q. How do you prove that?

A. I prove it, because the day in which Christ first gave the blessed sacrament, was, according to St. Matt. xxvi. 17, St. Mark xiv. 12, and St. Luke xxii. 7, 'the first day of unleavened bread.' Now upon that day, and for the whole following week, there was no other bread to be found in Israel; and it was even death to use any other but unleavened bread, as we learn from Exodus xii. 15. 'Seven days shall ye eat unleavened bread, even the first day ye shall put away leaven out of your houses ; for whosoever eateth leavened bread from the first day until the seventh day, that soul shall be cut off from Israel ;' ver. 19. 'Seven days shall there be no leaven found in your houses,' &c. So that it is plain that our Saviour made use of unleavened bread at his last supper, and that there was no other bread used at that time.

Q. Is there any other reason why we should prefer unleavened bread?

A. Yes, unleavened bread is an emblem or symbol of sincerity and truth. Hence *St. Paul* admonishes us, 1 Cor. v. 7 and 8, 'to purge out the old leaven of malice and wickedness, and to feast with the unleavened bread of sincerity and truth.'

Q. What kind of wine do you make use of for this sacrament?

A. Wine of the grape, with which by apostolical tradition we mingle a little water.

Q. Has the practice of mingling water with wine been always observed from the apostles' days?

A. It certainly has, and that throughout the whole church: see *St. Justin, Apolog.* 2, *St. Irenæus, L.* 5, *c.* 2, *St. Cyprian, Epistola* 63, *ad. Cæcillium,* &c.

Q. Did Christ, when he gave the cup to his disci ples, mingle water with wine?

A. It is probable he did: though the scripture neither mentions the water nor the wine: but only speaks of his giving them the cup: However, the ancient and universal practice of the church in all probability comes originally from the example of Christ.

Q. Is there not some mystery or secret meaning in the mingling the water with the wine in the chalice?

A. Yes, it represents to us, first the union of the human and divine nature in the person of the Son of God; 2dly, the union of the faithful with Christ their head; 3dly, the water and blood that flowed from the side of Christ.

Q. Why did our Lord appoint bread and wine for the matter of this sacrament?

A. 1st, Because bread and wine, being most nourishing to the body, were the most proper to represent the grace of this sacrament, which is the food and nourishment of the soul. 2dly, Because bread and wine are both composed of many individuals, (viz. Grains or Grapes,) made one by a perfect union of them all; and therefore, as the holy fathers take notice, are a most proper type or symbol of Christ's mystical body the Church, and of that unity which our Lord would recommend to the faithful by this sacrament—According to that of *St. Paul,* 1 Cor. x. 17. ' We being many are one bread, and one body, for we are all partakers of that one bread.'

Q. What other things are signified or represented by the outward forms of bread and wine in this sacrament?

A. They are chiefly designed to signify or represent to us three things; the one now past, viz. the passion of Christ, of which they are the remembrance: another really present, viz. the body and blood of Christ of which they are the *veil*: a third to come, viz. everlasting life, of which they are the pledge

---

SECTION VI.

Of Communion in one Kind.

Q. WHY do not the faithful in the Catholic Church receive under the form of wine, as well as under the form of bread?

A. The Catholic Church has always looked upon it to be a thing indifferent, whether the faithful receive in one kind or both; because she has always believed that they receive Jesus Christ himself, the fountain of all grace, as much in one kind as in both: but her custom and discipline for many ages has been to administer this sacrament to the laity only in one kind, viz. under the form of bread, by reason of the danger of spilling the blood of Christ, if all were to receive the cup, which discipline was confirmed by the general Council of Constance in opposition to the Hussites, who had the rashness to condemn, in this point, the practice of the universal Church.

Q. Did the Catholic Church never allow of the communion in both kinds?

A. She did, and may again, if she pleases; for this is a matter of discipline, which the Church may regulate or alter, as she shall see most expedient for the good of her children.

Q. What do you mean, when you say, this is a matter of discipline; I thought communion of one kind had been looked upon in the Catholic Church as a matter of faith?

A. You must distinguish in this case between that which is of faith, and that which is of discipline only

It is a matter of faith, that under one kind we receive Christ whole and entire, and the true sacrament; and that there is no command of Christ for all the faithful to receive in both kinds: So far both is and ever was the faith of the Catholic Church; for her faith is unalterable. But then, whether the blessed sacrament should actually be administered to the laity in one kind or in both, that is to say, what is most proper or expedient for the Church to practise or ordain in this particular, considering the circumstances of time, place, &c.; this is what I call a matter of discipline, which may be different in different ages, without any alteration of the faith of the Church.

Q. But did not Christ command the receiving in both kinds, St. Matt. xxvi. 27, ' Drink ye all of it?'

A. These words were addressed to the twelve Apostles, who were all that were then present; and the precept was by them all fulfilled; 'And they all drank of it.' St. Mark xiv. 23. Now it is certain, that many things were spoken in the gospel to the Apostles in quality of pastors of the Church, which were not directed to the laity; as when they were commissioned to preach and baptize, St. Matt. xxviii. 19, 20, and to absolve sinners, St. John xx. 22, and upon this very occasion to do what Christ had done; that is, to consecrate and administer this sacrament in remembrance of him, St. Luke xxii. 19. And consequently, it is no argument that all are obliged to drink of the cup, because Christ commanded all the Apostles to drink of it. no more than that all are obliged to consecrate the sacrament, because Christ commanded all the Apostles to do it. For both these commands were delivered at the same time, upon the same occasion, and to the same persons.

Q. But why should the Apostles, and their successors, the bishops and priests of the Church, be commanded to drink of the cup rather than the laity? Or why should Christ, at the first institution of the sacrament, consecrate and give it in both kinds, if all Christians were not always to receive it in both kinds?

A. To satisfy both these queries at once, you are to

7 *

take notice that the blessed eucharist, according to the faith of the Catholic Church, and as we shall show hereafter, is a sacrifice as well as a sacrament; and of this sacrifice, by the institution of Christ, the Apostles, and their successors, the bishops and priests of the Church, are the ministers; whom he has commanded to offer it in remembrance of his death, St. Luke xxii. 19.   Now this sacrifice in remembrance of Christ's death, for the more lively representing the separation of Christ's blood from his body, requires the separate consecration of both kinds, and therefore the priests, that are the · ministers of this sacrifice, receive at that time in both kinds, and Christ, in the first institution of this sacrifice, consecrated and gave both kinds, designing without doubt that it should be so received, at least by the ministers.

Q. But why should not the nature of the sacrament as much require both kinds to be received by all, as the nature of the sacrifice requires both kinds to be consecrated?

A. Because the nature of the sacrament consists in being the sign and cause of grace; now under either kind there is both a sufficient sign of grace, viz. of the nourishment of the soul, and at the same time the fountain and cause of all grace, by the real presence of Christ, in whom are locked up all the treasures of grace; so that the nature of the sacrament sufficiently subsists in either kind.   But the nature of the sacrifice particularly requires the exhibiting to God, the body and blood of his Son, under the veils that represent the shedding of his blood, and his death; and therefore, the nature of the sacrifice requires the separate consecration of both kinds; which, being consecrated, must be received by some one, and by no one more properly than by the minister.

Q. Does not Christ say, St. John vi. 53, 'Except ye eat of the flesh of the Son of man, and drink his blood, ye shall not have life in you?'

A. He does: and in the same chapter, ver. 57, 58, he tells us, 'He that eateth me, even he shall live by me; and, he that eateth of this bread shall live forever'

Which texts are easily reconciled, if we consider, that according to the Catholic doctrine, and according to the truth, whosoever receives the body of Christ, most certainly receives his blood at the same time; since the body, which he receives, is a living body, (for Christ can die no more, Rom. vi. 9,) which cannot be without the blood. There is no taking Christ by pieces; whoever receives him, receives him whole.

Q. But are not the faithful deprived of a great part of the grace of this sacrament, by receiving only in one kind?

A. No: because the grace of this sacrament being annexed to the real presence of Christ, who is the fountain of all grace; and Christ, being as truly and really present in one kind as in both, consequently he brings with him the same grace to the soul, when received in one kind, as he does when received in both.

Q. Is it not then a privilege, granted to the priests above the laity, to receive in both kinds?

A. No. Their receiving in both kinds, as often as they say Mass, is no privilege, but the consequence of the sacrifice which they have been offering, as you may gather from what I have told you already: For, as for other times, when they are not saying Mass, no priest, bishop or pope, even upon his death-bed, ever receives otherwise than in one kind.

Q. Have you any thing more to add in favour of communion in one kind?

A. Yes; 1st, That the scripture in many places, speaking of the holy communion, makes no mention of the cup. See St. Luke xxiv. 30, 31. Acts ii. 42, 46, xx. 7. 1 Cor. x. 17. 2dly, That the scripture promises life eternal to them that receive in one kind, St. John vi. 51, 57, 58. 3dly, That the ancient Church most certainly allowed of communion in one kind, and practised it on many occasions. See Tertullian, L. 2 ad Uxorem, c. 5; St. Denys of Alexandria, Epist. ad Fabium Antioch, recorded by Eusebius, L. 6, Histor. c. 34; St. Cyprian, L. de Lapis; St. Basil, Epist. 269; St. Ambrose de Satyro Fratre; Paulinus in Vita Ambrosii, &c. 4thly, That many learned Protestants have acknowledged, that there is no command in scripture for all to receive in both kinds.   See Luther, in his epistle to the Bohemians ; Spalatensis de Rep. Eccles. L. 5. c. 6 ; Bishop Forbes, L. 2 de Eucharist, c. 1, 2; White, Bishop of Ely, Treatise on the Sabbath, p. 79 ; Bishop Montagu, Orig. p. 79.

Q. But what would you say further to a scrupulous soul, which, through the prejudice of a Protestant education, could not be perfectly easy upon this article?

A. I should remit such a person to the Church and her authority, and to all those divine promises recorded in scripture, by which we are assured, that in hearing the Church and her pastors, we are secure; that Christ and his holy Spirit shall be always with them, to guide them into all truth; and that the gates of hell shall never prevail against this authority.   So that a Christian soul has nothing to fear, in conforming herself to the authority and practice of the Church of God; but very much in pretending to be wiser than the Church, or making a scruple to hear and obey her spiritual guides.

SECTION VII.

Of the Manner of administering this blessed Sacrament: Of Devotion before and after Communion: Of the Obligations of receiving it; and of its Effects.

Q. In what manner is the blessed eucharist administered to the people?

A. After the communion of the priest in the Mass, such of the people as are to communicate, go up to the rail before the altar, and there kneel down; and taking the towel, hold it before their breasts, in such manner, that if, in communicating, it should happen that any particle should fall, it may not fall to the ground, but be received upon the towel.   Then the clerk, in the name of all the communicants, says the Confiteor, or the gen-

eral form of confession, by which they accuse themselves of all their sins to God, to the whole court of
heaven, and request the prayers and intercession ot
both the triumphant and militant Church.   After which
the priest, turning towards the communicants, says:

'May the Almighty God have mercy on you, and
forgive you your sins, and bring you to everlasting life.
Amen.'

'May the Almighty and merciful Lord grant you
pardon, absolution and remission of all your sins.
Amen.'

Then the priest, taking the particles of the blessed
sacrament, which are designed for the communicants,
and holding one of them, which he elevates a little over
the pix or paten, pronouncing the following words:
'*Ecce Agnus Dei, &c.*' that is, 'Behold the Lamb of
God : behold he who taketh away the sins of the world.'
Then he repeats three times, '*Domine non sum dignus,
&c.*' that is, 'Lord, I am not worthy that thou shouldst
enter under my roof: speak but only the word, and my
soul shall be healed.'   After which he distributes the
holy communion, making the sign of the cross with the
consecrated particle upon each one, and saying to each
one, '*Corpus Domini nostri, &c.*' 'The body of our
Lord Jesus Christ preserve thy soul unto life everlasting. Amen.'

Q. In what manner is the blessed sacrament admin
istered to the sick ?

A. The Catholic Church has always practised the
reserving some consecrated particles of the blessed
eucharist for communicating the sick ; and where she
enjoys free exercise of religion, takes care that this
blessed sacrament be carried to them with a religious
solemnity, attended with lights, &c. When the priest
comes into the chamber where the sick person lies, he
says, 'peace be to this house.' Ans. 'And to all
that dwell therein.'   Then setting down the pix with
the blessed sacrament upon the table, which must be
covered with a clean linen cloth, he takes holy water
and sprinkles the sick person and the chamber, saying,
Asperges, &c.' 'Thou shalt sprinkle me, O Lord,

with hyssop, and I shall be cleansed : thou shalt wash me, and I shall be made whiter than snow.' Psal. l.

Have mercy on me, O God, according to thy great mercy.   Glory be to the Father, &c.,   Then he again repeats the Anthem, ' Thou shalt sprinkle me, &c.' After which he adds, ' Our help is in the name of the Lord. Ans. Who made heaven and earth. Priest. O Lord, hear my prayer. Ans. And let my cry some unto thee. Priest. The Lord be with you. Ans. And with thy spirit. Priest. Let us pray.

THE PRAYER.

O Holy Lord, Almighty Father, everlasting God, graciously hear us ; and vouchsafe to send thy holy angel from heaven, to guard, to cherish, protect, visit, and defend all that dwell in this habitation, through Christ our Lord.   Amen.

Then the priest. coming to the sick person, endeavors to dispose him, and to prepare him for receiving the blessed sacrament; and, if he has any sin upon his conscience, hears his confession, and absolves him. After which the sick person, or some other in his name, says the Confiteor ; and the priest says, ' May the Almighty God have mercy on thee, &c.' as above. ' Behold the Lamb of God, &c.' ' Lord, I am not worthy, &c.'   And in giving the blessed sacrament, if it be by way of Viaticum, or preparation for death, he says, ' Receive, brother, (or sister,) the Viaticum of the body of our Lord Jesus Christ, who may guard thee from the wicked enemy, and bring thee to everlasting life.   Amen.'   But if the sick person be not in danger of death, the priest, in giving the blessed sacrament, pronounces the usual form ; ' May the body of our Lord Jesus Christ preserve thy soul to life everlasting Amen.'

After which the priest says the following prayer.

O Holy Lord, Almighty Father, eternal God, we beseech thee with faith, that the sacred body of our

Lord Jesus Christ thy Son may be available to this our brother (or sister) that has received it as a medicine to eternity, both for body and soul; through the same Lord Jesus Christ thy Son, who liveth and reigneth with thee in the unity of the Holy Ghost, forever and ever   Amen.

Then, if there remain in the pix any other particles of the blessed sacrament, the priest gives the benediction therewith to the sick person: otherwise he pronounces the usual blessing, making the sign of the cross, and saying, 'May the blessing of Almighty God, the Father, and the Son, and the Holy Ghost, descend upon thee, and remain always with thee.   Amen.'

Q. In what disposition of soul is a person obliged to be, in order to receive worthily the blessed sacrament?

A. He is obliged to be in the state of grace, and free at least from the guilt of mortal sin; that is to say, from the guilt of any wilful transgression, in any matter of weight, of the commandments of God, or his Church. The reason of this is, because a soul that is under the guilt of mortal sin is an enemy to God, and a slave to the devil; and therefore it would be a grievous crime for a soul in that state to presume to receive the body and blood of Christ, which, according to the doctrine of St. Paul, 1 Cor. xi. 29, would be receiving damnation to herself.

Q. What then is a person to do in order to prevent so great an evil?

A. St. Paul tells you, 1 Cor. xi. 28, that he is to 'try himself;' that is, to search and examine diligently his own conscience before he ventures to approach to this blessed sacrament.

Q. And what, if upon examination, he finds his conscience charged with any weighty matter?

A. He must take care to discharge it, in the manner that Christ has appointed, viz. by a hearty repentance and sincere confession; laying open the state of his soul to those sacred judges to whom Christ said, St. John xx. 23, 'Whose sins you shall forgive, they are

forgiven; and whose sins you shall retain, they are retained.'

Q. What else is required of a person that is to receive the blessed sacrament?

A. He must be fasting, at least from midnight; for so the Church commands, agreeable to a most ancient and apostolical tradition. So that if, through inadvertence, a person has taken any thing, though it were no more than one drop or crumb, after twelve o'clock at night, he must by no means receive that day; it would be a crime to attempt it.

Q. Is there no exception from this rule?

A. Yes, the case of danger of approaching death is excepted; for then persons are permitted to receive the blessed sacrament by way of Viaticum, though they are not fasting.

Q. What kind of devotion do you recommend to a Christian that is preparing himself for the holy communion?

A. Besides the clearing his conscience from sin by a good confession, I recommend to him, 1st, To think well on the great work he has in hand, to consider attentively who he is, and who it is that he is preparing to receive, and earnestly to beg of God to make him worthy. 2dly, To propose to himself a pure intention, viz. the honour of God, and the health of his own soul; and in particular, that by worthily receiving Christ, he may come to a happy union with him, according to that of St. John vi. 56, 'He that eateth my flesh, and drinketh my blood, dwelleth in me, and I in him.' 3dly, To meditate on the sufferings and death of his Redeemer, in compliance with that command of our Lord, St. Luke xxii. 19, 'Do this in remembrance of me.' 4thly, To prepare himself by acts of virtue, more especially of faith, love, and humility; that so he may approach to his Lord with a firm belief of his real presence in this sacrament, and of his death and passion, with an ardent affection of love to him who has so much loved us, and with a great sentiment of his own unworthiness and sins, joined with a firm confidence in the mercies of his Redeemer

Q. What ought to be a Christian's behavior at the time of receiving this blessed sacrament?

A. As to the interior, he ought to have his soul at that time full of the sentiments we have just now mentioned of faith, love, and humility. And as to the exterior, he ought to have his head erect, his eyes modestly cast down, his mouth moderately open, and his tongue a little advanced on his under-lip, that so the priest may conveniently put the sacred host on his tongue, which he must gently convey into his mouth, and after having moistened it for a moment or two on his tongue, swallow it as soon as he can, in all which he is carefully to avoid, 1st, The putting his mouth to the towel; 2dly, The chewing with his teeth, or raising the host to the roof of his mouth; 3dly, The letting the sacred particle quite dissolve in his mouth; 4thly, The spitting soon after communion. But if the particle should happen to stick to the roof of his mouth, let him not be disturbed, nor put his finger in his mouth to remove it; but gently remove it with his tongue as soon as he can, and so convey it down.

Q. What devotion do you recommend after communion?

A. 1st, Adoration, praise and thanksgiving, in order to welcome our dear Saviour upon his coming under our roof. Here then let the soul cast herself at the feet of her Lord: let her, like Magdalen, wash them in spirit with her tears; or, if she dares presume so high, let her embrace him with the Spouse in the Canticles, and say, ' I have found him whom my soul loves, I will hold him, and shall not let him go.' Let her, like the royal prophet, invite all heaven and earth to join with her in praising her Lord; and let her excite all her powers to welcome him. 2dly, I recommend to the devout communicant to make a present or offering to Christ, in return for his having given himself. The present that he expects is our heart and soul, which, with all its faculties, ought on this occasion to be offered and consecrated to our Lord. 3dly, At this time the soul ought to lay all her necessities before her Redeemer, and not neglect so favorable a conjuncture of suing for his mercy and grace, both for herself and the whole world; for those more especially whom she is in particular obliged to pray for: and above all things let her pray, that nothing in life or death may ever separate her from the love of him whom she has here received, and chosen for her Lord and Spouse forever.

Q. What do you think of those that spend little or no time in recollection and devotion after communion?

A. I think they put an affront upon Christ in so quickly turning their backs upon him; and that they wrong their own souls, which by this neglect are robbed of those graces and comforts which they would have received if they had staid in his company.

Q. Have you any thing more to recommend after communion?

A. I have this to recommend with regard to the whole following day, that a person take care to be more than ordinarily recollected, and very much upon his guard against the snares of the enemy, who is never more busy than upon this occasion to fling some temptation or provocation in a Christian's way, by which he may disturb the soul, and rob her of the treasure which she has received; and therefore it behoves Christians to be cautious against this wicked enemy and all his stratagems, lest by putting us into a passion, or otherwise drawing us into sin, he quickly put Christ out of our souls.

If you desire to be more perfectly instructed in what relates to this blessed sacrament, and the devotion that is proper before and after communion, I refer you to Father Lewis de Granada's Memorial of a Christian Life, book III. Dr. Gobinet's second volume of the Instruction of Youth; or Mr. Gother's little book of Instructions and Devotions for Confession and Communion.

Q. Are all Christians that are come to the years of discretion, under an obligation of receiving this sacrament?

A. They certainly are, 1st, By a divine precept or

commandment of Christ, St. John vi. 54. 'Except you eat the flesh of the Son of man, and drink his blood, you shall not have life in you.' Which precept obliges to the receiving sometime at least in our life, and at our death. 2dly, By a precept or commandment of the Church published in the great Council of Lateran, anno 1215; by which all the faithful are obliged to receive at least once a year, and that within the Easter-time, (which begins on Palm-Sunday and lasts till Low-Sunday) except the person, by the advice of his pastor, should, for some just reason, be permitted to put off his communion till another time.

Q. What is the penalty imposed by this council on such as neglect their Easter communion?

A. The council orders that such offenders should be excluded the Church, and, if they die in this transgression, be deprived of Christian burial.

Q. Are persons then actually excommunicated that neglect their Easter communion?

A. No, they are not, till superiors pronounce the sentence of excommunication against them: because the council does not actually inflict this penalty, but only orders or authorizes the inflicting of it.

Q. If a person has passed by the time of Easter, or was hindered from communicating at that time, is he obliged to communicate afterwards, as soon as he can?

A. Yes, he is; at least if you speak of one that has been a whole year without communicating; for the Church precept obliges to the receiving at least once a year. For the same reason, a person that has not been at communion within a year, and foresees that he shall be hindered at Easter, ought to anticipate his paschal communion, by receiving beforehand.

Q. And what if a person has made a sacrilegious communion at Easter, has such a one satisfied the precept of the Church?

A. No, certainly. (See the 55th proposition condemned by Innocent XI.) And there fore such a one remains obliged to communion, in the same manner as if he had not communicated at all.

Q. At what age are Christians obliged by the pre cept of the Church to communicate?

A. As soon as they come to the years of discretion, as it is expressed in the Council of Lateran: that is, when they have that perfect use of reason, and are so well instructed in their duty as to be able to discern the body of the Lord, and to receive it with due reverence and devotion. Now this happens in some earlier, in others later; but seldom earlier than about ten years of age.

Q. But what if a child, that is between seven and ten years of age, should be in evident danger of death?

A. Many divines are of opinion, if such a one be come to the use of reason (which is commonly presumed after seven years of age) that he may, or even ought to receive, because of the command of Christ, St. John vi. 54. So Saurez, Navarrus, &c.

Q. What are the effects of this blessed sacrament in the worthy receivers?

A. It is the food, nourishment, strength, and life of the soul, by supplying it with sanctifying grace, by repairing its forces, by arming it against its passions and concupiscences, by maintaining it at present in the life of grace, and bringing it to life and glory everlasting; according to that of St. John vi. 51, 'The bread that I will give is my flesh, for the life of the world;' and ver. 58, 'He that eateth of this bread shall live forever.'

SECTION VIII.

Of the Worship of Christ in this Sacrament: where also of Benedictions and Processions.

Q. WHAT kind of honor is due to this blessed sacrament?

A. Divine honour and adoration, inasmuch as it contains truly and really the divine Person of Jesus Christ, the Son of God ; who, as he is truly God, ought most certainly to be adored, wheresoever he is.

Q. Is there no danger of idolatry in this practice ?

A. No, certainly ; because this honour is not paid to the outward veil, or the sacramental signs, but to Jesus Christ, who lies hidden there : now Jesus Christ is no idol, but the true and living God.

Q. But if the doctrine of the real presence and transubstantiation should not be true, should we not then at least be guilty of idolatry?

A. We are as positively certain, by divine faith, of the truth of the doctrine of the real presence, and of transubstantiation, as Protestants can be of the divinity of Jesus Christ; and therefore we are as much out of the reach of the danger of idolatry, in worshipping Christ in this sacrament, as they are in worshipping him in heaven. I shall add, for their further satisfaction, that some of their best divines have discharged us from all danger of idolatry in worshipping Christ in this sacrament; as they may find in Dr. Jeremy Taylor's Liberty of Prophesying, sect. 20, numb. 26, and Mr. Thorndike's Just Weights and Measures, ch. 19, p. 125. Dr. Taylor's words on this subject deserves to be remarked. He writes as follows, " Idolatry is a forsaking the true God, and giving divine worship to a creature, or to an idol ; that is, to an imaginary God. — Now it is evident that the object of their (the Catholics') adoration, in the blessed sacrament, is the only true and eternal God, hypostatically joined with his holy humanity, which humanity they believe actually present, under the veil of the sacramental signs. And if they thought him not present, they are so far from worshipping the bread in this case, that themselves profess it idolatry to do so. Which is a demonstration that their soul has nothing in it that is idolatrical ; the will has nothing in it but what is a great enemy to idolatry ; and nothing burns in hell but proper will." So far this learned Protestant prelate.

Q. Why does the Catholic Church reserve the blessed sacrament in her churches ?

A. She reserves the blessed sacrament in tabernacles

8 *

upon her altar partly that she may have it there to carry to the sick at all hours, whenever they shall be in need of it; and partly for the comfort of her children, who by this means have Jesus Christ always amongst them, and may come when they please to visit him. This custom of reserving the blessed sacrament, is as ancient as Christianity, as appears from the most* certain monuments of antiquity. And it is upon account of the blessed sacrament, reserved in the tabernacle, that a lamp hangs before the altar to burn there day and night, and that we kneel as often as we pass before the tabernacle.

Q. Why is the blessed sacrament, upon certain days, exposed to the view of the people in remonstrance set up upon the altar?

A. It is to invite the people to come there to adore Jesus Christ, and to excite in them a greater devotion by the sight of their Lord, veiled in these sacred mysteries.

Q. What is the meaning of the benediction given on certain days?

A. It is a devotion practised by the Church, in order to give adoration, praise and thanksgiving to God, for his infinite goodness and love, testified to us in the institution of this blessed sacrament, and to receive at the same time the benediction or blessing of our Lord here present.

Q. Why is the blessed sacrament sometimes carried in solemn procession through the streets?

A. To honour our Lord there present with a kind of triumph, and thereby to make him some sort of amends for the injuries and affronts which are so frequently offered to this divine sacrament; and to obtain his bless ing for all those places through which he passes.

* Tertullian l. 2, ad Uxorem, c. 5; St. Cyprian, l. de Lapsis, &c.

CHAPTER VI.

Of the Sacrifice of the Mass.

Q. WHAT do you mean by the Mass?

A. The Mass is the liturgy of the Catholic Church, and consists in the consecration of the bread and wine into the body and blood of Christ, and the offering up of the same body and blood to God, by the ministry of the priest, for a perpetual memorial of Christ's sacrifice upon the cross, and a continuation of the same to the end of the world.

Q. Why is this liturgy called the Mass?

A. Some think this word is derived from the Hebrew word *missach*, Deut. xvi. which signifies a voluntary offering ; others are of opinion, that it is derived from the *misla*, or *missio*, that is, from the dismission of the catechumens and others, who were not permitted anciently to be present at this sacrifice.   But be this as it will, the name is of very ancient use in the Church, as appears from St. Ambrose, l. 2, Epist. 14, ad Soronem; St. Leo, Epist. 81, ad Dioscorum; and St. Gregory. Hom. 6, in Evangelia.

Q. Is the Mass properly a sacrifice?

A. Yes, it is.

Q. What do you mean by a sacrifice?

A. A sacrifice, properly so called, is an oblation or offering of some sensible thing made to God by a lawful minister, to acknowledge by the destruction or other change in the thing offered, the sovereign power of God, and to render him the homage due to his supreme Majesty.

Q. How then is the Mass a sacrifice?

A. Because it is an oblation of the body and blood of Jesus Christ, offered under the outward and sensible signs of bread and wine to God, by the ministry of the priests of the Church, lawfully consecrated and empowered by Christ; and this oblation is accompanied with a real change and destruction of the bread and wine, by the consecration of them into the body and

blood of Christ, and a real exhibiting of Christ our victim, heretofore immolated upon the cross, and here
mystically dying in the separate consecration of the
two different species; and this oblation is made to God
to acknowledge his sovereign power, to render him our
homage, and for all the other ends for which the sacrifice is offered to his divine Majesty

Q. What are the ends for which sacrifice of old was
offered, and is still to be offered to God?

A. For these four ends: 1st, For God's own honour
and glory, by acknowledging his sovereignty and paying him our homage; 2dly, To give God thanks for all
his blessings; 3dly, To beg pardon for our sins: 4thly,
To obtain grace and all blessings from his divine Majesty.

Q. Have the servants of God, from the beginning of
the world, been always accustomed to honour him with
sacrifices?

A. Yes, they have. Witness the sacrifice of Abel,
Gen. iv. the sacrifice of Noah, Gen. viii. the sacrifice
of Melchisedec, Gen. xiv. the sacrifices of Abraham,
Gen. xv. and xxii. the sacrifices of Job, ch. i. and xlii.
and the many different kinds of sacrifices prescribed in
the law of Moses. Of these ancient sacrifices some
were holocausts, or whole burnt-offerings, in which the
victim or host was wholly consumed by fire, and thereby
given fully to God without reserve for the more perfect acknowledgment of his sovereignty. Others were
sin-offerings or sacrifices offered for sins: others were
pacific or peace-offerings; and these were either offered in thanksgiving for blessings received, or for obtaining of graces and favours from the divine Majesty
Again, some were bloody sacrifices, in which the vic
im was slain; others unbloody, as the sacrifice of Melchisedec, which was bread and wine, Gen. xiv. the sacrifices of fine flour with oil and frankincense, of unleavened cakes, &c., prescribed Levit. ii. of the scape
goat, Levit. xvi. &c.

Q. Were these sacrifices of the law of nature, and
of the law of Moses agreeable to the divine Majesty?

A. They were, as often as they were accompanied

with the inward sacrifice of the heart; not for any virtue or efficacy that they had in themselves, as being but weak and needy elements, but in view of the sacrifice of Christ, of which they all were types and figures, and in consideration of the faith of those that offered them, by which they believed in a Redeemer to come, whose blood alone was capable to reconcile them to God.

Q. Why are all these sacrifices now abolished?

A. Because they were but figures of the sacrifice of Christ, and therefore were to give place to his sacrifice, as figures to the truth.

Q. How do you prove that these ancient sacrifices had no power nor efficacy of themselves, and were to make way for another sacrifice, viz. that of Christ?

A. This is evident from many texts of scripture; I shall only alledge one at present, viz. Psalm xxxix. spoken in the person of Christ to his Father: ' Sacrifice and oblation thou wouldst not; but ears thou hast perfected to me, (or as St Paul reads it, Heb. x. 5, a body thou hast prepared for me) holocaust and sin offering thou didst not require, then said I, behold I come.'

Q. What is then the sacrifice of Christians under the new law?

A. We have no other sacrifice but that of Christ, which he once offered upon the cross; and daily offers by the ministry of his priests upon the altar in the eucharist.

Q. Is the sacrifice of the cross and that of the eucharist the same sacrifice, or two distinct sacrifices?

A. It is the same sacrifice; because the victim is the selfsame, viz. Jesus Christ; and the priest or principal offerer is also the selfsame Jesus Christ: it was he that offered himself upon the cross: it is he that offers himself upon the altar. The only difference is in the manner of the offering; because in the sacrifice of the cross, Christ really died, and therefore that was a bloody sacrifice; in the sacrifice of the altar, he only dies mystically, and therefore this is an unbloody sacrifice; I say he dies mystically, inasmuch as his death

is represented in the consecrating apart the bread and wine, to denote the shedding of his sacred blood, from his body, at the time of his death.

Q. Why do you say, that Jesus Christ is the priest that offers the sacrifice of the altar, since there is always another priest to perform this office?

A. Because the priest that officiates in the Mass, officiates as Christ's vicegerent, and in his Person; and therefore when he comes to the consecration of the elements, in which this sacrifice essentially consists, he speaks not in his own name, but in the name and person of Christ, saying, 'This is MY body, this is the chalice of MY blood, &c.' So that Christ himself is the principal priest; the officiant only acts by his authority, in his name and person.

Q. But what need was there of the sacrifice of the altar, since we are fully redeemed by the sacrifice of the cross?

A. 1st, That we might have in the sacrifice of the altar a standing memorial of the death of Christ. 2dly, That by the sacrifice of the altar the fruit of his death might daily be applied to our souls. 3dly, That his children might have, till the end of the world, an external sacrifice, in which they might join together in the outward worship of religion, as the servants of God from the beginning of the world had always done. 4thly, That in and by this sacrifice they might unite themselves daily with their high-priest and victim Christ Jesus, and daily answer the four ends of sacrifice.

Q. What proofs have you that the Mass is properly a sacrifice?

A. Because as we learn from many plain texts of scripture, quoted in the foregoing chapter, and from the perpetual tradition of the universal church, in the consecration of the holy eucharist, the bread and wine are really changed into the body and blood of Christ; and consequently in and by this consecration, the real body and blood of Christ our victim, which for us was immolated upon the cross, is in the Mass exhibited and presented to God. Therefore the Mass is properly a sacrifice, and the same sacrifice as that which Christ offered upon the cross. And that this sacrifice is propitiatory for the obtaining of the remission of our sins, we learn from the very words of Christ our Lord, at the first institution of it at his last supper, when in the consecration of the elements, speaking in the present tense, he tells us, (as his words are in the original Greek,) 'This is my body which is broken or sacrificed for you,' 1 Cor. xi. 24; 'This is my blood of the New Testament which is shed for many for the remission of sins,' Matt. xxvi. 28, St. Mark xiv. 24, or, 'This cup is the New Testament in my blood, which (cup) is shed for you, viz. for the remission of your sins.'

Q. Have you any other texts of scripture for the sacrifice of the Mass?

A. Yes, besides many figures of this sacrifice in the Old Testament (of which the most evident is that of the bread and wine offered by Melchisedec the priest of the most high God, Gen. xiv. according to whose order Christ is said to be a priest forever, Psalm cx. and that as the holy fathers* take notice, by reason of this sacrifice of the eucharist) we have the prophecy of Malachy, chap. i. 10, 11, where God rejecting the Jewish sacrifices, declares his acceptance of the sacrifice or pure offering which should be made to him in every place among the Gentiles : which text the ancient fathers, both Greek and Latin, urge to show that the eucharist is a sacrifice. See St. Justin in dialog. cum Tryphone; St. Irenæus l. 4, c. 32; St. Chrysostome, in Psal. 92; St. Augustine, l. 18, *de civitate Dei*, c. 35, &c.

In the New Testament we have, Heb. xiii. 10, where the Apostle tells us, that under the new law we have an altar, (and consequently a sacrifice) whereof they have no right to eat who serve the tabernacle. That is they who continue in the service of the old law,

---

* St. Cyprian, Epist. 63; St. Chrysostome, Hom. 35, de Gen.; St. Epiphanius, Hier. 55; St. Jerome, Epist. 126, ad Evang.; St. Augustine, Conc. 1, in Ps. 33, l. 15; de Civ. D. c. 22; Lei. 18, c. 35 &c.; St. Cyril, l. 2; Glaphyrs Theodoret Qu. 64, in Gen.

and, 1 Cor. *x.* from ver. 14 to 21, the same apostle makes a parallel between the partakers of the Christian sacrifice and those that partake of the Jewish and heathenish victims, so as evidently to suppose, that the Christian table which he mentions, ver. 21, is an altar, where Christ is mystically immolated, and afterwards eaten by the faithful, as in the Jewish and heathenish sacrifices the victim was first offered on the altar, and then eaten by the people.   From whence the Apostle infers, that they who were partakers of this great sacrifice of the body and blood of Christ, ver. 16, ought not to be partakers with devils, by eating of the meats sacrificed to idols, ver. 21.   The sacrifice of the Mass is also mentioned in the 13th chapter of the Acts of the Apostles, ver. 2, where what we read in the Protestant Testament, ‘As they ministered to the Lord and fasted,’ &c. in the Greek original is, ‘as they were sacrificing to the Lord, and fasting, the Holy Ghost said, Separate me Barnabas and Saul for the work whereunto I have called them.’   Where the word which we have rendered in English, sacrificing, is the selfsame which to this day is used by the Greeks to express the sacrifice of the Mass.

Besides these arguments from scripture for the sacrifice offered to God in the blessed eucharist, we have the authority and the perpetual tradition of the Church of God, from the days of the Apostles.   Witness the most ancient liturgies of all the Churches and nations, Latins, Greeks, Goths, Syrians, Armenians, Egyptians, Ethiopians, Indians, &c.   Witness the manifold testimonies of councils and fathers of all ages; witness the frequent use in all Christian antiquity of the names of altar, sacrifice, oblation, priest, &c.   Witness, in fine, the universal consent of Christians of all denominations before Luther's time, in offering up the eucharist as a sacrifice; which is a matter of fact that cannot be contested.   To which, if we add another truth, no less notorious, viz. that no one of our adversaries can pretend to assign the time in which the use of this sacrifice first begun; we cannot have a more certain proof of an apostolical tradition. It is the rule which St. Augustine gives to discern apostolical traditions by, L 4, de Bapt. c. 24.

Q. But does not St. Paul say, Heb. x. 14. that Christ, by one offering, viz. that of the cross, hath perfected forever them that are sanctified? What room then can there be for the sacrifice of the Mass?

A. What the Apostle says is certainly true, that the sacrifice of Christ upon the cross, is that one offering by which we are perfected forever, because the whole world was redeemed by that one sacrifice, and all other means of our sanctification or salvation have their force and efficacy from that one offering. Yet as that one offering, by which Christ has perfected forever them that are sanctified, is no way injured by his supplications which as man he makes for us to his Father in heaven, where, as the same Apostle tells us, Heb. vii. 25, 'He ever liveth to make intercession for us;' so neither is it any ways injured, but highly honoured by the representing the same offering to God in the sacrifice of the altar.

Q. But the apostle tells us, Heb. xi. 25, that Christ does not offer himself often, what say you to this?

A. He speaks there of offering himself in a bloody manner, by dying for the redemption of the world · which was to be but once. But though the price of our redemption was to be paid but once, yet the fruit of it was to be daily applied to our souls, by those means of grace which Christ has left in his Church, that is, by his sacraments and sacrifice.

———◆———

CHAPTER VII.

Of hearing Mass: where also of the Order and Ceremonies of the Mass; and the Devotion proper for that Time.

.Q. ARE the faithful obliged to be present at the sacrifice of the Mass?

9

A. They are obliged by a precept of the Church to be present thereat upon all Sundays and holidays.

Q. Why does the Church oblige all her children to assist at the sacrifice of the Mass upon all Sundays and holidays?

A. That as Sundays and holidays are particularly set apart for the worship of God, and the sanctification of their souls, they may answer these ends by assembling together on these days, to commemorate the death of Christ, and to offer to God this most solemn worship of sacrifice, by the hands of the priest, and of their high-priest Christ Jesus: 1st, in testimony of God's sovereignty, and as a homage due to his divine majesty: 2dly, to give thanks for all his blessings general and particular: 3dly, to beg mercy and pardon for all their sins: 4thly, to obtain all necessary graces from the fountain of all grace.

Q. Why might not this as well be done without going to hear Mass?

A. Because, as we have seen in the foregoing chapter, the Mass is a sacrifice instituted by Christ to be offered for all those ends. And as in this sacrifice Christ himself is both the priest and the victim, who here presents to his eternal Father that same body and blood by which we were redeemed; it must be evident, that there can be no better means of adoring God, and offering our homage to him, than by uniting ourselves to this sacrifice of his only Son; no more acceptable thanksgiving than that which is here offered, by and through Jesus Christ; no means of obtaining mercy and pardon comparable to this oblation of the blood of the Lamb: in fine, no more seasonable time for obtaining the favours of heaven, than when we appear before the throne of grace with him and through him, in whom his Father is always well pleased.

Q. In what disposition of soul ought persons then to go to hear Mass?

A. They ought to go as if they were going to mount Calvary, to be present at the passion and death of their Redeemer; since the mass is indeed the same sacrifice as that which he there offered. And consequently there can be no better devotion for the time of the Mass than that which has relation to the passion of Christ, which is therein commemorated and represented to the eternal Father. And all the faithful, when they are at Mass, should endeavour to put their souls in the like dispositions of adoration, thanksgiving, love, and repentance for their sins, with which a good Christian would have assisted at the sacrifice of the cross, had he been present there.

Q. What think you of those, who, during the time of Mass, instead of attending to this great sacrifice, suffer themselves to be carried away with wilful distractions?

A. Such as these do not hear Mass, that is, they do not fulfil the Church precept, nor satisfy the obligation of the day, but rather mock God, whilst outwardly they pretend to honour him, and their heart is far from him.

Q. What then do you say to those who, during the time of the Mass, are laughing and talking, or pass that time in criminal amusements?

. A. These not only are guilty, like the former, of breaking the Church precept, but also must answer for the scandal that they give by their ill example, and for their hindering others from attending to their duty ; as well as for their profaning those most sacred mysteries, by such an unchristian behavior at this holy time.

Q. I should be glad if you would explain to me the order and ceremonies of the Mass : and first, pray what is the meaning of the priest's vestments?

A. The priest, in saying Mass, represents the person of Christ, who is the high-priest of the new law, and the Mass itself represents his passion ; and therefore, the priest puts on these vestments, to represent those with which Christ was ignominiously clothed at the time of his passion. Thus, for instance, the Amice represents the rag or clout with which the Jews muffled our Saviour's face, when at every blow they bid him prophesy who it was that struck him. St. Luke xxii. 64. The Alb represents the white garment with which he was vested by Herod. The Girdle, Maniple, and Stole, represent the cords and bands with which he was bound in the different stages of his passion. The

Chasuble, or outward vestment, represents the purple garment with which he was clothed as a mock king; upon the back of which there is a cross, to represent that which Christ bore on his sacred shoulders. Lastly, The priest's tonsure or crown, is to represent the crown of thorns which our Saviour wore. Moreover, as in the old law, the priests that were to officiate in sacred functions had, by the appointment of God, vestments assigned for that purpose, as well for the greater decency and solemnity of the divine worship, as to signify and represent the virtues which God required of his ministers, so it was proper, that in the Church of the New Testament, Christ's ministers should, in their sacred functions, be distinguished from the laity by their sacred vestments, which might also represent the virtues which God requires in them: thus the Amice, which is first put upon the head, represents divine hope, which the Apostle calls the helmet of salvation; the Alb, innocence of life; the Girdle, (with which the loins are begirt,) purity and patient-suffering, the labours of this mortal life; the Stole, the sweet yoke of Christ to be borne in this life, in order to a happy immortality in the next; in fine, the Chasuble, which as uppermost, covers all the rest, the virtue of charity.

In these vestments the Church makes use of five colours, the white, on the feast of our Lord, of the blessed Virgin, of the angels, and of the saints that were not martyrs; the red, on the feast of Pentecost, of the invention and exaltation of the cross, and of the Apostles and martyrs; the green, on the greatest part of the Sundays; the violet, in the penitential times of Advent and Lent, and upon Vigils and Ember-days; and the black upon Good-Friday, and in the Masses for the dead.

Q. Why is there always a crucifix upon the altar at the time of Mass?

A. That as the Mass is said in remembrance of Christ's passion and death, the priest and people may have always before their eyes the image that represents his passion and death.

Q. What is the meaning of having lighted candles upon the altar at the time of Mass?

A. 1st, To honour the triumph of our King, which is there celebrated by these lights, which are tokens of our joy, and of his glory. 2dly, To denote the light of faith, with which we are to approach him.

Q. What is the meaning of making a reverence to the altar?

A. 1st, because the altar is a figure of Christ, who is not only our sacrifice and our high-priest, but our altar too, inasmuch as we are to offer our prayers and sacrifices through him. 2dly, Because the altar is the seat of the divine mysteries, and therefore deserves our reverence.

Q. What is the meaning of the use of incense in the Mass and other offices of the Church?

A. Incense is an emblem of prayer, ascending to God from a heart inflamed with his love, as the smoke of incense ascends on high from the fire of the censer Hence the royal prophet, Psal. cxl. says, 'Let my prayer, O Lord, be directed like incense in thy sight.' And St. John in the Revelation, c. v. 8, and c. v. iii. 4, saw the four and twenty elders and the angel offering up to God odours and incense, which were the prayers of the saints. Moreover the incensing of the altar, of the priest, &c. is, according to the use of the Church, a token of honour to the thing that is incensed: not of divine honour, since we also incense the whole choir and the people, but of a due respect for the things of God, for his ministers and people.

Q. What is the use of singing, and of organs, in the divine service?

A. To help us to raise our hearts to heaven, and to celebrate with greater solemnity the divine praises.

Q. Tell me now, if you please, the different parts of the Mass, and the ceremonies thereof, that I may be the better instructed in this heavenly sacrifice.

A. 1st, The priest standing at the foot of the altar, having made a low reverence, begins with the sign of the cross, saying, *In Nomine Patris, &c.* In the name of the Father, and of the Son, and of the Holy Ghost,

9 *

and then recites alternately with the clerk the **42d** Psalm, *Judica me Deus, &c.* Judge me, O God, &c. composed by David, in the time that he was persecuted by Saul, and kept at a distance from the tabernacle or temple of God, and expressing his ardent desires and hopes of approaching to God's altar, and offering praise and sacrifice to him. And therefore this Psalm is most proper here, as expressing the sentiments of soul, with which we ought to come to this holy sacrifice.

2dly, The priest, bowing down at the foot of the altar, says the Confiteor, or general confession, acknowledging his sins to God, to the whole court of heaven, and to all the faithful there assembled. and begging their prayers to God for him : and the clerk repeats the same in the name of the people; to the end that both priest and people may dispose themselves for this great sacrifice, by a sincere repentance for their sins. Our adversaries object against this form of confession, because therein we confess our sins to the saints; as if this was giving them an honour that belongs to God alone, not considering that the confessing of our sins to any one, so far from being an honour peculiar to God, is what we are directed in scripture to do to one another, St. James, v. 16. And accordingly in this very form, which we call the Confiteor, we not only confess our sins to God, and to his saints, but the priest also confesses to the people, and the people to the priest.

3dly, The priest in going up to the altar begs for himself and the people, that God would take away their iniquities that they may be worthy to enter into his sanctuary. Then coming up to the altar he kisses it in reverence to Christ, of whom it is a figure ; and going to the book he reads what is called the Introit, or entrance of the Mass ; which is different every day, and generally an Anthem taken out of the scripture with the first verse of one of the Psalms, and the *Gloria Patri*, to glorify the blessed Trinity.

4thly, He returns to the middle of the altar, and says alternately with the clerk the *Kyrie Eleison*, or Lord have mercy on us, which is said three times to God the Father ; three times, *Christe Eleison*, or Christ have mercy on us, to God the Son; and three times again, *Kyrie Eleison,* to God the Holy Ghost. This frequently calling for mercy, teaches us the necessity of approaching to this sacrifice with a penitential spirit, and that the best devotion for this beginning of the Mass, is to offer up to God the sacrifice of a contrite and humble heart.

5thly, After the *Kyrie Eleison,* the priest recites the *Gloria in Excelsis,* Glory be to God on high, &c. being an excellent hymn and prayer to God, the beginning of which was sung by the angels at the birth of Christ. This being a hymn of joy, is omitted in the Masses for the dead, and in the penitential times of Advent, Lent, &c. After this the priest, turning about to the people, says, ' *Dominus vobiscum,*' 'the Lord be with you.' Answ. ' *Et cum Spiritu tuo,*' 'and with thy spirit.' Then returning to the book, he says, ' *Oremus,*' 'Let us pray ;' and then reads the collects or prayers of that day, concluding them with the usual termination, ' *Per Dominum nostrum,* &c.* 'Through our Lord Jesus Christ,' &c. with which the Church commonly concludes all her prayers, as hoping for no mercy, grace or blessing, but through our Saviour Jesus Christ.

6thly, After the collects, is read the lesson or epistle of the day, (and upon the Wednesdays and Saturdays in the Ember-weeks several lessons or epistles) at the end of which the clerk answers, ' *Deo Gratias,*' i. e. 'Thanks be to God ;' to give God thanks for the heavenly instructions contained in that divine lesson of holy writ. The lesson or epistle is followed by the gradual or tract, consisting of some devout verses taken out of scripture ; to which are joined the alleluias, to praise God with joy, excepting in the penitential time between Septuagesima and Easter, for then alleluia is not said.

7thly, After the epistle and gradual, the book is removed to the other side of the altar, in order to read the gospel of the day ; which removal of the book represents the passing from the preaching of the old law, figured by the lesson or epistle, to the gospel of Jesus Christ, published by the preachers of the new law. The priest before he reads the gospel, makes his

prayer, bowing down before the middle of the altar that God would cleanse his heart and his lips, that he may be worthy to declare his gospel. At the beginning of the gospel both priest and people make the sign of the cross, 1st, upon their foreheads, to signify that they will not be ashamed of the cross of Christ and his doctrine; 2dly, upon their mouth, to signify that they will profess it in words; 3dly, upon their breast, to signify that they will always keep it in their hearts. During the gospel the people stand, to show, by this posture, their readiness to go and do whatsoever they shall be commanded by their Saviour in his divine word. At the end the clerk answers, in the name of the people, '*Laus tibi Christe*,' 'Praise be to thee, O Christ;' to give praise to our Redeemer for his heavenly doctrine; and the priest kisses the book, in reverence to those sacred words which he has been reading out of it. In the high or solemn Mass, the gospel is sung by the deacon, and lighted candles are held by the acolyths on each side, to denote the light which Christ brought us by his gospel.

8thly, After the gospel upon all Sundays, as also upon the feasts of our Lord, of the blessed Virgin, of the Apostles, and of the doctors of the Church, the priest standing at the middle of the altar, recites the Nicene Creed and kneels down at these words, '*Et homo factus est*,' 'And was made man,' in reverence to the mystery of our Lord's incarnation. Then turning about to the people, he greets them with the usual salutation, '*Dominus vobiscum*,' 'The Lord be with you.' Ans. '*Et cum spiritu tuo*,' 'And with thy spirit.' After which he reads a short sentence of scripture called the Offertory, and then takes off the veil from the chalice, in order to proceed to the offering up the bread and wine for the sacrifice.

9thly, He offers first the bread upon the paten, or little plate; then pours the wine into the chalice, mingling with it a little water, and offers that up in like manner, begging that this sacrifice may be accepted of by the Almighty for the remission of his sins, for all there present, for all the faithful living and. dead, and for the salvation of the world. Then bowing down, he says, 'In the spirit of humility, and in a contrite mind, may we be received by thee, O Lord: and so may our sacrifice be made this day in thy sight, that it may please thee, O Lord God.'   Then he blesses the bread and wine with the sign of the cross, invoking the Holy Ghost, saying, 'Come thou, the Sanctifier, the Almighty, and eternal God, and bless ✝ this sacrifice prepared for thy holy name.'   After this he goes to the corner of the altar, and there washes the tips of his fingers, saying, '*Lavabo*,' &c. 'I will wash my hands among the innocent, and I will encompass thy altar, O Lord,' &c. as in the latter part of the 25th Psalm. This washing of the fingers denotes the cleanness and purity of soul with which these divine mysteries are to be celebrated ; which ought to be such, as not only to wash away all greater filth, but even the dust which sticks to the tips of our fingers, by which are signified the smallest faults and imperfections.

10thly, After washing his fingers the priest returns to the middle of the altar, and there bowing down, begs of the blessed Trinity to receive this oblation in memory of the passion, resurrection, and ascension of our Lord Jesus Christ, and for an honourable commemoration of the blessed Virgin and of all the saints, that they may intercede for us in heaven, whose memory we celebrate on earth.   Then turning about to the people, he says, '*Orate Fratres*,' &c. that is, 'Brethren, pray that my sacrifice and yours may be made acceptable in the sight of God the Father Almighty.'   The clerk answers in the name of the people, 'May the Lord receive this sacrifice from thy hands, to the praise and glory of his own name and for our benefit, and that of all his holy Church.'

11thly, Then the priest says, in a low voice, the prayers called the Secreta, which corresponds to the collects of the day, and are different every day. He concludes by saying aloud, '*Per omnia sæcula sæculorum*,' that is, 'World without end.'   Ans. Amen. Then after the usual salutation, 'The Lord be with you, Ans. 'And with thy spirit,' he admonishes the people to lift up their hearts to God (*Sursum corda*) and to join with him in giving thanks to our Lord. (*Gratias agamus Domino Deo nostro.*) To which the clerk answers, '*Dignum et justum est,*' 'It is meet and just.' Then follows the Preface, so called because it serves as an introduction to the Canon of the Mass; in which, after solemnly acknowledging ourselves bound in duty ever to give thanks to God, through his Son Jesus Christ, whose majesty all the choirs of angels ever praise and adore, we humbly beg leave to have our voices admitted together with theirs in that celestial hymn, '*Sanctus, Sanctus,*' &c. i. e. 'Holy, Holy, Holy, Lord God of hosts. The heavens and earth are full of thy glory. Hosanna in the highest. Blessed is he that comes in the name of the Lord, Hosanna in the highest.'

12thly, After the Preface follows the Canon of the Mass, or the most sacred or solemn part of this divine service, which is read with a low voice, as well to express the silence of Christ, in his passion, and his hiding at that time his glory and his divinity, as to signify the vast importance of that common cause of all mankind, which the priest is then representing as it were in secret to the ear of God, and the reverence and awe with which both priest and people ought to assist at these tremendous mysteries. The Canon begins by the invoking the Father of mercies, through Jesus Christ his Son, to accept this sacrifice for the holy Catholic Church, for the pope, for the bishop, for the king, and for all the professors of the Catholic and Apostolic faith, throughout the whole world. Then follows the *Memento*, or commemoration of the living, for whom, in particular, the priest intends to offer up that Mass, or who have been particularly recommended to his prayers, &c. To which is subjoined a remembrance of all there present, followed by a solemn commemoration of the blessed Virgin, the Apostles and martyrs, and all the saints, to honour their memory, by naming them in the sacred mysteries, to communicate with them, and to beg of God, the help of their intercession, through Jesus Christ our Lord.

Then the priest spreads his hands over the bread

and wine, which are to be consecrated into the body and blood of Christ, (according to the ancient ceremony prescribed in the Levitical law, Levit. i. 3, 4, 16, that the priest or persons who offered sacrifice, should lay their hands upon the victim, before it was immolated,) and he begs that God would accept this oblation which he makes in the name of the whole Church, and that he would grant us peace in this life, and eternal salvation in the next.   Then he blesses the bread and wine with the sign of the cross (a ceremony frequently repeated in the Mass, in memory of Christ's passion, of which this sacrifice is the memorial; and to give us to understand that all grace and sanctity flow from the cross of Christ, that is, from Christ crucified) and he prays that God would render this oblation blessed, received, approved, reasonable, and acceptable, that it may be made to us the body and blood of his most beloved Son our Lord Jesus Christ.   Then he proceeds to the consecration, first of the bread into the body of our Lord, and then of the wine into his blood; which consecration is made by the words of Christ pronounced by the priest in his name, and as bearing his person and this is the chief action of the Mass, in which the very essence of this sacrifice consists; because, by the separate consecration of the bread and wine, the body and blood of Christ are really exhibited and presented to God, and Christ is mystically immolated.

Immediately after the consecration follows the elevation, first of the host, then of the chalice, in remembrance of Christ's elevation upon the cross, and that the people may adore their Lord veiled under these sacred signs.   At the elevation of the chalice the priest recites these words of Christ, 'As often as you shal. do these things, you shall do them in remembrance of me.'   Then he goes on making a solemn commemoration of the passion, resurrection, and ascension of Christ, and begging of God to accept this sacrifice as he was pleased to accept the oblation of Abel, Abraham, and Melchisedec; and to command that it may by his holy angel, be presented upon the altar above, in presence of his divine majesty, for the benefit of all those that shall partake of these mysteries here below.

Then the priest makes the Memento or remembrance for the dead; praying for all those that are gone before us with the sign of faith, and rest in the sleep of peace; and in particular for those for whom he desires to offer this sacrifice, that God would grant them a place of refreshment, light and peace, through Jesus Christ our Lord. Then raising his voice at *Nobis quoque peccatoribus*, and to us sinners, &c. he strikes his breast in token of repentance, like the humble publican in the gospel, and begs of God mercy and pardon, and to be admitted into some part and society with the holy Apostles and martyrs, through Christ our Lord. He goes on, ‘By whom, O Lord, thou dost always create, sanctify, enliven, bless and give us all these good things. Then kneeling down, and taking the sacred host in his hand, he makes the sign of the cross with it over the chalice, saying, ‘Through him, and with him, and in him, is to thee, God the Father in the unity of the Holy Ghost, all honour and glory;’ which last words he pronounces elevating a little the host and chalice from the altar; and then kneels down, saying, with a loud voice, ‘ *Per omnia sæcula sæculorum.*’ ‘For ever and ever.’ Answer, Amen.

13thly, After this follows the ‘*Pater Noster*,’ or ‘Lord’s Prayer,’ which is pronounced with a loud voice; and in token of the people’s joining in this prayer, the clerk in their name says aloud, the last petition, ‘*Sed libera nos a malo*,’ ‘But deliver us from evil.’ The priest answers, Amen: and goes on with a low voice, begging that we may be delivered from all evils past, present and to come; and by the intercession of the blessed Virgin, and of all the saints, be favoured with peace in our days, and secured from sin and all disturbances, through Jesus Christ our Lord. Then he breaks the host, in imitation of Christ’s breaking the bread before he gave it to his disciples, and in remembrance of his body being broken for us upon the cross; and puts a particle of it into the chalice, saying to the people. ‘The peace of the Lord be always with you.' Answer, 'And with thy spirit.' This ceremony of mixing a particle of the host with the species of wine in the chalice represents the re-uniting of Christ's body, blood, and soul at his resurrection; and the priest's wish or prayer for peace, at the time of this ceremony, puts us in mind of that 'Pax vobis.' or 'Peace be unto you,' which our Lord spoke to his disciples when he first came to them after his resurrection, St. John xx. 19, 21, 26.

14thly, Then follows the 'Agnus Dei, &c.' which the priest pronounces three times, striking his breast in token of repentance; the words are, 'Lamb of God, who takest away the sins of the world, have mercy on us.' At the third time, instead of, have mercy on us, he says, grant us peace. After the Agnus Dei, follow three prayers, which the priest says to himself by way of preparation for receiving the blessed sacrament. After which kneeling down, and then rising and taking up the blessed sacrament, he three times strikes his breast, saying, 'Domine, non sum dignus, &c.' 'Lord, I am not worthy that thou shouldst enter under my roof; but only thou say the word, and my soul shall be healed.' Then receiving the sacred host he says, 'The body of our Lord Jesus Christ preserve my soul to life everlasting, Amen.' Having paused awhile, he proceeds to the receiving of the chalice, using the like words, 'The blood of our Lord Jesus Christ, &c.' Then follows the communion of the people, if any are to receive.

15thly, After the communion, the priest takes first a little wine into the chalice, which is called the first ablution, in order to consummate what remains of the consecrated species in the chalice; and then takes a little wine and water, which is called the second ablution, upon his fingers, over the chalice, to the end that no particle of the blessed sacrament may remain sticking to his fingers, but that all may be washed into the chalice and so received. Then wiping the chalice, and covering it, he goes to the book and reads a versicle of the holy scripture, called the Communion, because it was used to be sung in the high Mass, at the time

10

that the people communicated. After this, he turns about to the people with the usual salutation, *Dominus vobiscum;* and then returning to the book, reads the collects, or prayers called the Post-communion: after which he again greets the people with *Dominus vobiscum;* and gives them leave to depart, with ' *Ite Missa est,*' i. e. ' Go, the Mass is done.'   Here, bowing before the altar, he makes a short prayer to the blessed Trinity; and then gives his blessing to all there present, in the name of the same blessed Trinity, ' *Bene dicat vos, &c.*'   ' May the Almighty God, the Father, ✠ and the Son, and the Holy Ghost, bless you.'   He concludes, reading at the corner of the altar, the beginning of the gospel according to St. John, which the people hear standing; but at these words, *Verbum caro factum est,* The word was made flesh, both priest and people kneel, in reverence to the mystery of Christ's incarnation.   The clerk at the end answers, ' *Deo gratias,*' 'thanks be to God.'   And then the priest departs from the altar, reciting to himself the *Benedicite,* or the canticle of the three children, inviting all creatures in heaven and earth to bless and praise our Lord.

Q. In what manner ought the people to be employed during the Mass?

A. In such prayers and devotions as are most suitable to that holy sacrifice; which having so close a relation to the passion of Christ, is then best heard when the assistants turn the attention and affections of their souls towards the mysteries of the passion of our Lord, which are there represented.

Q. Is it not a good way of hearing Mass to accompany the priest through every part of it, so as to accommodate one's devotion to what he is then about?

A. It is a very good and profitable way: Not that the very prayers of the priest, in the Canon and Consecration, are always proper for the people, but that in every part of the Mass it is proper that the people should use such prayers as are adapted to what the priest is then doing.

Q. What kind of prayers and devotions then do you

esteem the best adapted to the several parts of the Mass ?

A. I should recommend, 1st, In the beginning of the Mass an earnest application of the soul to God, by way of begging his divine grace for the worthily and profitable assisting at this sacrifice.

2dly, At the Confiteor, and what follows until the *Kyrie Eleison* inclusively, I should advise the assistants to an humble confession of their sins to God, with a most hearty repentance and earnestly begging his mercy.

3dly, At the *Gloria in excelsis*, let them join in that heavenly hymn, and excite their souls to the affections expressed therein.

4thly, At the Collects, let them recommend to God their own necessities and those of the whole Church.

5thly, At the Epistle, Gradual, and Gospel, either let them attend to the heavenly lessons contained in them; or, if they have not the convenience for this, let them employ themselves in giving thanks to God for revealing to us his divine truths, and instructing us not only by his servants the prophets and Apostles, but also by his son; and begging of God that their lives may be always conformable to the maxims of his gospel.

6thly, At the Credo, let them recite it to themselves, with a lively faith of these great truths contained in it.

7thly, At the Offertory, let them join with the priest in offering up first the host, and then the chalice, for themselves and for the whole Church; but let them at the same time unite themselves closely with their High-Priest Christ Jesus, and with him, through him, and in him, offer up their hearts and souls to God, to be consecrated to his divine service, and changed into him; and in particular at the mingling of the water with the wine in the chalice, let them pray for this happy union with God.

8thly, At the Lavabo, when the priest washes his fingers at the corner of the altar, let them excite in their souls a hearty act of repentance, and beg to be washed from their sins in the blood of the Lamb.

9thly, When the priest turns about and says, *Orate Fratres*, let them pray that God would accept of that oblation for his own honour and their salvation.

10thly, At the Preface, let them raise up their hearts to God at *Sursum Corda*, and pour forth their souls in thanksgiving to him; joining themselves with the heavenly choirs, and with them humbly and fervently pronouncing that sacred hymn, ' *Sanctus, &c.*' Holy, Holy, Holy, Lord God of Hosts, &c.'

11thly, During the Canon of the Mass, let them, together with the priest, and together with the invisible priest, Christ Jesus, offer up the sacrifice, for the four ends of sacrifice, viz. 1. For God's honour, adoration and glory. 2. In thanksgiving for all his benefits, and especially for our redemption through Jesus Christ. 3. To obtain mercy and pardon through him for all their sins. 4. To obtain all graces and blessings of which they stand in need. Let them all join in the solemn commemoration that is here made of the passion, resurrection and ascension of the Son of God, and of the glory of his Church triumphant in heaven.

12thly, At the *Memento* for the living, let them earnestly recommend to God their parents, friends, benefactors, &c. their superiors, spiritual and temporal; those that have particularly desired their prayers; those that are in agony, or other great necessities, temptation, or affliction; those to whom they have given scandal or ill example; their enemies, and all unbelievers and sinners, that God may convert them; in fine, all true servants of God, and all such, for whom God would have them to pray.

13thly, At the Consecration and Elevation, let them again offer themselves to God with and through Christ, and with all the reverence of their souls adore their Lord there really present under the sacramental veils

14thly. At the *Memento* for the dead, let them represent to the eternal Father this victim which takes away the sins of the world, in behalf of all the faithful departed in the communion of the Church, and particularly of their relations, friends, &c. and those who stand most in need of prayers, or for whom God is best pleased that they should pray.

15thly, At the *Pater Noster*, let them join in that heavenly prayer; begging in the first petition (Hallowed be thy name) the honour and glory of God's name; in the second petition, the propagation of his kingdom here upon earth, and that they may have a share in his kingdom in Heaven; in the third petition, the perfect accomplishment of his will by all, and in all in the fourth, the participation of the bread of life in the fifth, the forgiveness of their sins; in the sixth, the grace of God against temptations; and in the seventh, a deliverance from all evils.

16thly, At the breaking of the host, let them remember Christ's body broken for them upon the cross, and let them pray for that peace which the priest wishes them, with God, with their neighbours, and with themselves.

17thly, At *Agnus Dei, &c.* let them, in the spirit of humility and contrition, beg mercy and pardon for their sins.

18thly, During the following prayers, and whilst the priest is receiving, let them make a spiritual communion. 1. By a lively faith, of the real presence of the Lamb of God slain for our sins, and of the abundance of grace which he brings to those that receive him worthily. 2. By an ardent desire of partaking of this life-giving food. 3. By humbly acknowledging at the *Domine, non sum dignus*, and heartily bewailing their unworthiness and sins, which hinder them from daring to approach to this heavenly table. 4. By fervent prayer, begging that Christ would communicate to them some share in those graces which he brings with him to the worthy receiver, and that he would come at least spiritually to their souls, and take possession of them, and unite them to himself by an indissoluble band of love.

19thly, After the communion, let them return thanks to God for the passion and death of his Son, and for having been permitted to assist at these divine mysteries, let them receive with humility the bene

10 *

diction given by the priest in the name of the blessed Trinity; let them beg pardon for their negligences and distractions; and so offering themselves and all their undertakings to God, depart in peace.

Q. What advice would you give to those who through indisposition, or other unavoidable impediments, are not able to assist at Mass upon a Sunday or Holy-Jay?

A. I would advise them to endeavour to hear Mass at least in spirit, according to the method prescribed by Mr. Gotner, for the absent, in the little book of instructions and devotions for hearing Mass.

Q. What if a person, through the absolute necessity of his unhappy circumstances, should be tied to a place where he can never hear Mass, do you think he might not then be allowed to join in prayer with those of another communion, by way of supplying this defect?

A. No, certainly. It is a misfortune, and a great misfortune, to be kept like David, when he was persecuted by Saul, at a distance from the temple of God, and his sacred mysteries; but it would be a crime to join one's self upon that account with an heretical or schismatical congregation, whose worship God rejects as sacrilegious and impious. In such a case therefore a Christian must serve his God alone to the best of his power, by offering to him the homage of prayer, adoration, contrition, &c. And must frequently hear Mass in spirit, by joining himself with all the faithful throughout the earth, wherever they are offering to God that divine sacrifice; ever sighing after these heavenly mysteries, and praying for his delivery from that Babylon, which keeps him at a distance from the temple of God.

———◆———

CHAPTER VIII.

Of the saying Mass in LATIN.

Q. Is it not a great prejudice to the faithful, that the Mass is said in Latin, which is a language that the generality of them do not understand?

A. It is no prejudice to them at all, provided they be well instructed in the nature of this sacrifice, and taught (as we have explained above) how to accompany the priest with prayers and devotions adapted to every part of the Mass; such as they commonly have of their manuals or other prayer-books. Hence it is visible to any unprejudiced eye, that there is far more devotion amongst Catholics at Mass, than there is at Protestants' common-prayer.

Q. But is not the Mass also a common prayer, that ought to be said alike by all the faithful?

A. It is a common sacrifice that is offered for all, and in some manner by all; but as for the particular form of prayers used by the priest in the Mass, there is no obligation for the faithful to recite the same; all that God or his Church expect from them is to assist at that sacrifice with attention and devotion; and this they fully comply with, when they endeavour to follow the directions given above, and use such prayers as are best adapted to each part of the Mass; though they be not the selfsame as the priest uses.

Q. Can you explain to me by some example how a person may devoutly and profitably assist at this sacrifice, though he be ignorant of the prayers which the priest is saying?

A. Yes. What do you think if you or any good Christian had been present upon Mount Calvary, when Christ was offering himself upon the cross a sacrifice for the sins of the whole world; would not the very sight of what was doing (provided that you had the same faith in Christ as you have) have sufficed to excite in your soul most lively acts of love of God, thanksgiving for so great a mercy, detestation of your sins, &c. though you could neither hear any word from the mouth of Christ your high-priest, nor know in particular what passed in his soul? Just so in the Mass, which is the same sacrifice as that which Christ offered upon the cross, because both the priest and the victim are the same; it is abundantly sufficient for the people's devotion, to be well instructed in what is then doing, and to excite in their souls suitable acts of adoration, thanksgiving repentance, &c. though they understand not the particular prayers used by the priest at that time.

I must add, that for the devoutly and profitably concurring in sacrifice offered to God, it is not even necessary that the people should hear or recite the same prayers with the priest, but that the very seeing of him is more than God was pleased to require in his law. Hence we find, St. Luke i. 10, that the whole multitude of the people were praying without, when Zacharias went into the temple to burn incense. And Levit. xvi. 17, it was expressly ordered, that there should be no man in the tabernacle or temple, when the high-priest went with the blood of the victims into the sanctuary to make atonement.

Q. But does not St. Paul, 1 Cor. xiv. condemn the use of the unknown tongues in the liturgy of the Church?

A. He has not one word in that whole chapter of the liturgy of the Church; but only reprehends the abuse of the gift of tongues, which some amongst the Corinthians were guilty of, who out of ostentation affected to make exhortations or extemporary prayers in their assemblies, in languages utterly unknown, which for want of an interpreter could be of no edification to the rest of the faithful. But this is far from being the practice of the Catholic Church, where all the exhortations, sermons, and such like instructions, are made in the vulgar language; where no new unknown extemporary prayers are recited but the ancient public liturgy and office of the Church, which, by long use are well known, at least as to the substance, by all the faithful; where, in fine, there is no want of interpreters, since the people have the Church offices interpreted into their ordinary prayer-books; and the pastors are commanded to explain to them the mysteries contained in the Mass. Council of Trent, Sess. 22. chap. 8.

Q. But why does the Church celebrate the Mass in Latin, rather than in vulgar language?

A. 1st, Because it is her ancient language, used in all her sacred offices even from the Apostles' days throughout all the western parts of the world: and therefore the Church, which hates novelty, desires to celebrate her liturgy in the same language as the saints have• done for so many ages. 2dly, For a greater uniformity in the public worship; that so a Christian, in whatsoever country he chances to be, may still find the liturgy performed in the same manner, and in the same language to which he is accustomed at home: and the Latin is certainly of all languages the most proper for this, as being the most universally studied and known. 3dly, To avoid the changes to which all vulgar languages, as we find by experience, are daily exposed. For the Church is unwilling to be chopping and changing her liturgy at every turn of language.

Q. Have any other Christians, besides Roman Catholics, ever celebrated their liturgy in a language which the greater part of the people did not understand?

A. Yes: it is the practice of the Greeks, as we learn from Alex. Ross, in his View of the Religions of Europe, p. 481; and Mr. Breerwood in his Inquiries, chap. 2. p. 12. It is the practice of all other sects of Christians in the east and south, viz. of the Armenians, of the Syrians, of the Nestorians, of the Cophts or Egyptians, of the Abassians or Ethiopians, who all use in their liturgies their ancient languages, which have long since ceased to be understood by the people: as we learn from Monsieur Renaudot in his Dissertation upon the Oriental Liturgies; chap. 6. And as for Protestants, we learn from Dr. Heylin's History of the Reformation, p. 128, &c. that in Queen Elizabeth's time, " The Irish parliament passed an act for the uniformity of common prayer; with permission of saying the same in Latin, where the minister had not the knowledge of the English tongue. But for translating it into Irish there was no care taken. The people are required by that statute, under several penalties, to frequent their Churches, and to be present at the reading the English liturgy, which they understood no more than they do the Mass. By which means——we have furnished the Papists with an excellent argument against ourselves, for having the divine service ce e-

brated in such a language as the people do not under-stand." Thus Dr. Heylin.

CHAPTER IX.

Of the Sacrament of Penance : Of Confession, and the Preparation for it : Of Absolution, &c.

Q. WHAT do you mean by a sacrament of penance?

A. An institution of Christ, by which our sins are forgiven ; which we fall into after baptism.

Q. In what does this institution consist ?

A. On the part of the penitent it consists in these three things, viz. contrition, confession, and satisfaction: and on the part of the minister, in the absolution pronounced by the authority of Jesus Christ. So that penance is a sacrament by which the faithful that have fallen into sins, confessing the same with a true repentance, and a sincere purpose of making satisfaction to God, are absolved from their sins by the ministers of God.

Q. How do you prove that the ministers of God have any such power as to absolve sinners from their sins ?

A. I prove it from St. John xx. 22, 23, where Christ said to his ministers, 'Receive ye the Holy Ghost; whose soever sins ye forgive, they are forgiven unto them, and whose soever sins ye retain, they are retained.' And St. Matt. xviii. 18. 'Verily I say unto you, whatsoever ye shall bind on earth shall be bound in heaven, and whatsoever ye shall loose on earth shall be loosed in heaven.'

Q. But was this power given to any besides the Apostles ?

A. It was certainly given to them and to their successors till the end of the world; no less than the commission of preaching, baptizing, &c. which, though addressed to the Apostles, was certainly designed to continue with their successors, the pastors of the Church for ever, according to that of Christ, Matt. xxviii 20.

'Lo 1 am with you always even till the end of the world.' And so the Protestant Church understands these texts, in the order for the visitation of the sick, in the common prayer book, where she prescribes a form of absolution the same in substance as that used in the Catholic Church, viz.

'Our Lord Jesus Christ, who hath left power to his Church to absolve all sinners who truly repent and believe in him, of his great mercy forgive thee thine offences: and by his authority committed to me, I absolve thee from all thy sins, in the name of the Father, and of the Son, and of he Holy Ghost. Amen.'

Q. Is it then your doctrine that any man can forgive sins?

A. We do not believe that any man can forgive sins by his own power, as no man by his own power can raise the dead to life: because both the one and the other equally belong to the power of God. But as God has sometimes made men his instruments in raising the dead to life; so we believe that he has been pleased to appoint that his ministers should in virtue of his commission, as his instruments, and by his power absolve repenting sinners: and as this is evident from the texts above quoted, it must be false zeal, under pretext of maintaining the honour of God, to contradict this commission which he has so evidently given to his Church.

Q. But will not sinners thus be encouraged to go on in their evil ways, upon the confidence of being absolved by the pastors of the Church, whenever they please, from their sins?

A. The pastors of the Church have no power to absolve any one without a sincere repentance, and a firm purpose of a new life; and therefore, the Catholic doctrine of absolution can be no encouragement to any man to go on in his sins.

Q. What then is required on the part of the sinner in order to obtain forgiveness of his sins in the sacrament of penance?

A. Three things, viz. contrition, confession, and satisfaction. By contrition we mean, 'a hearty sorrow for having offended so good a God, with a firm purpose of amendment.' By confession we mean, 'a full and sincere accusation made to God's minister, of all mortal sins, which after a diligent examination of conscience, a person can call to his remembrance.' By satisfaction, we mean, 'a faithful performance of the penance enjoined by the priest.'

Q. What preparation then do you recommend before confession, in order to discharge one's self well of this important duty?

A. A person that is preparing himself for confession has four things to do before he goes to confession. 1st,. He must pray earnestly to God for his divine grace, that he may be enabled to make a true and good confession. 2dly, He must carefully examine his own conscience, in order to find out what sins he has committed, and how often. 3dly, He must take due time and pains to beg God's pardon, and to procure a hearty sorrow for his sins. 4thly, He must make firm resolutions with God's grace to avoid the like sins for the future, and to fly the immediate occasions of them.

Q. Why must he begin his preparation by praying earnestly to God for his divine grace?

A. Because a good confession is a work of the utmost importance, and withal a difficult task, by reason of the pride of our hearts, and that fear and shame which is natural to us, and which the Devil, who is a mortal enemy to confession, seeks to improve with all his power. And therefore a Christian, that desires to make a good confession, ought in the first place to address himself to God by fervent prayer for his divine assistance. And the more he finds the enemy busy to instil into him an unhappy fear or shame, the more earnestly must he implore the mercy and grace of God upon this occasion.

Q. In what manner must a person examine his conscience in order to make a good confession?

A. He must use a moral diligence to find out the sins he has committed; which requires more or less time and care, according to the length of time from his last confession, and the greater or less care that he usually takes to the state of his conscience. The common method of examination, is to consider what one has done against any of the commandments of God; what neglects there may have been of Church precepts; how one has discharged one's self of the common duties of a Christian, and of the particular duties of one's respective station of life; how far one has been guilty of any one of the seven sins, which are commonly called capital, because they are the springs or fountains from whence all our sins flow, &c. And for the helping of a person's memory in this regard, the table of sins which is found in the manual, or other prayer-books, may be of no small service.

Q. Is a person to examine himself as to the number of times that he has been guilty of this or that sin?

A. Yes: because he is obliged to confess as near as he can, the number of his sins. But in sins of habit, which have been of long standing and very numerous, it will be enough to examine and confess the length of time that he has been subject to such a sin, and how many times he has fallen into it, in a day, in a week, or month, one time with another.

Q. What method do you prescribe to a person, in order to procure that hearty sorrow for sin, which is the most necessary part of the preparation for confession?

A. The best method to procure it is to beg it heartily of God; for it must be his gift. None but God can give that change of heart, which is so essential to a good confession, and he has been pleased to promise, St. Matt. vii. 7, 'Ask and it shall be given you: seek and ye shall find: knock and it shall be opened unto you.' To this end also, pious meditation and consideration, and devout acts of contrition, which are found in books of devotion, will much contribute, if read leisurely and attentively, so as to sink into the heart. But because many persons content themselves in running over in haste the Prayers before Confession, which they meet with in their books, with little or no change in the heart, which perhaps is grown hard by sinful habits, it is to be feared their performances are too often nothing worth in the sight of God.

Q. What then do you advise in the case of habitual sinners, in order to procure a true change of heart?

A. I advise them to a spiritual retreat for some days, in which being retired as much as possible from the noise of the world, they may think on the great truths of religion, of the end for which they came into this world; of the benefits of God, of the enormity of sin, of the sudden passing away of all that this world admires, of the four last things, of the passion of Christ, &c.; that so the serious considerations of these great truths, joined to retirement and prayer, may make a due impression on their hearts, and effectually convert them to God. Those whose circumstances will not permit them to make a regular retreat, may at least endeavour, during some days, to think as often and as seriously as they can upon the truths above-mentioned; and by frequently and fervently calling upon the Father of mercies, in the midst of all their employments, may hope to procure to themselves the like grace.

Q. What must be the chief motive of a sinner's sorrow and repentance, in order to qualify him for absolution?

A. Divines are not perfectly agreed in the resolution of this query: but all are perfectly agreed in advising every one to aim at the best motive he can; and that the best and safest way is to renounce and detest our sins for the love of God above all things.

Q. What do you mean by the resolution of amendment, which you suppose to be a necessary ingredient in the preparation for confession?

A. I mean a full determination of the soul to fly for the future all wilful sin, and the immediate occasions of it.

Q. What do you mean by the immediate occasions of sin?

A. All such company, places, employment, diversions, books, &c. which are apt to draw a person to mortal sin, either in deed, word, or in thought.

Q. And is a person indispensably obliged to avoid all such immediate occasions of sin?

A. He is obliged to avoid them to the very utmost of his power, according to that gospel rule of parting even with a hand or an eye, that is an occasion of offence to the soul, St. Matt. xviii. 8, 9.

Q. What scripture do you bring to recommend the confession of our sins to God's ministers?

A. 1st, The precept of God in the Old Testament, Numb. v. 6, 7. 'When a man or woman shall commit any sin that men commit, to do a trespass against the Lord, and that person be guilty, then they shall confess their sin which they have done,' &c.' 2dly, The example of the people that hearkened to the preaching of St. John the Baptist, who were baptized by him, 'confessing their sins,' St. Matt. iii. 6. 3dly, The prescription of St. James v. 16. 'Confess your sins one to another;' that is, to the priests, or elders of the Church, whom the Apostle had ordered to be called for, v. 14. 4thly. The practice of the first Christians, Acts xix. 18. 'Many that believed came, and confessed and declared their deeds.'

Q. How do you prove that there is any command of Christ, for the confession of our sins to his ministers?

A. I prove it from the commission which Christ has given to his ministers, St. John xx. 22, 23. 'Receive ye the Holy Ghost; whose soever sins you remit they are remitted unto them, and whose soever sins you retain, they are retained.' And St. Matt. xviii. 18. Verily I say unto you, whatsoever you shall bind on earth, shall be bound in heaven: and whatsoever you shall loose on earth, shall be loosed in heaven.' For it is visible, that this commission of binding or loosing, forgiving or retaining sins, according to the merits of the cause and the disposition of the penitent, cannot be rightly executed without taking cognizance of the state of the soul of him who desires to be absolved from his sins by virtue of this commission; and consequently cannot be rightly executed without confession. So that we conclude with St. Augustine,* that to pre-

* Homil. 49. Inter. 50.

tend it is enough to confess to God alone, is making void the power of the keys given to the Church, St. Matt. xvi. 19; that it is contradicting the gospel, and making void the commission of Christ.

Q. Are Christians then obliged to confess all their sins to the ministers of Christ?

A. They are obliged to confess all such sins as are mortal, or of which they have reason to doubt, lest they may be mortal; but they are not obliged to confess venial sins, because as these do not exclude eternally from the kingdom of heaven, so there is not a strict obligation of having recourse for the remission of them to the keys of the Church.

Q. But by what rule shall a person be able to make a judgment whether his sins be mortal or venial?

A. All those sins are to be esteemed mortal which the word of God represents to us as hateful to God, against which he pronounces a wo, or of which it declares, that such as do those things shall not enter into the kingdom of heaven: of these we have many instances, Rom. i. 29, 30, 31. 1 Cor. vi. 9, 10. Galat. v. 19, 20, 21. Ephes. v. 5. Apocalypse xxi. 8.; and in the Old Testament, Isai. v. Ezek. xviii. &c. But though it be very easy to know that some sins are mortal, and others but venial, yet to pretend to be able always perfectly to distinguish which are mortal and which are not, is above the reach of the most able divines; and therefore a prudent Christian will not easily pass over sins in confession, under the pretence of their being venial, unless he be certain of it. And this caution is more particularly necessary in certain cases, where persons being ashamed to confess their sins, are willing to persuade themselves they are but venial; for in such cases it is much to be feared, lest their self-love should bias their judgment.

Q. Is it a great crime to conceal through shame or fear, any mortal sin in confession?

A. Yes, it is a great crime; because it is telling a lie to the Holy Ghost; for which kind of sin Ananias and Saphira were struck dead, by a just judgment of God, Acts v. It is acting deceitfully with God, and that in a matter of the utmost consequence. It is a sacrilege, because it is an abuse of the sacrament of penance, and is generally followed by another greater sacrilege, in receiving unworthily the body and blood of Christ. And what is still more dreadful, such sinners seldom stop at the first bad confession and communion, but usually go on for a long time in these sins, and very often die in them. But it is not only a great crime to conceal one's sins in confession, it is a great folly and madness too; because, such offenders, if they have not renounced their faith, know very well that these sins must be confessed, or that they must burn for them; and they cannot be ignorant, that these bad confessions do but increase their burden, by adding to it the dreadful guilt of repeated sacrileges which they will have far more difficulty of confessing, than these very sins of which they are now so much ashamed.

Q. Have you any instances in Church History, of remarkable judgments of God, upon those that have presumed to approach to the blessed sacrament, without making a sincere confession of their sins?

A. Yes, we have several recorded by St. Cyprian, (L. de Lapsis,) and other grave authors; but the most common, and indeed the most dreadful punishments of these sins, is a blindness and hardness of heart, which God justly permits such sinners to fall into, and which is the broad road to final inpenitence.

Q. Have you any thing to offer by way of encouragement to sinners to confess their sins sincerely?

A. Yes, 1st, The great benefit that their souls will reap in the remission of their sins, promised by Christ, St. Matt. xviii. 18. and St. John xx. 22, 23. and the other advantages which an humble confession of sins brings along with it; such as a present comfort and ease of conscience, a remedy against future sins, directions and prescriptions from the minister of God, for the curing the spiritual maladies of the soul, &c. 2dly, That by this short passing confusion, which will last but a moment, they will escape the dreadful shame of having their sins written on their foreheads at the last day to their eternal confusion. 3dly, That the greater

11 *

their sins have been, the greater will be the joy, as of the whole court of heaven, so of their confessor here upon earth, to see their sincere conversion to God testified by the humble confession of their shameful sins : Upon which account, so far from thinking worse of them, he will conceive far greater hopes of their future progress, and a more tender affection for them. 4thly, That by the law of God and his Church, whatever is declared in confession can never be discovered directly or indirectly to any one, upon any account whatsoever, but remains an eternal secret betwixt God and the penitent soul ; of which the confessor cannot, even to save his own life, make any use at all to the penitent's discredit, disadvantage or any other grievance whatsoever. *Vide Decretum Innocentii* XI. *die* 18 *Novemb. Anno* 1682.

Q. But suppose it has been the sinner's misfortune to have made a bad confession, or perhaps a great many bad confessions, what must he do to repair this fault, and to reinstate himself in God's grace?

A. He must apply himself to God by hearty prayers for his grace and mercy ; and so prepare himself to make a good general confession of all his sins, at least from the time of his going astray : Because all the confessions that he has made since he began to conceal his sins were all sacrilegious, and consequently null and invalid; and therefore must be all repeated again.

Q. But is he obliged in this case to confess again those sins which he has confessed before?

A. He is, because the concealing of any one mortal sin in confession makes the whole confession nothing worth ; and all the following confessions, until this fault is repaired, are all null; and therefore they must all be made again. But if it be to the same confessor who has a confused remembrance of the sins before confessed, it may suffice for the penitent to accuse himself in general terms of all that has been confessed before ; and then to specify in particular the sins that have been omitted, together with the number of the bad confessions and communions that have been made by him.

Q. Are there any other cases in which the confession is nothing worth, and consequently must be made again, besides this case of concealing mortal sin?

A. Yes, if the penitent has taken no care to examine his conscience, or to procure the necessary sorrow for his sins, or a true purpose of amendment, his confession is good for nothing, and must be repeated; and also, if the priest to whom he has made this confession has not had the necessary faculties and approbation.

Q. What if the penitent, through forgetfulness, pass over some mortal sin in confession?

A. This omission, provided there was no considerable negligence which gave occasion to it, does not make the confession invalid. But then the sin that has been thus omitted must be confessed afterwards, when the penitent remembers it: and if he remembers it before communion, it ought to be confessed before he goes to communion; if he remembers it not till after communion, he must confess it in the next confession.

Q. Is a person obliged to confess the circumstances of his sins?

A. He is obliged to confess such circumstances as alter the kind or nature of the sin; and also, such as notably aggravate the guilt; but in modest and decent terms, particularly in confessing the circumstances of sins against chastity.

Q. Would it be a crime to neglect the penance or satisfaction enjoined by the priest?

A. Yes, it would; the more because we ought to regard the penance enjoined as an exchange which God makes of the eternal punishments, which we have deserved by sin, into these small penitential works.

Q. Has the Church of God always enjoined penances to sinners?

A. Yes, she has, and in the primitive times much more severe than now-a-days, when three, seven, or ten years of penance used to be imposed for sins of impurity, perjury, &c.

Q. Does the Church at present approve of giving ordinarily very slight penances for very great sins?

A. So far from it, that the Council of Trent, Sess.

14, chap. 8, gives us to understand, that a confessor, by such excessive indulgence, is in danger of drawing upon his own head the guilt of his penitent's sins, and declares that a priest ought to enjoin a suitable penance according to the quality of the crime and the penitent's ability.

Q. Ought the penitent to content himself with performing the penance enjoined, so as to take no further thought about making satisfaction to God for his sins?

A. No, by no means; for it is to be feared, that the penance enjoined is seldom sufficient to take off all the punishment due to God's justice upon account of her sins; and it is certain, that the more a penitent is touched with a hearty sorrow for his offences against God, the more he will be desirous of making satisfaction, and revenging upon himself by penitential severities the injury done to God by his sins. Hence the life of a good Christian ought to be a perpetual penance.

Q. What then do you recommend to a penitent, besides the performance of his penance, in order to cancel the punishment due to his sins, and to make satisfaction to the divine Justice?

A. I recommend to him, 1st, Ever to maintain in himself a penitential spirit, and in that spirit to perform all his prayers; daily offering up to God the sacrifice of a contrite and humble heart. 2dly, I recommend to him almsdeeds, both corporal and spiritual, according to his ability. 3dly, Fasting, and other mortifications; especially the retrenching all superfluities in eating, drinking, and sleeping; all unnecessary diversions, and much more all such as are dangerous; all idle curiosity, vanity, &c. 4thly, I recommend to him to have recourse to indulgences, and to perform with religious exactitude the conditions thereunto required. 5thly, In fine, I recommend to him to take from the hands of God, in part of penance for his sins, all sicknesses, pains, labors, and all other crosses whatsoever, and daily to offer them up to God to be united to and sanctified by the sufferings and death of Jesus Christ.

Q. What is the form and manner of confession?

A. The penitent, having duly prepared himself by

prayer, by a serious examination of his conscience, and a hearty contrition for his sins, kneels down at the confession chair on one side of the priest, and making the sign of the cross upon himself, asks the priest's blessing, saying, 'Pray, Father, give me your blessing.' Then the priest blesses him in the following words: 'The Lord be in thy heart, and in thy lips, that thou mayest truly and humbly confess all thy sins, in the name of the Father, and of the Son, and of the Holy Ghost, Amen.' After which the penitent says the Confiteor, in Latin, or in English, as far as *Meâ Culpâ; &c.* and then accuses himself of all his sins, as to the kind, number, and aggravating circumstances; and concludes with this or the like form: 'Of these, and all other sins of my whole life, I humbly accuse myself; I am heartily sorry for them, I beg pardon of God, and penance and absolution of you my ghostly father.' And so he finishes the Confiteor, 'Therefore, I beseech thee,' &c. And then attends to the instructions given by the priest, and humbly accepts the penance enjoined.

Q. What is the form of absolution?

A. 1st, The priest says, 'May the Almighty God nave mercy on thee, and forgive thee thy sins, and bring thee to life everlasting, Amen.'

Then stretching forth his right hand towards the penitent, he says, 'May the Almighty and merciful Lord give thee pardon, absolution, and remission of thy sins, Amen.'

'Our Lord Jesus Christ absolve thee, and I, by his authority, absolve thee, in the first place, from every bond of excommunication or interdict, as far as I have power and thou standest in need: in the next place, I absolve thee from all thy sins, in the name of the Father, ✠ and of the Son, and of the Holy Ghost, Amen.'

'May the passion of our Lord Jesus Christ, the merits of the blessed Virgin Mary, and of all the saints, and whatsoever good thou shalt do, or whatsoever evil thou shalt suffer, be to thee unto the remission of thy sins, the increase of grace, and the recompense of everlasting life, Amen.

Q. In what case is a confessor to defer or deny absolution?

A. The rule of the Church is to defer absolution, excepting the case of necessity, to those of whose disposition the confessor has just cause to doubt, and to deny absolution to those who are certainly indisposed for it; which is the case of all such as refuse to forgive their enemies, or to restore ill-gotten goods, or to forsake the habits or immediate occasions of sin, or, in a word, to comply with any part of their duty, to which they are obliged under mortal sin. *Rit. Rom. de Sacramento Pœnitentiæ.*

Q. How do you prove, from all that has been said, that penance, i. e. the confession and absolution of sinners is properly a sacrament?

A. Because it is an outward sign of inward grace, ordained by Jesus Christ; which is the very notion and definition of a sacrament: the outward sign is found in the sinner's confession, and the form of absolution pronounced by the priest; the inward grace is the remission of sins promised by Jesus Christ, St. John xx. 22, 23, and the ordinance of Christ is gathered from the same place, and from St. Matt. xviii. 18.

CHAPTER X.

Of Indulgences and Jubilees.

Q. WHAT do you mean by indulgences?

A. There is not any part of the doctrine of the Catholic Church that is more grossly misrepresented by our adversaries than this of indulgences; for the generality of Protestants imagine that an indulgence is a leave to commit sin, or, at least, that it is a pardon for sins to come; whereas, indeed, it is no such thing. There is no such power in heaven or earth that can give leave to commit sin; and consequently there is no giving pardon beforehand for sins to come. All this is far from the belief and practice of the Catholic Church. By an indulgence, therefore, we mean no more than a releasing to true penitents the debt of temporal punishment, which remained due to their sins, after the sins themselves, as to the guilt and eternal punishment, had been already remitted by the sacrament of penance, or by perfect contrition.

Q. Be pleased to explain this a little farther.

A. That you may understand this the better, take notice, that in sin there are two things; there is the guilt of the sin, and there is the debt of the punishment due to God upon account of the sin. Now upon the sinner's repentance and confession, the sin is remitted as to the guilt, and likewise as to the eternal punishment in hell, due to every mortal sin; but the repentance and conversion is seldom so perfect as to release the sinner from all debt of temporal punishment due to God's justice, which the penitent must either discharge by the way of satisfaction and penance; or, if he be deficient therein, he must expect to suffer hereafter, in proportion to this debt which he owes to the divine Majesty. Now an indulgence, when duly obtained, is a release from this debt of temporal punishment.

Q. How do you prove, that after the guilt of sin and the eternal punishment has been remitted, there remains oftentimes a debt of temporal punishment due to the divine Justice?

A. I prove it, 1st, from scripture; where, to omit other instances, we find in the case of king David, 2 Sam. xii. that although upon his repentance the prophet Nathan assured him, v. 13, that the Lord hath put away his sin, yet he denounced unto him many temporal punishments. which should be inflicted by reason of this sin. which accordingly after ensued. See v. 10, 11, 12, 15. 2dly, I prove it from the perpetual practice of the Church of God, of enjoining penances to the repenting sinners, in order to cancel this punishment due to their sins.

Q. How do you prove that the Church has received

a power from Christ of discharging a penitent sinner from this debt of temporal punishment, which remains due upon account of his sins ?

A. I prove it by that promise of our Lord, made to St. Peter, St. Matt. xvi. 19. 'I will give unto thee the keys of the kingdom of heaven: and whatsoever thou shalt bind on earth shall be bound in heaven: and whatsoever thou shalt loose on earth shall be loosed in heaven.' Which promise, made without any exception, reservation, or limitation, must needs imply a power of loosing or releasing all such bonds as might otherwise hinder or retard a Christian soul from entering heaven.

Q. Did the primitive Church ever practise any thing of this nature ?

A. Yes, very frequently, in discharging penitents, when there appeared just cause for it, from a great part of the penance due to their sins, as may be seen in Tertullian, St. Cyprian, and other ancient monuments: And of this nature was what St. Paul himself practised in forgiving, as he says, 2 Cor. ii. 10, in the person of Christ, that is, by the power and authority received from him, the incestuous Corinthian, without waiting his going through a longer course of penance.

Q. But were these primitive indulgences understood to release the punishment due to sin in the sight of God, or only that which was enjoined in the Church in her penitential canons ?

A. Both one and the other, as often as they were granted upon a just cause: according to what our Lord had promised, St. Matt. xviii. 18. 'Verily I say unto you, whatsoever you shall bind on earth shall be bound in heaven, and whatsoever you shall loose on earth shall be loosed in heaven.'

Q. What conditions are necessary for the validity of an indulgence ?

A. 1st, On the part of him that grants the indulgence, besides sufficient authority, it is necessary that there be a just cause or motive for the grant; for, according to the common doctrine of the best divines, indulgences, granted without cause, will not be ratified by Almighty God. 2dly, On the part of him that is to obtain the indulgence, it is requisite that he duly perform the conditions prescribed, such as going to confession and communion, fasting, alms, prayers, &c. and that he be in the state of grace; for it is in vain to expect the remission of the punishment due to sin, whilst a person continues in the guilt of mortal sin.

Q. Does the indulgence so far remit all temporal punishment as to free a penitent from all obligation of doing penance for his sins?

A. No; for the obligation of doing penance for sin and leading a penitential life, is an indispensable duty. Hence the Church usually enjoins penitential works, in order for the obtaining of indulgences. And the opinion of the learned Cardinal Cajeran, and others, is highly probable that one condition for attaining to the benefit of an indulgence, in the release of the punishment of the next life, is a disposition to do penance in this life; for the treasure of the Church, out of which indulgences are granted, is intended by our great master for the relief of the indigent; yet not so as to encourage the lazy, who refuse to labour at all for themselves.

Q. Are you then of opinion, that a Christian receives no farther benefit by an indulgence, than he would do by the penitential works which he performs for the obtaining of that indulgence?

A. I am far from being of that opinion: for, according to that way of thinking, no benefit would be reaped from the indulgence, but only from the works, performed for the obtaining of it: whereas, the Church of God has declared, in the Council of Trent, that 'Indulgences are very wholesome to Christian people.' Sess. 25. But what many divines maintain is that, regularly speaking, there is required, though not an equality, ye some proportion at least between the works to be done for the obtaining of an indulgence, and the indulgence itself: and this I believe to be true. See Soto in 4tum. Dist. 21. Q. 2, Art. 2. and Sylvius in Sup. Q. 25, Art. 2. Quæsito 2. Conclus. 5.

Q. What is meant by the treasure of the Church, out of which indulgences are said to be granted?

A. The treasure of the Church, according to divines, are the merits and satisfaction of Christ and his saints, out of which the Church, when she grants an indulgence to her children, offers to God an equivalent for the punishment which was due to the divine Justice. For the merits and satisfaction of Christ are of infinite value, and never to be exhausted, and the source of all our good; and the merits and satisfactions of the saints, as they have their value from Christ, and through him are accepted by the Father, so by the communion, which all the members of Christ's mystical body have one with another, are applicable to the faithful upon earth.

Q. What is meant by a plenary indulgence?

A. That which, when duly obtained, releases the whole punishment that remained due upon account of past sins.

Q. What is meant by an indulgence of seven years, or of forty days?

A. By an indulgence of so many years or days is meant the remission of the penance of so many years or days, and consequently of the punishment corresponding to the sins, which, by the canons of the Church, would have required so many years or days of penance, Bellarmin, l. 1. de Indulg. c. 9. And thus, if it be true, that there ever were any grants of indulgence of a thousand years or more, they are to be understood with relation to the punishment corresponding to the sins, which according to the penitential canons would have required a thousand or more years of penance. For since, by these canons, seven or ten years of penance were usually assigned for one mortal sin of lust, perjury, &c. it follows, that habitual sinners, according to the rigour of the canons, must have been liable to great numbers of years of penance, and perhaps some thousands of years. And though they could not be expected to live so long as to fulfil this penance; yet, as by their sins, they had incurred a debt of punishment proportionable to so long a time of penance, these indulgences, of so many years, if ever granted, which some call in question) were designed to release them from the debt.

Q. What is the meaning of indulgences for the dead?

A. They are not granted by way of absolution, since the pastors of the Church have not that jurisdiction over the dead: but they are only available to the faithful departed, by way of suffrage, or spiritual succour applied to their souls out of the treasure of the Church.

Q. What is the meaning of a jubilee?

A. A jubilee is so called from the resemblance it bears with the jubilee-year in the old law, Levit. xxv. and xxvii. (which was a year of remission, in which bondsmen were restored to liberty, and every one returned to his possessions) is a plenary indulgence granted every twenty-fifth year, as also upon other extraordinary occasions, to such as being truly penitent, shall worthily receive the blessed sacrament, and perform the other conditions of fasting, alms and prayer usually prescribed at such times.

Q. What then is the difference betwixt a jubilee and any other plenary indulgence?

A. A jubilee is more solemn, and accompanied with certain privileges, not usually granted upon other occasions, with regard to the being absolved by any approved confessor from all excommunications and other reserved cases, and having vows exchanged into the performance of other works of piety. To which we may add, that as a jubilee is extended to the whole Church, which at that time joins as it were in a body in offering a holy violence to heaven by prayers and penitential works; and as the cause for granting an indulgence at such times is usually more evident, and more or greater works of piety are prescribed for the obtaining it, the indulgence of consequence is likely to be much more certain and secure.

Q. What are the fruits which usually are seen amongst Catholics at the time of a jubilee?

A. As at that time the Church most pressingly invites all sinners to return to God with their whole hearts, and encourages them by setting open her

spiritual treasure in their favour, so the most usua,
effects of a jubilee are the conversions of great numbers
of sinners, and the multiplying of all sorts of good
works amongst the faithful.   So far it is from being
true, that indulgences are an encouragement to sin,
or an occasion of a neglect of good works as our
adversaries unjustly object.

CHAPTER XI.

Of the Sacrament of Extreme Unction.

Q. WHAT do you mean by extreme unction ?

A. I mean the anointing of the sick, prescribed St.
James v. 14, 15. 'Is any one sick among you, let him
call for the priests of the Church, and let them pray
over him, anointing him with oil in the name of the
Lord: and the prayer of faith shall save the sick man,
and the Lord shall ease him; and if he be in sins, they
shall be forgiven him.'

Q. How do you prove that this anointing of the sick
is a sacrament ?

A. Because it is the outward sign of an inward
grace, or a divine ordinance, to which is annexed a
promise of grace in God's holy word.   The anointing,
together with the prayers that accompany it, are the
outward sign; the ordinance of God is found in the
words of St. James above quoted: the inward grace is
promised in the same place, 'The prayer of faith shall
save the sick man—and if he be in sins, they shall be
forgiven him.'

Q. How do you prove that this ordinance was designed for all ages, and not only for the time of the
apostles ?

A. Because the words of the scripture in which this
ordinance is contained are no way limited to the
Apostles' time, no more than the words of the ordinance
of baptism, St. Matt. xxviii. and because the Church of

God, the best interpreter of his words and ordinances, nas practised it in all ages.

Q. To what kind of people is the sacrament of ex treme unction to be administered?

A. To those who, after having come to the use of reason, are in danger of death by sickness; but not to children under the age of reason, nor persons sentenced to death, &c.

Q. Can the same person receive the sacrament of extreme unction more than once?

A. Yes, but not in the same illness, except it should be of long continuance, and that the state of the sick man should be changed so as to recover out of the danger, and then fall into the like case again.

Q. What are the effects and fruits of the sacrament of extreme unction?

A. 1st, It remits sins, at least such as are venial, for mortal or deadly sins must be remitted, before receiving extreme unction, by the sacrament of penance and confession. 2dly, It heals the soul of her infirmity and weakness, and a certain propension to sin contracted by former sins, which are apt to remain in the soul, as the unhappy relics of sin; and it helps to remove something of the debt of punishment due to past sins. 3dly, It imparts strength to the soul, to bear more easily the illness of the body, and arms her against the attempts of her spiritual enemies. 4thly, If it be expedient for the good of the soul, it often restores the health of the body.

Q. What kind of oil is that which is made use of in the sacrament of extreme unction?

A. The oil of olives, solemnly blessed by the bishop every year on Maunday-Thursday.

Q. What is the form and manner of administering this sacrament?

A. 1st, The priest, having instructed and disposed the sick person to this sacrament, recites, if the time permits, certain prayers prescribed in the Ritual, to beg God's blessing upon the sick, and that his holy angels may defend them, that dwell in that habitation, from all evil. 2dly. Is said the Confiteor, or general form

12 *

of confession and absolution ; and the priest exhorts all present to join in prayer for the person that is sick and if opportunity permit, according to the quality of number of persons there present, to recite the seven penitential Psalms with the Litanies, or other prayers upon this occasion. 3dly, The priest, making three times the sign of the cross upon the sick person, at the name of the blessed Trinity, says, ' In the name of the Father, and of the Son, and of the Holy Ghost, may all power of the devil be extinguished in thee, by the laying on of our hands, and the invocation of all the holy angels, archangels, patriarchs, prophets, Apostles, martyrs, confessors, virgins, and all the saints. Amen.'   4thly, Dipping his thumb in the holy oil, he anoints the sick person in the form of the cross, upon the eyes, ears, nose, mouth, hands and feet; at each anointing making use of this form of prayer: ' Through this holy unction, and his own most tender mercy, may the Lord pardon thee whatever sins thou hast committed by thy sight. Amen.' And so of the hearing, and the rest, adapting the form to the several senses.   5thly After this the priest goes on ; ' Lord have mercy on us Christ have mercy on us.   Lord have mercy on us Our Father, &c.   And lead us not into temptation. R. But deliver us from evil.   V. Save thy servant. R. Trusting in thee, O my God.   V. Send him O Lord, help from thy sanctuary.   R. And do thou defend him from Sion.   V. Be to him, O Lord, a tower of strength.   R. From the face of the enemy.   V Let not the enemy have any power over him.   R. Nor the Son of iniquity be able to hurt him.   V. Lord, hear my prayer.   R. And let my cry come unto thee. V. The Lord be with you.   R. And with thy spirit

Let us pray.

O Lord God, who hast said by thy Apostle James. Is any one sick among you? Let him call for the priests of the Church, and let them pray over him, anointing him with oil in the name of the Lord; and the prayer of faith shall save the sick, and the Lord shall ease him; and if he be in sins they shall be remitted to him; heal, we beseech thee, O our Redeemer by the grace of the Holy Ghost, the maladies of this sick man, cure his wounds, and forgive him his sins, and expel from him all pains of mind and body, and mercifully restore unto him perfect health, both as to the interior and exterior, that being recovered by thy mercy, he may return to his former duties. Who with the Father and the Holy Ghost, livest and reignest one God, for ever and ever. Amen.

Let us pray.

Look down, we beseech thee, O Lord, on thy servant N. fainting under the infirmity of his body, and refresh a soul which thou hast created: that he, being improved by thy chastisements may be saved by thy medicine. Through Christ our Lord. Amen.

Let us pray.

O Holy Lord, Almighty Father, everlasting God, who, by imparting the grace of thy benediction to sick bodies, preservest, according to the multitude of thy mercies, the work of thy hands; favourably attend to the invocation of thy name, and deliver thy servant from his illness, and restoring him to health, raise him up by thy right hand, and strengthen him by thy virtue, defend him by thy power, and restore him with all desired prosperity to thy holy Church. Through Christ our Lord. Amen.

As to what belongs to the order of the visitation of the sick, and the prayers and devotions proper upon that occasion, as also the manner of assisting those that are dying, consult the Roman Ritual; out of which I shall present you with the following form of the recommendation of a departing soul.

CHAPTER XII.

The Order of the Recommendation of a Soul that is just departing.

Q. WHAT is the form or order of the recommenda
tion of a soul to God in its last passage?

A. 1st, There is a short Litany recited, adapted to
that occasion; then the following prayers.

Go forth, O Christian soul, from this world, in the
name of God the Father Almighty, who created thee;
in the name of Jesus Christ the Son of the living God,
who suffered for thee; in the name of the Holy Ghost,
who sanctified thee; in the name of the angels and the
archangels; in the name of the thrones and domina-
tions; in the name of the principalities and powers;
in the name of the cherubims and seraphims; in the
name of the patriarchs and prophets; in the name of
the holy apostles and evangelists; in the name of the
holy martyrs and confessors; in the name of the holy
monks and hermits; in the name of the holy virgins,
and of all the saints of God: Let thy place be this
day in peace, and thy abode in the holy Sion
Through Christ our Lord.   Amen.

O God most merciful, O God most clement, O God,
who, according to the multitude of thy tender mercies,
blottest out the sins of the penitent, and graciously
remittest the guilt of their past offences; mercifully
regard this thy servant N. and vouchsafe to hear him,
who with the whole confession of his heart begs for
the remission of all his sins.   Renew, O most merciful
Father, whatever has been corrupted in him through
human frailty, or violated through the deceit of the
enemy; and associate him as a member of redemption
to the unity of the body of the Church.   Have compassion, O Lord, on his sighs; have compassion on his
tears, and admit him, who has no hope but in thy mercy,
to the sacrament of thy reconciliation.   Through
Christ our Lord.   Amen.

I recommend thee, dear brother, to the Almighty God, and commit thee to his care, whose creature thou art; that when thou shalt have paid the debt of all mankind by death, thou mayest return to thy Maker, who formed thee of the slime of the earth. When thy soul therefore shall depart from thy body, let the resplendent multitude of the angels meet thee: let the triumphant army of the martyrs, clad in their white robes, conduct thee: let the glorious company of illustrious confessors encompass thee: let the choir of joyful virgins receive thee: and mayest thou meet with a blessed repose in the bosom of the patriarchs: Let Christ Jesus appear to thee with a mild and cheerful countenance, and order thee a place amongst those that are to stand before him for ever: mayest thou never know the horror of darkness, the gnashing in flames or racking torments. May the most wicked enemy, with all his evil spirits, be forced to give way: may he tremble at thy approach in the company of angels, and fly away into the vast chaos of eternal night. Let God arise, and his enemies be dispersed: and let them that hate him fly before his face: let them, like smoke, come to nothing, and as wax that melts before the fire, so let sinners perish in the sight of God, but may the just feast and rejoice in his sight. Let then all the legions of hell be confounded and put to shame, and may none of the ministers of satan dare to stop thee in thy way. May Christ deliver thee from torments, who was crucified for thee. May Christ deliver thee from eternal death, who vouchsafed to die for thee. May Christ the Son of God place thee in the delightful garden of his Paradise, and may he, the true Shepherd, number thee amongst his sheep. May he absolve thee from all thy sins, and place thee at his right hand in the lot of his elect. Mayest thou see thy Redeemer face to face, and standing always in his presence, behold with joyful eyes the most clear truth. Mayest thou be placed amongst the companies of the blessed, and enjoy the sweetness of the contemplation of thy God, for ever. Amen.

Receive thy servant, O Lord, into the place of salvation, which he hopes for from thy mercy. R. Amen.

Deliver, O Lord, the soul of thy servant from all the perils of hell, from pains and all tribulations. Amen.

Deliver, O Lord, the soul of thy servant, as thou deliveredest Enoch and Elias from the common death of the world. R. Amen.

Deliver, O Lord, the soul of thy servant, as thou deliveredest Noah from the flood. R. Amen.

Deliver, O Lord, the soul of thy servant as thou deliveredest Abraham from Ur of the Chaldeans. R Amen.

Deliver, O Lord, the soul of thy servant, as thou deliveredest Job from his sufferings. R. Amen.

Deliver, O Lord, the soul of thy servant, as thou deliveredest Isaac from being sacrificed by the hand of his father Abraham. R. Amen.

Deliver, O Lord, the soul of thy servant, as thou deliveredst Lot from Sodom and the flames of fire. R. Amen.

Deliver, O Lord, the soul of thy servant, as thou deliveredest Moses from the hands of Pharaoh king of Egypt. R. Amen.

Deliver, O Lord, the soul of thy servant, as thou deliveredest Daniel from the lions' den. R. Amen.

Deliver, O Lord, the soul of thy servant, as thou deliveredest the three children from the fiery furnace, and from the hands of a wicked king. R. Amen.

Deliver, O Lord, the soul of thy servant, as thou deliveredest Susannah from her false accusers. R. Amen.

Deliver, O Lord, the soul of thy servant, as thou deliveredest David from the hands of king Saul and from the hands of Goliah. R. Amen.

Deliver, O Lord, the soul of thy servant, as thou deliveredest Peter and Paul out of prison. R. Amen.

And as thou deliveredest the most blessed St. Thecla, virgin and martyr, from three most dreadful torments, so vouchsafe to deliver the soul of this thy servant, and make it rejoice with thee in the joys of heaven. R. Amen.

We commend to thee, O Lord, the soul of thy servant N And we beseech thee, O Lord Jesus Christ, the Saviour of the world, that thou wouldst not refuse to admit into the bosom of thy patriarchs. a soul for which, in thy mercy, thou wast pleased to come down upon earth. Own him for thy creature, not made by any strange gods, but by thee the only living and true God; for there is no other God but thee, and none that can equal thy works. Let his soul rejoice in thy presence, and remember not his former iniquities and excesses, the unhappy effects of passion or evil concupiscence, for although he has sinned he has not renounced the Father, or the Son, or the Holy Ghost; but believed, and had a zeal for God, and faithfully worshipped him who made all things.

Remember not, O Lord, we beseech thee, the sins of his youth, and his ignorance ; but according to thy great mercy, be mindful of him in thy heavenly glory. May the heavens be opened to him, and may the angels rejoice with him. Receive, O Lord, thy servant into thy kingdom. Let St. Michael the archangel of God, conduct him, who is chief of the heavenly host. Let the holy angels of God come to meet him, and carry him to the city of the heavenly Jerusalem. May St. Peter the Apostle receive him, to whom God has given the keys of the kingdom of heaven. May St. Paul the Apostle assist him, who was a vessel of election. May St. John the chosen Apostle of God intercede for him, to whom were revealed the secrets of heaven. May all the holy Apostles pray for him, to whom our Lord gave the power of binding and loosing. May all the saints and elect of God intercede for him, who in this world had suffered torments for the name of Christ ; that he, being delivered from the bonds of the flesh, may deserve to be admitted into the glory of the kingdom of heaven: through the merits of our Lord Jesus Christ, who with the Father and the Holy Ghost liveth and reigneth for ever and ever. Amen.

After which, if the sick person still continues to labour in his agony, it may be proper, as the Ritual prescribes, to continue reciting other Psalms and prayers adapted to those circumstances.

Q. What is the meaning of the lighting of a blessed candle, and keeping it burning during a person's agony?

A. This light represents the light of faith in which a Christian dies, and the light of glory which he looks for. Besides, these candles are blessed by the Church, with a solemn prayer to God, to chase away the devils from those places where they shall be lighted.

Q. What is the form of blessing candles?

A. The Ritual prescribes the following prayer:

V. Our help is in the name of the Lord.
R. Who made heaven and earth.

Let us pray.

O Lord Jesus Christ, Son of the living God, bless ✝ by our prayers these candles; pour forth upon them by the virtue of the holy ✝ cross thy heavenly benediction, who hast given them to mankind to chase away darkness; and may they receive such a blessing, by the sign of the holy ✝ cross, that in what place soever they shall be lighted or set up, the rulers of darkness, with all their ministers, may depart, and trembling fly away from those dwellings; nor presume any more to disturb or molest those that serve thee the Almighty God, who livest and reignest for ever and ever Amen.

Q. What is the meaning of tolling the passing bell when a person is expiring?

A. To admonish the faithful to pray for him, that God may grant him a happy passage.

CHAPTER XIII.

Of the Office for the Burial of the Dead.

Q. WHAT is the manner and order of burying the dead in the Catholic Church?

A. The pastor or parish priest, accompanied by his clerics, goes to the house of the deceased, and having sprinkled the body or coffin with the Holy water, recites the Anthem, ‘If thou observe iniquities, O Lord, O Lord who shall sustain it;’ with the 129th Psalm. *De profundis,* ‘From the depth, I have cried,’ &c. in the end of which he says, ‘Eternal rest give to him, O Lord.’ R. ‘And let perpetual light shine upon him.’ Then he repeats the Anthem, ‘If thou shalt observe iniquities,’ &c.

After this, the body is carried to the Church, the clergy going before, two and two, after the manner of a procession, and singing the 50th Psalm, ‘*Miserere,*’ Have mercy on me, O God, according to thy great mercy,’ &c. and the people following the corpse, and praying in silence for the deceased. When they are come to the Church, the corpse is set down in the middle of the Church, with the feet towards the altar (except the deceased was a priest, in which case the head is to be towards the altar) and wax tapers are lighted and set up round the coffin. Then, if time and opportunity permit, is recited the Dirge, that is, the office of the matins and lauds for the dead, followed by a solemn Mass for the soul of the deceased, according to the most ancient custom of the universal Church.

The Dirge and Mass being finished, the priest standing at the head of the deceased, begins the office of the burial as follows:

Enter not into judgment with thy servant, O Lord, for no one shall be justified in thy sight, except thou vouchsafe to grant him the remission of all his sins. Let not therefore, we beseech thee, the sentence of thy

13

judgment fall upon him, whom the true supplication of Christian faith recommendeth to thee: but by the assistance of thy grace let him escape the judgment of thy vengeance, who, whilst he was living, was marked with the sign of the holy Trinity: who livest and reignest for ever and ever.   Amen.

Then the Choir sings the following Responsary.

Deliver me, O Lord, from eternal death, at that dreadful day, when the heavens and earth shall be moved, when thou shalt come to judge the world by fire. V. I am struck with trembling, and I fear, against the day of account, and of the wrath to come; when the heavens and earth shall be moved. V That day, a day of wrath, of calamity and misery, a great and most bitter day, when thou shalt come to judge the world by fire. V. Eternal rest give to him, O Lord, and let perpetual light shine upon him. Deliver me, O Lord, &c. *as before, till the Verse,* 'I am struck,' &c.

Lord have mercy on us. Christ have mercy on us Lord have mercy on us. Our Father, &c. (Here the priest puts incense into the thurible, and then going round the coffin, sprinkles with Holy water, and afterwards incenses the body, and then concludes the Lord's Prayer.) V. Lead us not into temptation. R. But deliver us from evil. V. From the gate of hell. R. Deliver his soul, O Lord. V. Let him rest in peace. R. Amen. V. O Lord, hear my prayer R. And let my cry come to thee. V. The Lord be with you. R. And with thy spirit.

Let us pray

O God, to whom it belongs always to show mercy, and to spare, we humbly beseech thee for the soul of thy servant N. which thou hast this day commanded to depart out of this world, that thou wouldst not deliver it up into the hands of the enemy, nor put it out of thy memory for ever, but that thou wouldst order it to be

received by the holy angels, and conducted to Para·
dise, its true country: that since it has believed and
hoped in thee, it may not suffer the pains of hell, but
take possession of everlasting joys, through Christ our
Lord. Amen.

After this, whilst the body is carried towards the
place of its interment, is sung or said he following
Anthem.

May the angels conduct thee into Paradise, may the
martyrs receive thee at thy coming, and bring thee to
the holy city of Jerusalem, may the choir of angels
receive thee, and mayest thou have eternal rest with
Lazarus, who was formerly poor.

When they are come to the grave, if it has not been
blessed before, the priest blesses it by the following
prayer, which is the same that we make use of in this
kingdom, in blessing the mould or earth, which we put
in the coffin with the corpse, in the private burial
office.

O God, by whose tender mercy the souls of the
faithful find rest, vouchsafe to bless this tomb, and
depute thy holy angel to guard it, and absolve from all
the bonds of sin the souls of those whose bodies are
here interred, that with thy saints they may ever
rejoice without end in thee.   Through Christ our Lord.
Amen.

Then the priest sprinkles with Holy water, and
afterwards incenses both the corpse of the deceased
and the grave. Then, whilst the body is put in the
earth, is sung or said the following Anthem, with the
Canticle *Benedictus*, or the song of Zacharias, St.
Luke i. 65, &c.

I am the resurrection and the life, he that believeth
in me, although he be dead, shall live; and every one
that liveth, and believeth in me, shall not die for ever.
St. John xi. 25.

Or else (as it is the custom in many places) when the body is put in the earth, the priest, with the assistants, recites the penitential Psalm, *Miserere.*

Then the priest says, Lord have mercy on us. Christ have mercy on us. Lord have mercy on us. Our Father, &c. (Here he sprinkles the body with Holy water.) V. And lead us not into temptation. R. But deliver us from evil. V. From the gate of hell. R. Deliver his soul, O Lord. V. Let him rest in peace. R. Amen. V. O Lord, hear my prayer. R. And let my cry come unto thee. V. The Lord be with you. R. And with thy spirit.

Let us pray.

Grant, O Lord, this mercy to thy servant deceased, that he (or she) may not receive a return of punishment for his (or her) deeds, who in his (or her) wishes has held fast by thy will; that as here true faith has joined him (or her) to the company of thy faithful, so thy mercy there may associate him (or her) to the choirs of angels. Through Christ our Lord, Amen.

V. Eternal rest give to him, O Lord. R. And let perpetual light shine upon him. V. Let him rest in peace. R. Amen. May his soul, and the souls of all the faithful departed, through the mercy of God, rest in peace.

Then the priest, returning from the grave, recites the Psalm, ' *De profundis,*' with the Anthem, ' If thou shalt observe iniquities, O Lord, O Lord who shall sustain it ?'

———◆———

CHAPTER XIV

Of Prayers for the Dead, and of Purgatory.

Q. WHAT is the meaning of prayers for the dead?

A. Praying for the dead is a practice as ancient as Christianity received by tradition from the Apostles, as appears by the most certain monuments of antiquity and observed by the Synagogue or Church of God in the Old Testament, as appears from 2 Machab. xii. written long before Christ's coming, and followed by the Jews to this day. A practice grounded upon Christian charity, which teaches us to pray for all that are in necessity, and to implore God's mercy for all that are capable of mercy; which we have reason to be convinced is the case of many of our deceased brethren, and therefore we pray for them.

Q. How do you prove that the practice of praying for the dead is as ancient as Christianity?

A. From Tertullian, in his book of the Soldier's Crown, chap. 3, written about a hundred years after the death of the Apostles; where he reckons the obligations for the dead upon their anniversary days amongst the immemorial traditions observed by all Christians: and in his book de Monogamià, chap. 10, where he affirms it to be the duty of a Christian widow to pray for the soul of her husband, and to beg a refreshment for him, and to keep his anniversaries. See St. Cyprian, epist. 66. Arnobius, l. 4. Eusebius, l. 4. de Vità Constantini, c. 71. St. Cyril of Jerusalem, Catech. Mystag. 5. St. Gregory Nazianzen, Orat. 10 &c. Hence, St. John Chrysostom, Hom. 3, upon the epistle to the Philippians, tells us, that it was ordained by the Apostles that the dead should be commemorated in the sacred mysteries; and St. Augustine, serm. 32, 'de Verbis Apost. § 2,' that it was a practice received from the fathers, and observed by the universal Church. And it appears from St. Epiphanius, Hær. 75, that Aerius was ranked amongst the heretics by the Church in the fourth century, for denying that the prayers of the living did the dead any good.

Q. Is it any argument, in favour of prayers for the dead, that it was practised by Judas Machabæus, and by the Jews before the coming of Christ?

A. Yes, a very great argument; 1st, Because this practice is expressly approved in the 12th chapter of the second book of Machabees; which books, by many councils and fathers, are ranked amongst the divine scriptures. 2dly. Because the Jews in those days

13 *

were undoubtedly the people of God. 3dly, Because as Dr. Taylor writes, Lib. of Prophesying, sect 20, numb. 11, p. 265. " We find by the history of the Machabees that the Jews did pray and make offerings for the dead, which also appears by other testimonies, and by their form of prayers still extant, (which they used in the captivity.) Now it is very considerable, that since our blessed Saviour did reprove all the evil doctrines and traditions of the Scribes and Pharisees, and did argue concerning the dead and the resurrection against the Sadducees, yet he spake no word against this public practice, but left it as he found it ; which he who came to declare to us all the will of his Father would not have done, if it had not been innocent, pious, and full of charity."

Q. But what reason is there to believe that our prayers can be of any service to the dead ?

A. The same reason as there is to believe that our prayers are of service to the living ; for whether we consult the scripture, or primitive tradition, with relation to the promises or encouragements given in favour of our prayers, we shall nowhere find the dead excepted from the benefit of them ; and the perpetual practice of the Church of God, which is the best interpreter of the scripture, has, from the very beginning, ever authorized prayers for the dead, as believing such prayers beneficial to them.

Q. But are not they that have past this mortal life arrived to an unchangeable state of happiness or misery, so that they either want not our prayers, or cannot be bettered by them?

A. Some there are, though I fear but few, that have before their death so fully cleared all accounts with the Divine Majesty, and washed away all their stains in the blood of the Lamb, as to go straight to heaven after death ; and such as those stand not in need of our prayers. Others there are, and their numbers are very great, who die in the guilt of deadly sin, and such as these go straight to hell, like the rich glutton in the gospel, St. Luke xvi. and therefore cannot be bettered by our prayers. But, besides these two kinds, there are many Christians, who, when they die, are neither so perfectly pure and clean, as to exempt them from the least spot or stain, nor yet so unhappy as to die under the guilt of unrepented deadly sin. Now such as these the Church believes to be, for a time, in a middle state, which we call purgatory; and these are they who are capable of receiving benefit by our prayers. For though we pray for all that die in the communion of the Church, because we do not certainly know the particular state in which each one dies, yet we are sensible that our prayers are available for those only that are in this middle state.

Q. But what grounds have you to believe that there is any such place as a purgatory, or middle state of souls?

A. We have the strongest grounds imaginable from all kind of arguments, from scripture, from perpetual tradition, from the authority and declaration of the Church of God, and from reason.

Q. What grounds have you for purgatory from scripture?

A. 1st, Because the scripture teaches us in many places, that it is the fixed rule of God's justice, 'to render to every man according to his works.' See Psalm lxii. 12. St. Matt. xvi. 27. Rom. ii. 6. Rev. xxii. 12, &c. So that according to the works which each man has done in the time of his mortal life, and according to the state in which he is found at the moment of his departure out of this life, he shall certainly receive reward or punishment from God. Hence it evidently follows, that as by this rule of God's justice, they that die in great and deadly sins, not cancelled by repentance, will be eternally punished in hell; so by the same rule, they that die in lesser or venial sins (which is certainly the case of a great many) will be punished somewhere for a time, till God's justice be satisfied, and this is what we call purgatory.

2dly, Because the scripture assures us, Rev. xxi. 27, that 'there shall in no wise enter into the heavenly Jerusalem any thing that defileth, or that is defiled.' So that if the soul is found to have the least spot or stain, at the time of her departure out of this life, she cannot in that condition go straight to heaven. Now, how few are there that depart this life perfectly pure from the dregs and stains to which we are ever subject in this state of mortality? and yet God forbid that every little spot or stain should condemn the soul to the everlasting torments of hell. Therefore, there must be a middle place for such souls as die under these lesser stains.

3dly, Because the scripture assures us, St. Matt. xii. 36, that we are to render an account hereafter to the great Judge, even 'for every word' that we have spoken; and, consequently, every idle word, not cancelled here by repentance, is liable to be punished by God's justice hereafter. Now no one can think that God will condemn a soul to hell for every idle word; therefore there must be another place of punishment for those that die guilty of these little transgressions.

4thly, Because St. Paul informs us, 1 Cor. iii. 13, 14, 15, that 'every man's work shall be made manifest,' by a fiery trial; and that they who have built upon the foundation, which is Christ, wood, hay, and stubble, (that is, whose works have been very imperfect and defective, though not to the degree of losing Christ) 'shall suffer loss; but themselves shall be saved, yet so as by fire.' Which place cannot be well explained otherwise than by the fire of purgatory.

5thly, Because our Lord tells us, St. Matt. xii. 32, that 'whosoever speaketh against the Holy Ghost, it shall not be forgiven him, neither in this world, neither in the world to come.' Where our Lord (who could not speak any thing absurd, or out of the way) would never have mentioned 'forgiveness in the world to come,' if sins not forgiven in this world could never be forgiven in the world to come. Now if there may be forgiveness of any sin whatsoever in the world to come, there must be a middle place or purgatory; for no sin can enter heaven to be forgiven there, and in hell there is no forgiveness.

Add to these texts of scripture the prison mentioned, St. Matt. v. 26, out of which a man 'shall not come till be nas paid the uttermost farthing;' and 'the spirits in prison, to which our Saviour is said to have gone to preach, 1 Pet. iii. 18, 19, 20.

Q. What grounds have you for purgatory from perpetual tradition?

A. Because, as we have seen already, the Jewish Church, long before our Saviour's coming, and the Christian Church, from the very beginning, have offered prayers and sacrifice for the repose and relief of the faithful departed, as appears from innumerable testimonies of the fathers, and from the most ancient liturgies of all Christian Churches and nations, Romans, Greeks, Syrians, Armenians, Nestorians, Egyptians, Ethiopians, Indians, Mosarabes, &c. Which consent, so ancient and so universal, of all ages, and of all nations, before protestantism, is a most convincing argument that this practice came by tradition from the Apostles; and consequently that the belief of a purgatory is an apostolic tradition; for what sense could there be in praying for the repose and relief of the souls of the faithful departed, if there were no middle place, but all went straight to heaven or hell?

Q. What grounds have you for the belief of a purgatory from the authority of the Church?

A. Because the Church of Christ has declared that there is a purgatory, as well by condemning of old Aerius for a heretic, for denying that the prayers of the living did the dead any service, as also by the express definitions of her general Councils. Now the Scripture most evidently teaches us, in many places, that we are to hear and obey the Church, and that Christ and the Holy Ghost will be always with the Church to guide her into all truth, and that the gates of hell shall not prevail against her. So that what the Church has thus declared, can be no error, but must absolutely be a most certain truth.

Q. What grounds have you for the belief of a purgatory from reason?

A. Because reason teaches these two things; 1st. That every sin, be it ever so small, is an offence of God, and consequently deserves punishment from the justice of God; and therefore that every person that dies under the guilt of any such offence unrepented, must expect to be punished by the justice of God. 2dly, That there are small sins, in which a person may happen to die, that are so small, either through the levity of the matter, or for want of a full deliberation in the act, as not to deserve everlasting punishments. From whence it plainly follows, that, besides the place of everlasting punishments, which we call hell, there must be also a place of temporal punishment for such as die in those lesser offences, and this we call purgatory.

Q. But does not the blood of Christ sufficiently purify us from all our sins, without any other purgatory?

A. The blood of Christ purifies none that are once come to the use of reason, from any sin without repentance; and therefore such sins as have not been here recalled by repentance, must be punished hereafter, according to their gravity, by the divine Justice, either in hell, if the sins be mortal; or, if venial, in purgatory.

Q. Do you then think, that any repentance can be available after death?

A. No; but God's justice must take place after death, which will render to every man according to his works. So that we do not believe that the repentance of the souls that are in purgatory, or any thing else that they can do, will cancel their sins; but they must suffer for them till God's justice be satisfied.

Q. Are they not then capable of relief in that state?

A. Yes, they are, but not from any thing that they can do for themselves, but from the prayers, alms, and other suffrages offered to God for them by the faithful upon earth, which God in his mercy is pleased to accept of by reason of that communion which we have with them, by being fellow members of the same body of the church, under the same head, which is Christ Jesus.

Q. But what do you say to that text of scripture, Eccles. xi. 3. ' If the tree fall towards the south, or towards the north, in the place where the tree falleth there shall it lie?'

A   I say that it is no way evident that this text has relation to the state of the soul after death ; but if it be so understood as to have relation to the soul, it makes nothing against purgatory, because it only proves what no Catholic denies ; viz. that when once a soul is come to the south, or to the north, that is, to heaven or hell, its state is unchangeable.

Q. But does not the scripture promise rest after death to such ' as die in the Lord,' Rev. xiv. 13 ?

A. Yes, it does, but then we are to understand, that those are said to die in the Lord, who die for the Lord by martyrdom ; or at least those who, at the time of their death, are so happy as to have no debts nor stains to interpose between them and the Lord.   As for others who die but imperfectly in the Lord, they shall rest indeed from the labours of this world ; but as their works that follow them are imperfect, they must expect to ' receive from the Lord according to their works.'

Q. Christ said to the thief upon the cross, St. Luke xxiii. ' this day thou shalt be with me in Paradise ;' what appearance then is there that any one dying in God's grace should go to purgatory ?

A. The case of this penitent thief, to whom Christ was pleased to give a full discharge at once of all his sins, was extraordinary, as his faith and confession was extraordinary ; and therefore to make a general rule from this particular instance is a bad way of arguing ; the more, because we have reason to be convinced, that not one in a thousand dies so perfectly penitent as to be perfectly purified before death from all the dregs of sin, which was the particular grace granted to this penitent thief.

If you ask me, what is meant by Paradise in that text, and how the penitent thief could be with Christ that day in Paradise, before our Lord had taken possession of heaven for himself and us, by his resurrection and ascension ? I answer, that our Lord descending after death into limbo, to the holy fathers, made that place a Paradise, by manifesting his glory to those happy souls : and this was the Paradise into which he introduced the penitent thief immediately after his death.

CHAPTER XV.

Of the Sacrament of Holy Orders.

Q. WHAT do you mean by the sacrament of holy Orders?

A. A sacrament by which the ministers of Christ are consecrated to their sacred functions, and receive grace to discharge them well.

Q. How do you prove that holy Orders are a sacrament?

A. Because they are a visible sign of an invisible grace, and that by divine institution, or by the ordinance of Christ, which alone can annex the gift of grace to any outward rite or ceremony. The outward and visible sign is found in the imposition or laying of the bishop's hands and prayer: after which sort we find the seven deacons ordained, Acts vi. 6, and St. Paul, and St. Barnabas, Acts xiii. 3. The invisible grace conferred by this imposition of hands, is attested, 2 Tim. i. 6. 'Stir up the grace of God, which is in thee by the imposition of hands.' And the divine institution of holy Orders is gathered, as well from the use of the Apostles, and the perpetual tradition of the Church, as from those texts in which Christ bequeathed the whole power of the priesthood to his disciples, and to their successors, St. Luke xxii. 19. 'Do this in remembrance of me;' and St. John xx. 22, 23. 'Receive ye the Holy Ghost: whose soever sins ye remit, they are remitted unto them; and whose soever sins ye retain, they are retained.'

Q. By what steps do persons ascend in the Catholic Church to the Order of priesthood?

A. 1st. They must be initiated by the clerical tonsure, which is not properly an Order, but only a preparation for Orders. The bishop cuts off the extremities of their hair, to signify their renouncing the world, and its vanities; and he revests them with a surplice, and so receives them into the clergy; they making at the same time a solemn profession of taking the Lord for their inheritance and portion for ever.

2dly, They must pass through the minor or lesser orders, which have been received from the primitive Church, viz. the Orders of porter or doorkeeper of the Church; lector, or reader of the lessons in the divine Office; exorcist, whose function is to read the exorcisms and prayers of the Church over those who are possessed or obsessed by the devil; and acolyth, whose function is to serve the Mass, light the candles in the Church, &c. All these are ordained by receiving from the bishop the instruments or books belonging to their respective offices, and solemn prayers prescribed in the Pontifical.

3dly, From the minor Orders they are promoted to the Order of subdeacon, which is the first of those that are called holy. In the conferring this Order, the bishop puts the candidates in mind, that hitherto they have had their liberty to quit the ecclesiastical calling, and engage themselves by marriage in the world; but if they will be ordained subdeacons, which he leaves to their choice, they are thereby tied for ever to the service of God and his Church in the state of perpetual continence. Subdeacons also are obliged to the canonical hours of the church office, and in the High Mass assist the deacon in his ministry.

4thly, From the Order of subdeacons they are advanced to the Order of deacon, which is conferred upon them by the imposition of the bishop's hand, and by delivering to them the book of the gospels. The deacon's office is to assist the bishop or priest in the sacrifice of the Mass, to sing and preach the gospels, to baptize, &c.

5thly, From the Order of deacon the next ascent is to the Order of priest, or presbyter, above which is the Order of bishops, amongst whom the chief is called the Pope.

Q. In what manner is the Order of priesthood administered?

A. The person that is to be ordained is presented to the bishop by the archdeacon, desiring, in the name of

14

the Church, that he may be promoted to priesthood, and
bearing testimony of his being worthy of that office.
Then the bishop publishes to the clergy and people
there present the designed promotion, that if any one
has any thing to allege against the person that is to
be ordained, he may freely declare it. If no one ap-
bears to allege any thing against him, the bishop proceeds to admonish him of the duties and functions of
the priesthood, and to exhort him to a diligent discharge
thereof. After which, both the bishop and the person
that is to be ordained, prostrate themselves in prayer,
whilst the litanies are sung or said by the choir or clergy there present; which being ended, the bishop stands
up, and the person that is to be ordained kneeling, the
bishop first, and then all the priests there present, one
after another, lay both their hands on his head, which imposition of hands is immediately followed by the solemn
prayers of consecration, and by revesting him with the
priestly ornaments; then the Holy Ghost is invoked
by the hymn, Veni Creator. After which the bishop
anoints the hands of the person ordained, and then de-
livers into his hands the chalice with the wine and water, and the patent with the bread, saying, 'Receive the
power to offer sacrifice to God, and celebrate Mass, as
well for the living as for the dead, in the name of the
Lord.' Then the person ordained says Mass with the
bishop, and receives the holy communion at his hands.
At the end of the Mass the bishop again imposes his
hands upon him, saying those words of Christ: St. John
xx. 22, 23, 'Receive the Holy Ghost: whose sins thou
shalt forgive. they are forgiven them; and whose sins
thou shalt retain, they are retained.' After which he
receives from him the promise of obedience, and gives
him the kiss of peace.

CHAPTER XVI.

Of the Superiority of the Bishops, and of the Supremacy of the Pope.

Q. How do you prove that besides priests or presbyters, there has been always in the Church the Order of bishops superior to that of priest?

A. I prove it both from scripture and perpetual tradition. The New Testament, in several places, mentions bishops, as Philip. i. 1. 1 Tim. iii. 2. Tit. i. 7 Acts xx. 28. And it is visible that the angels of the seven Churches of Asia, mentioned in the 1st, 2d, and 3d chapters of the Revalation, were the bishops of those sees, and accordingly had a jurisdiction over them. It is no less visible, from the epistles of St. Paul to Timothy and Titus, that both one and the other were bishops, with power of ordaining inferior priests; and Timothy, in particular, is instructed by the Apostles, in what manner he is to comport himself to the priests under him, 1 Tim. v. 17, 19. And as for perpetual tradition, it is evident from all kind of monuments, and from the most ancient Church history, that the Church has always been governed by bishops, and that the Apostles every where established bishops. Thus St. Irenæus, L. 3. C. 3. Tertullian, L. de Prescrip. and other ancients assure us, that Linus and Clement were ordained bishops by St. Peter and St. Paul for the See of Rome. Thus Eusebius, and other ancient monuments, inform us, that St. Mark was the first bishop of Alexandria, and was succeeded by Anianus; that Evodius and Ignatius, disciples of the Apostles, were, after St. Peter, the first bishops of Antioch; that St. James was constituted by the Apostles the first bishop of Jerusalem, and had for successor Simeon the son of Cleophus; th t St. Polycarp was made bishop of Smyrna by St. John, &c.

Q. How do you prove that amongst bishops one should be head, and have a jurisdiction over the rest?

A. Because Christ has so appointed, who gave that

preëminence to St. Peter with respect to the rest of the apostles; as appears from St. Matt. xvi. 18, 19, when, in reward of his faith and confession, he confirmed to him the name of Peter, or Rock; and promised to him, that upon this rock he would build his Church, and the gates of hell should not prevail against it; and that he would give him the ' keys of the kingdom of heaven,' &c. And from St. John xxi. 15, &c. when our Lord, after having asked St. Peter, 'Dost thou love me more than these?' three times, committed to him the charge of all his lambs and sheep, without exception; that is, of his whole Church. Hence, St. Matthew, chap. x. 2, reckoning the names of the twelve Apostles, says, 'The first, Simon, who is called Peter.' Now, it does not appear that he could be said the first, upon any other account but by reason of his supremacy; for that he was first in age is more than appears, and that he was first in calling is not true; for St. Andrew came to Christ before Peter, and was probably the elder brother; and certain it is, that the Evangelists, in reckoning up the names of the Apostles, upon several occasions, neither follow the order of their age nor of their calling; yet we always reckon Peter in the first place, and sometimes more clearly to intimate his preëminence, name him alone as chief or prince; as, St. Mark i. 36, 'Simon, and they that were with him;' St. Luke ix. 32, 'Peter, and they that were with him:' Acts ii. 14, 'Peter standing up with the eleven:' Acts v. 29, 'Peter and the Apostles answered and said,' &c. where the Protestant translation has put in the word 'other Apostles,' as clearly seeing that the former expression (which is that of the original) too clearly expressed St. Peter's being something more than the rest.

It is also worth observing, that our Lord was pleased to teach the people out of St. Peter's ship, St. Luke v. 3; that he ordered the same tribute to be paid for himself and Peter, St. Matt. xvii. 27; that he particularly prayed for Peter, that his faith should not fail, and ordered him to confirm or strengthen his brethren, St. Luke xxii. 32. &c.

Hence St. Peter's supremacy is acknowledged by the perpetual tradition of the holy fathers. See Origen, on the 6th chapter to the Romans, and in his 5th Homily upon Exodus; St. Basil, of the Judgment of God, t. 2, p. 402; St. Cyril, of Jerusalem, in his 2d Catechesis: St. Epiphanius, Hær. 51, § 17, & Hær. 54, § 7, and in his Anchoratus, § 6, p. 14, 15: St. John Chrysostom in his 2d Homily on the 50th Psalm, in his 54th Homily upon St. Matthew, &c. St. Cyril, of Alexandria, in his 12th Book upon St. John: St. Austerius, Bishop of Amasæa, in his sermon upon St. Peter and St. Paul; and among the Latins, St. Cyprian, Epist. 70, to Januarius: St. Optatus of Milevis, l. 2, and 7: St. Ambrose, l. 10, upon St. Luke: St. Hierome, in his 1st book against Jovinian: St. Augustine, l. 2 de Baptismo, c. 1: St. Leo, Epist. 84, to Anastasius: St. Gregory the Great, l. 4, Epist. 32, &c.

Q. How do you prove that St. Peter was to have a successor in this office of chief bishop of the Church?

A. Because as Christ established his Church to remain till the end of the world, St. Matt. xxviii. 20, so most certainly he designed that the form of government which he established in his Church should remain for ever. Hence, supposing the supremacy of St. Peter, which we have proved above from scripture, it cannot be questioned, but that our Lord designed that this supremacy, which he appointed for the better government of his Church, and the preserving of unity, should not die with Peter, no more than the Church, (with which he promised to remain for ever,) but should descend, after Peter's decease, to his successors. For it is not to be imagined, that Christ should appoint a chief bishop for the government of his church, and maintaining unity in the Apostles' time, and design another kind of government for succeeding ages, when there was like to be so much greater danger of schism, and consequently so much greater need of one head to preserve all in one faith and one communion.

Q. But how do you prove that the Pope or bishop of Rome is the successor of St. Peter?

A. I prove it, 1st, Because the Church never ac-
14 *

knowledged any other for her chief pastor: and no
other does, or ever did, put in a claim to the spiritual
supremacy in quality of St. Peter's successor; so that,
supposing what has been proved, that Christ appointed
a chief pastor for his Church, the bishop of Rome must
be the man.

2dly, I prove it from the current sense of the holy
fathers and councils that have acknowledged this
supremacy in the see of Rome and her bishops. See
St. Ignatius, disciple of the Apostles, in the beginning
of his epistle to the Romans, where he calls the Church
of Rome the presiding Church; St. Irenæus, l. 3, c.
3, who calls the same the greatest and most ancient
Church, founded by the two most glorious Apostles,
Peter and Paul; and adds, that all sectaries are confounded by the Roman tradition; for to this Church,
by reason of its more powerful principality, says he, it
is necessary that every Church resort, or have recourse;
in which (Church) the apostolical tradition has always
been preserved by those that are in every place ; and
St. Cyprian, in his 55th epistle to pope Cornelius, where
he calls the see of Rome, the chair of Peter, and the
principal Church from which the priestly unity has its
origin. *Ecclesiam Principalem, unde Unitas Sacerdo
talis exorta est.*

See also St. Optatus, Bishop of Milevis, in his 2d
Book against Parmenianus, the Donatist Bishop of
Carthage : where he thus addresses himself to his adversary.   You cannot pretend to be ignorant that Peter
held first the bishop's chair in the city of Rome, in
which Peter, head of all the Apostles sat; in which one
chair unity might be maintained by all, lest the rest
of the apostles should each one claim his own separate
chair.   So that he is now a schismatic, and an offender,
who against this single chair erects any other.   In this
one chair, which is the first of the properties of the
Church, Peter first sat ; to him succeeded Linus, to
him Clement, &c. Give you now an account of the
origin of your chair, you who claim to yourselves the
holy Church.

And St. Jerome, writing to pope Damasus, Epist.

57, tells him, I am joined in communion with your holiness, that is, with the chair of Peter: upon that rock I know the Church is built: whoever eats the lamb out of this house is profane: whosoever is not in (this) Ark shall perish in the deluge, &c.

And St. Augustine in his Psalm against the Donatists thus addresses himself to these schismatics. Come brethren, says he, if you have a mind to be ingrafted in the vine, it is a pity to see you lopped off in this manner from the stock. Reckon up the prelates in the very see of Peter; and in that order of fathers see which has succeeded which. This is the rock over which the proud gates of hell prevail not. And in his 162d Epistle he tells the Donatists, that in the see of Rome the principality (or supremacy) of the apostolic Church was ever acknowledged. *Semper Apostolicæ Cathe Iræ viguit Principatus.*

And St. Prosper, in his dogmatic Poem against the enemies of grace, calls Rome the see of Peter, which being made to the world the head of pastoral dignity, rules by religion all that which she possesses not by her arms. And to the same effect St. Leo the Great, in his first Sermon upon St. Peter and St. Paul, thus addresses himself to Rome: these are they who have advanced thee to this glory, that being made the head of the world, by being St. Peter's see, thou hast a wider extent of religious empire than of earthly dominion. For though by thy many victories thou hast extended thy dominions far and near, by sea and land, yet that which has been subdued by the labour of thy arms is not so much as that which has been made subject to thee by Christian peace. All these fathers hitherto quoted, flourished within four hundred years after the passion of Christ.

The supremacy of the bishops of Rome has also been acknowledged by many general Councils: as by the general Council of Ephesus, in the sentence of deposition against Nestorius, anno 431, by the general Council of Chalcedon, in their epistle to St. Leo, anno 451, by the general Council of Constantinople, anno 680, in their epistle to pope Agatha: not to mention the decrees of later general Councils, especially the fourth of Lateran, anno 1215. the second of Lyons, anno 1274, and that of Florence, anno 1439. Though as pope Galasius, long ago, in the council of Rome of seventy bishops, anno 494, has declared, ' The Roman See hath not its preëminence over other Churches from any ordinances of Councils, but from the words of our Lord and Saviour in the gospel, ' Thou art Peter, and upon this rock I will build my Church,' &c.

Q. But has the pope or bishop of Rome, in every age since the days of the Apostles, exercised this supremacy over other Churches ?

A. Yes, most certainly : in the very age immediately after the Apostles, that is, in the second century, pope Victor threatened to excommunicate the bishops of Asia Minor, for keeping Easter at an undue time, Eusebius, l. 5, Histor. Eccles. c. 25. And though it is probable he relented upon the remonstrances of St. Irenæus and others, yet no one of them all charged him with usurping an authority which did not of right belong to him. In the third century, St. Cyprian, epist 67, wrote to pope Stephen, desiring him to despatch his letters into the province and to the people of Arles, by which they might be authorized to depose Marcianus the bishop of Arles, and substitute another in his place. *Dirigantur in Provinciam——à te literæ, quibus absente Marciano, alius in locum ejus substituatur.*

In the fourth century, pope Julius cited St. Athanasius, bishop of Alexandria, that is to say, the second patriarch of the Church, to his Council at Rome, to answer the accusations of his adversaries ; who accordingly did appear, and was there cleared. See St. Athanasius's Apology against the Arians, num. 29, p. 148, of the new edition ; and Theodoret, l. 2, Histor. c. 3. The same pope, as we learn from the historian Socrates, l. 2, c. 15, and Sozomenus, l. 3, c. 8, about the same time restored by his authority to their respective Sees, from whence they had been deposed by the Eusebians, St. Paul, bishop of Constantinople, St. Lucius, bishop of Adrianople, Marcellus, bishop of

Ancyra in Galatia, and Asclepas, bishop of Gaza in Palestine; and this, as Sozomenus expressly words it, because, by reason of the dignity of his See, the care of all belonged to him. In the fifth century, pope Celestine deputed St. Cyril, Patriarch of Alexandria, to proceed as his delegate to the excommunication of Nestorius, patriarch of Constantinople, tom. 3, Concil. Labbe, p. 349. And in the same century, St. John Chrysostom, and St. Flavian, both Patriarchs of Constantinople, unjustly deposed by numerous Councils in the East, appealed from their judgment, the one to pope Innocent I., the other to pope Leo the Great. See the epistle of St. John Chrysostom to pope Innocent, and the 23d epistle of St. Leo. In the sixth century, pope Agapetus deposed Anthymus, patriarch of Constantinople; not to mention many other instances in all these centuries of the exercise of the pope's jurisdiction over other Churches; and as for the following ages there is no dispute.

From all which it follows, that the Protestant pretences of the Pope's having received the supremacy from Phocas, the emperor of Constantinople, who began to reign anno 602, is a groundless fiction, like the idle tale of pope Joan.

Q. But does not our Lord intimate, St. Luke xxii. 24, 25, 26, that amongst his disciples none should be the chief or head?

A. No; but only that ' he that is the greatest should be as the younger, and he that is chief as he that doth serve,' ver. 26. Which words, so far from denying, evidently suppose a chief; which is farther confirmed by our Lord's alleging himself for an example in the following verse, who was most certainly chief. So that what is here recommended, is not equality of jurisdiction, but humility in superiors.

Q. But does not St. Paul say, 2 Cor. xii. 11, ' In nothing am I behind the very chiefest Apostle, though I be nothing;' where was then St. Peter's supremacy?

A. It is visible that St. Paul speaks with regard to his labours, miracles and doctrine, in which he was inferior to none; but whether St. Peter or he had a supe rior jurisdiction, was foreign to the matter he had then in hand, and therefore no wonder that he takes no notice of it.

Q. If St. Peter was head, how came St. Paul to withstand him to his face at Antioch, Gal. ii. 11?

A. Because, as the Apostle tells us in the same place, he was to blame, viz. in withdrawing himself from the table of the Gentiles, for fear of giving offence to the Jews: and this it was that St. Paul reprehended, because of the danger of the Gentiles taking scandal thereby. But this no way disproves St. Peter's superiority, since no one doubts, but that a superior, when in fault, may sometimes lawfully be reprehended by an inferior.

And, after all, do our adversaries imagine that the enhancing the dignity and authority of St. Paul makes any thing against the bishop of Rome, who indeed inherits the succession both of St. Peter and St. Paul, who both honoured Rome with their preaching and with their death.

Q. But some Protestants doubt whether St. Peter ever was at Rome. What say you to this?

A. Grotius, a learned Protestant, writes that, 'no Christian ever doubted but St. Peter was at Rome.' In Synopsi Criticorum, p. 1540. H. And Chamierus, another learned Protestant, tells us, that ' all the fathers with great accord have asserted that Peter went to Rome, and governed that Church.' *Omnes Patres magno consensu asseruerunt Petrum Romam esse profectum, eamque Ecclesiam administrasse:* l. 13, c. 4, § 2. And Dr. Pearson, the Protestant bishop of Chester, one of the most eminent men amongst the Protestant writers ever known, has demonstrated, by innumerable arguments, that Peter was at Rome, and that the bishops of Rome are his successors. See Pearson's Opera Posthuma, printed at London, anno 1688, p. 27, &c.

Q. Does the scripture any where affirm that St. Peter was at Rome?

A. St. Peter's first epistle seems to affirm it, chap. v. 13, where, by Babylon, the best interpreters understand Rome, so called by the Apostle, as afterwards by

St. John in the Apocalypse, because of its being then the chief seat both of the empire and of heathenish idolatry, as formerly Babylon had been.   And so this place is understood by S. Papias, disciple of the apostles, and Clement of Alexandria, alleged by Euseb. l. 2, Hist. c. 15, and by St. Hierome, l. de Scriptor. in Marco ; by venerable Bede, Œcumenius, and others. Nor is there any probability that the Babylon here mentioned could be that in Chaldæa, which at this time was nothing but a heap of ruins ; nor that in Egypt, which was but a very inconsiderable place in those days, and in which no monuments of antiquity give us the least hint that St. Peter ever preached.

But if the scripture had been entirely silent in this matter, we have it proved by universal tradition, which is the means by which we come to the knowledge of the scripture itself. And, indeed, there is a more universal tradition for St. Peter's being at Rome, than there is for many parts of the scripture which Protestants receive : for whereas many of the ancient fathers have called in question some books of scripture ; for instance the Revelation, the epistle to the Hebrews, &c. and there is scarce any part of the Bible or New Testament, but what has been rejected by some heretics of old ; yet we cannot find that St. Peter's being at Rome was ever called in question by any single man, infidel or Christian, Catholic or heretic, for thirteen or fourteen hundred years after Christ. Though all heretics and schismatics, as being always enemies of the Church of Rome, would have been most glad to have called in question this succession of St. Peter (which the bishops of Rome ever gloried in) had not the matter of fact been out of dispute.

The ancient fathers that have attested St. Peter's being at Rome, besides many others, are St. Irenius, l. 3, c. 3.   St. Denys, Bishop of Corinth, Caius and Origen, alleged by Eusebius in his Church History, p. 71, 78 ; Tertullian, l. de Præscript. c. 36, and in Scorpiaco, c. 5. St. Cyprian, Epist. 52, and 55. Arnobius, L 2, contra Gentes. Lactantius, l. de Morte

Persecutorum, c. 2.   Eusebius, l. 2,   Hist. c. 14, p.
52, l. 3. c. 4, p. 74.   St. Athanasius, in Apolog. de
fugâ suâ, p. 331.   St. Cyril, of Jerusalem, Catech. 6, p.
54.   St. Ambrose, l. 4.   Hexam. c. 8.   St. Jerome de
Scriptoribus Eccles. in Petro & in Marco, and in his
Chronicon ad Annum 43 and 69.   Sulpitius Severus,
l. 2.   Hist. St. Augustine, l. de Hær. c. 1, Epist. 53.
l. 2. contra Lit. Petil. c. 51.   St. John Chrysostom, Tom.
5, Hom. 12.   Orositus, l. 7, c. 6.   St. Peter Chrysologus,
Epist. ad Eutych.   St. Optatus, l. 2, contra Parmenia.
Theodoret. in Epist. ad Rom. and l. 1.   Hæret. Fab. c
1. &c.

CHAPTER XVII.

Of the Celibacy of the Clergy.

Q. WHAT is the reason why the Catholic Clergy are
not allowed to marry?

A. Because at their entering into holy Orders, they
make a solemn promise to God and the Church to live
continently.   Now the breach of such a promise as this
would be a great sin: witness St. Paul, 1 Tim. v. 11,
12, where, speaking of widows, that are for marrying,
after having thus engaged themselves to God, he says,
'They have damnation, because they have cast off their
first faith;' that is, their solemn engagement made to
God.

Q. But why does the Church receive none to holy
Orders, but such as are willing to make this solemn
engagement?

A. Because she does not think it proper that they,
who by their office and functions, ought to be wholly
devoted to the service of God, and the care of souls,
should be diverted from these duties by the distractions
of a married life. 1 Cor. vii. 32, 33, 'He that is unmarried, careth for the things that belong to the Lord,
how he may please the Lord: but he that is married,

careth for the things that are of the world, how he may please his wife.'

Q. But was it always a law in the Church that the clergy should abstain from marriage?

A. It was always a law in the Church, that bishops, priests and deacons, should not marry after having received holy Orders : and we have not one example, in all antiquity, either in the Greek or Latin Church, of any such marriage : but it has been at some times, and in some places, as at present among the Greeks, permitted for priests and deacons to continue with their wives which they had married before their ordination, though even this was disallowed by many ancient canons.

The 27th of the apostolic canons allows none of the clergy to marry but those that are in the minor orders, that is, Lectors and Cantors. The Council of Neocæsarea, which was more ancient than that of Nice, in its first canon orders, that if a priest marries he would be deposed. The Council of Ancyra, which was held about the same time, orders the same thing with regard to deacons, except they protested at the time of their ordination that they could not live unmarried, and were therefore presumed to be dispensed with by the bishop. Concil. Ancyra, Can. 10.

The great Council of Nice, in the third canon, forbids clergymen to have any women in their house, except it be mother, sister, or aunt, &c. A caution, which would never have been thought on, if they had been allowed to have wives.

In the West, the Council of Illiberis, which was held about the close of the third century, canon 33, commands bishops, priests, deacons, and subdeacons to abstain from their wives, under pain of degradation. The second Council of Arles, can. 2, ordains that no married man be made priest, unless he promise conversion, that is, to live continently. The second Council of Carthage, can. 2, ordains, that bishops, priests, and deacons, should live continently, and abstain from their wives; and this because the Apostles so taught, and all antiquity observed. *Ut quod Apostoli docuerunt,*

15

& ipsa servavit antiquitas nos quoque custodiamus. And the fifth Council of Carthage, anno 398, can. 2, ordains in like manner, that all bishops, priests, and deacons should abstain from their wives, or be deposed. There are many other ancient canons to the like effect, as well as decrees of the ancient popes; as of Siricius, in his epistle to Himmerius bishop of Tarragona, c. 7; of Innocent I. in his epistle of Victricius bishop of Roan, c. 9; of St. Leo the Great, epist. 82, to Anastasius, c. 3 and 4.

Hence St. Epiphanius, who flourished in the East in the fourth century, in his great work, against all heresies, Hær. 59, writes thus: ' The Church does not admit him to be a deacon, priest, bishop, or subdeacon, though he be a man of one wife, who makes use of conjugal embraces.' He adds, that this ' is observed in those places chiefly in which canons of the Church are exactly kept, which being directed by the Holy Ghost, aims always at that which is most perfect; that those who are employed in divine functions may have as little as can be of worldly distractions.' And St. Jerome, epist. 50, ' Bishops, (says he,) priests, and deacons, are chosen either virgins or widowers, or from the time of their priesthood perpetually chaste.' He affirms the same in his book against Vigilantius, by the name of the Churches of the East, and of Egypt, and of the see Apostolic; and of all bishops, in his book against Jovinianus. See also Origen, Hom. 13, upon Numbers; Eusebius, l. 1, Demonstr. Evang. c. 9; and St. John Chrysostom, Homil. de Patientiâ Job.

If you ask the reason, why the Church has insisted so much in all ages upon this point of discipline? Besides the reason alleged above out of St. Paul, 1 Cor. vii 32, 33, ' The reason of single life for the clergy,' says Mr. Thorndyke, an eminent Protestant divine, in his letters at the end of Just Weights and Measures, p. 239, is firmly grounded by the fathers and canons of the Church upon the precept of St. Paul, forbidding man and wife to part, unless for a time to attend unto prayer, 1 Cor. vii. 5. For priests and deacons being continually to attend upon occasions of celebrating the eucharist. which ought continually to be frequented; if others be to abstain from the use of marriage for a time, then they always.' Thus far Mr. Thorndyke.

Q. But were not the Apostles married?

A. Some of them were, before they were called to the apostleship; but we do not find that they had any commerce with their wives after they were called by Christ. St. Jerome expressly affirms that they had not, Epist. 50. And this seems to be clear from St. Matt. xix. 27, where St. Peter says to our Lord, ' Behold we have forsaken all things and followed thee.' For that among the ALL, which they had forsaken, wives also were comprehended, is gathered from the enumeration made by our Saviour in the 29th verse, where he expressly nameth wives.

Q. But does not St. Paul say, 1 Cor. ix. 5. 'Have we not power to lead about a sister, a wife, as well as other Apostles,' &c.?

A. The Protestant translation has wilfully corrupted the text in this place; it should have been translated. a woman, a sister. The Apostle speaks not of his wife; for it is visible he had none, from 1 Cor. vii. 7, 8. But he speaks of such pious women, as, according to the custom of the Hebrew nation, waited upon the Apostles and other teachers, serving them in necessaries; as they had done also upon our Lord in the time of his mortal life, see St. Luke viii. 2, 3. Though St. Paul, that he might be less burthensome to the faithful, chose rather to serve himself, and live by the work of his own hands.

Q. Does not the Apostle, 1 Tim. iii. 2 and 12, require that bishops and deacons should be the ' husbands of one wife?'

A. The meaning of the Apostle is not that every bishop, priest, or deacon should have a wife; for he himself had none; and he declares, 1 Cor. vii. 8, '1 say to the unmarried and widows, it is good for them if they abide even as I.' But his meaning is. that none should be admitted to be a bishop, priest, or deacon that had been married more than once; which law has ever since been observed in the Catholic Church for since it was not possible in those days of the first preaching of the gospel (when there were few or no converts, either among the Jews or Gentiles, but such as were married) to have found a sufficient number of proper ministers if they had not admitted married men, they were consequently obliged to admit such to the ministry; but still with this limitation, provided they had not been twice married. But now the Church has a sufficient number of such as are trained up to a single life, and are willing to embrace perpetual continence; and therefore prefers such to the ministry, and is authorized so to do by the Apostle, 1 Cor. vii. 32, 33, 38. And if, after having consecrated themselves to God in this kind of life, they should be for looking back, and engaging in a married life, they are expressly condemned by the same Apostle, 1 Tim. v. 12.

Q. Is it not said, Heb. xiii. 5, ' Marriage is honourable in all ? '

A. The Protestant translation has strained the text to make it say more than the original, which may full as well be rendered in the imperative mood, thus : ' let marriage be honourable in all, and the bed undefiled ; for whoremongers and adulterers God will judge ; ' which is rendered in the Protestant translation by the imperative, ' let your conversation be without covetousness,' &c. So that the true meaning of this text is, that married persons should not dishonour their holy state by any liberties contrary to the sanctity of it; but not to allow marriage to those who have chosen the better part, and consecrated themselves by vow to God.

Q. But is not forbidding marriage called a doctrine of devils ? 1 Tim. iv. 3.

A. It certainly was so in those of whom the Apostle there speaks, viz. the Gnostics, the Marcionites, the Encratites, the Manicheans, and many other heretics, who absolutely condemned marriage as the work of the devil. For our part, no body reverences marriage more than we do, for we hold it to be a sacrament, and forbid it to none but those that have voluntarily renounced it to consecrate themselves more wholly to the divine service: and in such as these

St. Paul condemns i; as much as we; see 1 Tim. v. 12. That these same heretics also condemned absolutely the use of all kinds of meat. not on fasting days only, (as was also practised by the Church,) but at any time whatsoever; because they looked upon all flesh to be from an evil principle. So that it is evident these were the men of whom the Apostle, 1 Tim. iv. intended to speak.

Q. But do you think that a vow of continency so strictly obliges any person, that it would be a sin in such a person to marry?

A. Yes, most certainly; because the law of God and nature requires that we should keep our vows to God. Deut. xxiii. 21, 22, 23, 'When thou shalt vow a vow unto the Lord thy God, thou shalt not slack to pay it: for the Lord thy God will surely require it of thee; and it would be sin in thee. But if thou shalt forbear to vow, it shall be no sin in thee. That which is gone out of thy lips, thou shalt keep and perform.' Psalm lxxvi. 11, 'Vow and pray unto the Lord your God. Eccles. v. 4, 'Pay that which thou hast vowed. Better it is that thou shouldst not vow, than that thou shouldst vow and not pay.' For if it be a crime to break our faith with man, how much more with God? If you say, that the state of continency is not more acceptable to God than that of marriage, and therefore cannot be the proper matter of a vow, you contradict the doctrine of the Apostle, 1 Cor. vii. 38, 'He that giveth his virgin in marriage, doth well; but he that giveth her not, doth better.'

Hence St. Augustine, l. de Bono Viduitatis, c. 11, affirms, that the breach of such a vow of chastity is worse than adultery: and St. John Chrysostom, (ad Theodorum Lapsum,) 'Though you call it marriage a thousand times, yet I maintain it is much worse than adultery.' Hence the Council of Illiberis, can. 13; the fourth Council of Carthage, can. 104; and the great Council of Chalcedon, can. 15, excommunicate those who presume to marry after such a vow. What would the Church of those ages have thought of a religion introduced into the world by men that had notoriously

15 *

broke through those most solemn engagements, and who raised the fabric of their pretended reformation upon thousands of broken vows?

Q. But all have not the gift of continency; why then should the first reformers be blamed, if, finding they had not this gift, they ventured upon marrying with nuns?

A. Continency is not required of all, but such as have by vow engaged to keep it: and therefore, before a person engages himself by vow, he ought certainly to examine whether he has a call from God, and whether he can go through with what he thinks of undertaking: but after he has once engaged himself by vow, he is not now at liberty to go back: but may assure himself, that the gift of continence will not be denied him, so that he uses proper means to obtain and preserve it, particularly prayer and mortification, which, because Luther laid aside, by quitting his canonical hours of prayer and other religious exercises, to which he had been accustomed in his convent, no wonder if he had lost the gift of continency, which he owns he enjoyed whilst he was a popish friar. 'Whilst I was a religious (says he) I observed chastity, obedience and poverty: and, in short, being wholly disengaged from the cares of this present life, I wholly gave myself up to fasting, watching and prayer." In Gal. l. 15, t. 5 Witemb. fol. 291. 2. But as soon as he commenced reformer, to demonstrate that he was changed for the worse, he declares, he had so far lost this gift, that he could not possibly live without a woman. Sermon. de Matrim. t. 5, fol. 119. 1.

Q. But does not Christ say, concerning continency, St. Matt. xix. 11, 'All men cannot receive this saying:' and St. Paul, 1 Cor. vii. 9, 'If they cannot contain, let them marry: for it is better to marry than to burn?'

A. No: both these texts are wilfully corrupted in the Protestant Testament. Where he speaks not of such as have vowed chastity, but of other Christians, whom he advises rather to marry than to burn with unlawful lust here, and for unlawful lust hereafter And the same advice is most frequently inculcated by

Catholic divines.   But as for those that have vowed chastity, they must make use of other means to prevent this burning, particularly prayer and fasting.   But what a wretched case must that of the adversaries of the celibacy of the clergy be, when to maintain it they nave in so many places wilfully corrupted the scripture? and what a melancholy case it must be, that so many thousands of well-meaning souls should be wretchedly deluded with the pretence of God's pure word, when instead of this, they have nothing put in their hands but corrupted translations, which present them with a mortal poison, instead of the food of life?

CHAPTER XVIII.

Of Religious Orders and Confraternities.

Q. WHAT is the meaning of so many religious Orders in the Catholic Church, under different denominations? are not all Catholics of the same religion?

A. Yes, certainly, all Catholics, and consequently all these religious, though called by different denominations, are all of one religion, professing one and the same faith, acknowledging one and the same Church authority, and all the decisions of the Church; subject to one and the same head, and closely united together in one communion.

Q. In what then do these religious Orders differ one from another, if they are all of one religion?

A. They differ in having different rules and constitutions prescribed by their respective founders; different habits; different exercises of devotion and penance; different institutes; some wholly sequestered from the world, and addicted to prayer and contemplation; others employed in preaching, teaching and converting souls; others tending the sick, redeeming captives, &c. so as to make a beautiful variety in the Church of God of different companions, all tending towards Christian perfection, though by different exercises, according to the spirit of their respective institutes.

Q. Are not all these religious consecrated to God by certain vows?

A. Yes: there are three vows which are common to them all, viz. of poverty, chastity, and obedience. By the vow of poverty, they renounce all property to the things of this world, so as to have nothing at their own disposal; by the vow of chastity, they renounce all carnal pleasures; and by the vow of obedience, they give up their own will to follow that of God in the person of their superior.

Q. How do we know that this voluntary poverty, perpetual chastity, and entire obedience, are agreeable to God?

A. That voluntary poverty, or renouncing the goods and possessions of this world, is agreeable to God, is evident from St. Matt. xix. 21, 'If thou wilt be perfect, go and sell all thou hast, and give to the poor, and thou shalt have a treasure in heaven; and come and follow me.' That perpetual chastity is agreeable to God, is no less evident, from St. Matt. xix. 12, 'There be eunuchs, which have made themselves eunuchs for the kingdom of heaven's sake—he that is able to receive it, let him receive it.' And that an entire obedience to lawful superiors must needs be agreeable to the divine Majesty, is evident, because obedience is better than sacrifice; since by obedience we give up to God, and for God, that which is naturally most dear to us, viz. our liberty, and that which stands most in the way of our soul's welfare, viz. our own will and self love.

Q. Ought any Christians to embrace this state of life without a call from God?

A. No, certainly; it would be rashness to attempt it.

Q. How shall any person know if he have a call from God to this state of life?

A. By consulting God, his Director, and his own heart. In choosing a state of life every one ought to consult God, in the first place, by fervent prayer, begging daily of him like the convert, St. Paul, Acts ix. 6, 'Lord, what wilt thou have me to do?' He ought also to consult with a virtuous and prudent director, and to lay open to him the inclinations of his heart, and the motives upon which he is inclined to embrace this kind of life; for there is no better proof of a call from God than when a person, after having consulted God by prayer, finds in himself a strong inclination to a religious life, and that for a long time, and upon motives which have nothing in them of self love, but are such as could not be suggested but by the grace of God.

Q. What are the motives upon which a Christian should embrace a religious life?

A. To do penance for his sins; to fly from the dangers and corruptions of this wicked world; to consecrate himself wholly to the service of God, and sanctify himself by the exact observance of his vows, and all the exercises of a religious life; and to tend without ceasing to Christian perfection.

Q. But may it not be feared, that young persons may too rashly engage themselves by vows in a religious state for which they are not fit?

A. To prevent this inconvenience, the Catholic Church suffers none to be professed in any order of men or women without a year's noviceship, by way of probation or trial.

Q. Is a religious state of life very ancient in the Church of God?

A. Yes, very ancient; for not to mention St. John Baptist's life in the wilderness, St. Luke i. 30, and the lives of the first Christians of Jerusalem, who had all things common, and sold their possessions and goods, continuing daily with one accord in the temple, &c. Acts ii. 44, 45, 46, in which they exhibit a specimen of a religious life; we learn from the most certain monuments of antiquity, that even in the three first centuries there were religious men, whom Eusebius calls Ascetæ, and great numbers of nuns or virgins consecrated to God; though neither the one nor the other was as yet formed into the regular monasteries till the beginning of the fourth century.

About the middle of the third century, St. Paul the first hermit, flying from the fury of the persecution begun by Decius, in the year 289. retired into the desert of Thebais, and there passed ninety years and upwards in a lonesome cave, in conversation with God. His wonderful life is extant, written by St. Jerome.

About the year 271, St. Anthony, a young gentleman of Egypt, left his estate and the world to consecrate himself to a religious life. He found, at his first retirement, some others that had already undertaken that kind of life, though few in number, and those living near the towns or villages; but he, by his example, drew great numbers after him into the desert, and is generally looked upon as the author and father of a monastic life. His life is written by the great St. Athanasius, and is full of excellent lessons of spirituality.

About the year 313, St. Pachomius retired from the world, and, after having lived some time in solitude with St. Palemon, became the father of many religious, and the first founder of the famous congregation of Tabenne, to which he prescribed a rule which he had received from an angel.

From these beginnings, the deserts of Egypt and of Thebais soon were peopled with innumerable solitaries, and all those parts were full of religious of both sexes of admirable virtue; insomuch, that when Rufinus visited those countries in the latter end of the fourth century, he found in the city of Oxyrincus alone, ten thousand religious men, and twenty thousand nuns.

From Egypt, this kind of life, so agreeable to the principles of the gospel, and the spirit of Christianity, quickly spread itself though all parts of the world inhabited by Christians. St. Hilarian, having learned St. Anthony's way of living, began to practise the like in Palestine about the beginning of the fourth century; and that country also was quickly replenished with religious men and women: whilst St. James, afterwards bishop of Nisibis, St. Julian Sabas, and other great servants of God, whose lives and miracles are recorded by Theodoret in his Philotheus, propagated the same way of living in Syria and Mesopotamia. About the same time, or not long after, the deserts of Pontus and Cappadocia began also to be inhabited by religious men, whose manner of life was embraced by those two great lights of the Church, St. Gregory Nazianzen and

St. Basil; the latter of which composed an excellent rule for his religious, professed to this day by the Greek and Russian monks, and by some in Poland and Italy.

As for the Western parts of the Church, we find that the monastic life had already gained a great footing there in the fourth century. St. Augustine informs us of a monastery near the walls of Milan, full of good religious men, under the care of St. Ambrose, l. 8, Confess. chap. 6. And of several such religious societies at Rome, in his book of the Manners of the Catholic Church, chap. 33. Of a religious house near Treves, in Germany, where two courtiers, upon reading the life of St. Anthony, consecrated themselves to God, l. 8, Confess. c. 6. And the same St. Augustine, upon his return into Africa, after his conversion, propagated the same kind of life in that part of the world also.

In France, the great St. Martin, bishop of Tours, in the fourth century, whose apostolic life and miracles are recorded by Sulpicius Severus, founded the monastery of Marmoutier, in which he united together in one the clerical and monastical life, as St. Eusebius had done before him at Verceli in Piedmont. But the most famous monastery in all France was that of the isle of Lerines, founded towards the close of the fourth century, by St. Honoratus, afterwards bishop of Arles; which was the fruitful parent of many great saints and illustrious prelates.

As for our British islands, though we know not the particular time when the first monasteries began to be established, yet we are assured, that we were not long behind our neighbours in embracing this kind of life. The monastery of Bangor, in Wales, in which there were above two thousand monks, was very ancient; and we are told of an ancient monastery at Winchester, before the English Saxons came over into this land. As for Ireland, St. Patrick, who established Christianity there, settled also the monastic discipline amongst his converts; which from thence was propagated to the Picts in Scotland, by St. Columba, alias Columkil, the apostle of that nation, who having first

founded in Ireland the famous abbey of Dearmach, afterwards passing into Scotland, founded that of the isle of Hy; from which two monasteries many others, as well in Ireland as in Scotland, had their origin as following the institute of the aforesaid St. Columba, of whom Ven. Bede, in his third book of Ecclesiastical History of the English Church, chap. 4, writes thus·
'Of whose life and words (he speaks of St. Columba) some writings are said to be preserved by his disciples. But whatsoever he has himself, this we know of him for certain, that he has left successors renowned for much continency, the love of God, and regular observance.'

From this monastery of the isle of Hy, St. Aidan, the first bishop of Lindisfarn, and many other apostolic preachers came, who preached and established Christianity among the Northern English, as St. Augustine and his companions did amongst those of the South, St. Felix amongst the East English, and St. Birinus amongst those of the West.

Q. I should be glad to know which are the chief religious Orders that flourish at present in the Church of God; together with the names of their founders, the time of their first institution, &c.

A. I shall endeavour to satisfy you as briefly as I can. And, first as to the East. The Orders that flourish there, are those of St. Anthony, and of St. Basil, of which we have spoken already.

In the West, St. Augustine, upon his return into Africa, about the year 390, with divers others his companions, entered into a religious society, wherein he lived for three years before his coming to Hippo. And after his coming to that city, where he was first made priest, and afterward bishop, he erected a monastery within his own house, living there with his clergy in common; to which institute the Canon regulars of St. Augustine owe their original, who have flourished ever since in the Church of God, and have branched out into divers congregations, as that of St. John Lateran, that of St. Victor, of St. Genovefa, &c. As the hermits of St. Augustine's Order, commonly called Austin friars derive their institute from his first religious society, before his coming to Hippo. Those hermits were translated from the deserts into towns, by pope Innocent the Fourth, to the end that their godly conversation might be more profitable to their neighbours. From this Order Luther apostatized in the 16th century, and like the dragon, Revel. xii. 4, 'drew with him the third part of the stars of heaven,' (that is, great numbers of religious of all denominations,) 'and cast them to the earth.'

Towards the end of the 5th century, St. Benedict, *vulgo* Bennet, retired from the world; and after having practised for many years a religious life in a most eminent degree of perfection, founded twelve monasteries in Latium; and the thirteenth at Mount Cassim, in the kingdom of Naples, from which he happily passed to the mountain of eternity, in the sixth century. He composed an excellent rule, which was afterwards embraced by almost all the religious of the West, till towards the twelfth century, and has furnished the Church of God with innumerable prelates and apostolic men, and heaven with innumerable saints. The wonderful life of St. Benedict was written by St. Gregory the Great in his dialogues.

From the rule of St. Benedict many other Orders have sprung, besides the Benedictines, as the Cluniacenses, so called from their first abbey of Cluny in France. These were instituted by St. Odo, in the tenth century, and for a long time flourished in great sanctity. The Cumaldulenses, instituted by St. Romuald, amongst the Apennine mountains, about the year 1000, and to this day edifying the Church, yielding a sweet odour of sanctity to all that come near them. The monks of Valombrosa, instituted by St. John Gaulbert in the 11th century, and called from the place of their first institution. The Cistercians, so called from their first abbey, founded about the end of the eleventh century by St. Robert, abbot of Molesme in France. St. Robert being obliged to return to his abbey of Molesme, left for his successor, St. Albericus, who was succeeded by St. Stephen Harding, an Englishman,

16

who had the happiness to receive St. Bernard into his society, by whose preaching and miracles this Order was wonderfully propagated, and the religious of it, from him, are commonly called Bernardines. Of this Order is the famous abbey of La Trape in France, which in these, our days, has renewed the austerities and abstracted lives of the primitive religious. I pass over several other religious professing the rule of St. Benedict, as the Silvesterines, the Grandimontenses, the Celestines, so called from St. Peter Celestine their founder, the Olivetants, &c.

Towards the end of the eleventh century, St. Bruno, a doctor of Paris, with six companions, retired from the world to the desert mountains of Carthusia, in the diocess of Grenoble in Dauphine, and there laid the foundation of the Order of the Carthusians, formerly in England called the Charter-house monks; who to this day have happily preserved their primitive fervour, keeping perpetual silence, (only when they are singing the praises of God,) perpetual abstinence, wearing always a rough hair shirt, and continually employed in prayer and contemplation.

About the year 1120, St. Norbet, who had exchanged the court life for the voluntary poverty recommended by the gospel, founded an Order of Canon regulars, from him called Norbertines, and Premonstratenses, from Premonté, the place of their first abbey, in the diocess of Laon in France.

In the same age also was instituted in France, the Order of the blessed Trinity, for the redemption of captives out of the hands of infidels, by St. John de Matha, and St. Felix de Valois, two holy priests and solitaries invited to this charitable work by divine visions. As in the following age another Order was instituted in Spain for the same end, by St. Peter Nolascus. This is commonly called, the Order of our Lady de Mercede, or of the redemption.

About the year 1200, the Carmelites were first brought into Europe, and were quickly spread through all parts of Christendom, where they have flourished exceedingly: nowhere more than heretofore in England, where from the colour of their mantles they were called white friars. These were originally hermits living upon Mount Carmel, who whilst the Christians were in possession of Syria and the Holy Land, were assembled together by Aimeric the patriarch of Antioch, and received a rule from Albert patriarch of Jerusalem. This rule was afterwards mitigated by the pope; but embraced again in its full extent by St. Theresa, in the 16th century, and by the friars and nuns that follow her reform, and are called Discalced, or barefoot Carmelites.

Not long after the Carmelites' coming into Europe, God was pleased to raise two new Orders, which have flourished from that time to this day; and furnished the Church with several popes, innumerable cardinals, bishops, ecclesiastical writers, and apostolic men; and have both been very fruitful in saints, viz. The Order of St. Dominick, and that of St. Francis. The Dominicans, or Friars Preachers, were instituted for preaching the gospel to infidels and sinners, which they have done with great success. These were formerly in our country, called Black Friars, from the colour of their cloak or outward habit, which is black, as the Franciscans were called Gray Friars. St. Francis would have his religious, for humility, called Friars Minors, whom he trained up in great poverty and penance. And so great and speedy was the increase of this Order, that in a chapter held by the saint himself, at Assisium, there were assembled no less than five thousand religious. This Order at present is the most numerous in the Church of God, and is divided into three chief branches under their respective generals, viz. the Convensuals, the Observants, and the Capuchins. The Observants are again subdivided into Cordeliers, Recollects, &c. Besides which, there is the congregation of St. Peter of Alcantara, which is the strictest of all. The nuns who follow the rule of St. Francis, are commonly called Poor Clares, from St. Clare, who first received the habit from St. Francis and was the first abbess. Besides these there are Capuchinesses or Penitents, nuns of the third Order of St. Francis, &c.

Other Orders, that have been founded between the beginning of the thirteenth century and the sixteenth, are the Servites, or servants of the blessed Virgin, mstituted about 1232, by seven gentlemen of Florence, who retired themselves to a neighbouring mountain to do penance; the Crucigeri, or Crutched Friars, though these, by some, are supposed to have been much more ancient; the Jesuati, instituted by St. John Colombin, anno 1356; the Brigittins, by St. Brigit, anno 1360; the Hieronnimites, by Pedro Ferdinando, anno 1383 the Minims, by St. Francis of Paula, about the year 1450, &c.

The sixteenth century gave rise to several new Orders: the Theatins, or Regular Clerks, were insti tuted anno 1528, by St. Cajetanus Thianæus, a man of apostolic life. This Order flourishes very much in Italy, as well as the Barnabites, or Clerics Regular of St. Paul.

The Jesuits, or Society of Jesus, were instituted by St. Ignatius of Loyola, anno 1540, as a troop, or company of auxiliaries, to assist the pastoral clergy in that time of the Church's greatest necessity; to labour in the conversion and sanctification of souls; to train up youth in piety and learning; to defend the faith against heretics, and propagate it amongst infidels: in all which particulars, this Order has done signal services to the Church in these two last centuries.

About the same time, St. John de Deo founded an Order of religious brethren, to take care of the sick, and to provide for them all necessary assistance both for soul and body.

In the beginning of the seventeenth century, St Francis de Sales, bishop of Geneva, instituted the Order of the nuns of the Visitation of the blessed Virgin. And thus have I given you a short account of the chief orders that flourish in the Church.

Besides these religious Orders, there are certain regular congregations of clergy living in common, though not under the tie of religious vows: as the Oratorians, instituted by St. Philip Nerius, in the sixteenth century; the Fathers of the Christian Doctrine the Lazarians, or Fathers of the Mission, &c.

Q. Are there not also many confraternities amongst the Catholics, in which many of the laity are enrolled? pray what is the meaning of these confraternities?

A. These confraternities, or brotherhoods, are certain societies or associations, instituted for the encouragement of devotion, or for promoting of certain works of piety, religion, and charity; under some rules or regulations, though without being tied to them, so far as that the breach or neglect of them would be sinful. The good of these confraternities is, that thereby good works are promoted, the faithful are encouraged to frequent the sacraments, to hear the word of God, mutually to assist one another by their prayers, &c.

CHAPTER XIX.

Of the Sacrament of Matrimony, and of the Nuptial Benediction.

Q. When was matrimony instituted?

A. It was first instituted by God Almighty between our first parents in the earthly Paradise, Gen. ii. and this institution was confirmed by Christ in the New Testament, St. Matt. xix. 4, 5, 6, where he concludes, 'What God hath joined together, let no man put asunder.' And our Lord, to show that this state is holy, and not to be condemned or despised, was pleased to honour it with his first miracle, wrought at the wedding of Cana, St. John ii.

Q. What are the ends for which matrimony is instituted?

A. For the procreation of children, which may serve God here, and people heaven hereafter; for a remedy against concupiscence, and for the benefit of conjugal society, that man and wife may mutually help one another, and contribute to one another's salvation.

Q. How do you prove that matrimony is a sacrament?

A. Because it is a conjunction made and sanctified by God himself, and not to be dissolved by any power of man, as being a sacred sign or mysterious representation of the indissoluble union of Christ and his Church.

16 *

Hence St. Paul, Eph. v. 31, 32, expressly calls it a
'great sacrament or mystery,' with regard to Christ and
his Church; and as such it has been always acknowledged in the Catholic Church. See St. Ambrose,
l. 1, de Abraham, e. 7; St. Augustine, l. de Bono Con-
jug. c. 18 and 24. l. de Fide et Operibus, c. 17. .. de
Nuptis et Concep. 10, &c.

Q. Does matrimony give grace to those that receive it?

A. Yes, if they receive it in the dispositions that
they ought, it gives a grace to the married couple to
love one another according to God, to restrain the violence of concupiscence, to bear with one another's
weaknesses, and to bring up their children in the fear
of God.

Q. How comes it then that some marriages are unhappy, if matrimony be a sacrament which gives so
great a grace?

A. Because the greatest part do not receive it in the
dispositions they ought: they consult not God in their
choice, but only their own lust or temporal interest;
they prepare not themselves for it, by putting themselves in the state of grace; and too often are guilty of
freedoms before marriage, which are not allowable by
the law of God.

Q. In what dispositions ought persons to receive the
sacrament of matrimony?

A. They ought to be in a state of grace, by confession: their intention ought to be pure, viz. to embrace this holy state for the ends for which God instituted it · and if they be under the care of parents, &c.
they ought to consult them, and do nothing in this kind
without their consent.

Q. In what manner does the Catholic Church proceed in the administration of matrimony?

A. 1st, She orders that the banns should be proclaimed on three Sundays, or festival-days, before the
celebration of marriage; to the end, that if any one
knows any impediment why the parties may not by the
law of God, or his Church, be joined in matrimony he
may declare it.

2dly, The parties are to be married by their own parish priest, in the presence of two or three witnesses.

3dly, The parties express, in the presence of the priest, their mutual consent, according to the usual form of the Church; after which the priest says, I join you in matrimony, in the name of the Father and of the Son, and of the Holy Ghost. Amen.

4thly. The priest blesses the ring according to this form.

V. Our help is in the name of the Lord.

A. Who made heaven and earth.

V. O Lord hear my prayer.

A. And let my cry come to thee.

V. The Lord be with you.

A. And with thy spirit.

Let us pray.

Bless, ✠ O Lord, this ring, which we bless ✠ in thy name, that she that shall wear it, keeping inviolable fidelity to her spouse, may ever remain in peace and in thy will, and always live in mutual charity. Through Christ our Lord. Amen.

Then the priest sprinkles the ring with Holy water; and the bridegroom taking it, puts it on the fourth finger of the left hand of the bride, saying, 'In the name of the Father, and of the Son, and of the Holy Ghost. Amen.' Here also, according to the custom of Ireland, the bridegroom puts some gold and silver into the hand of the bride, saying, 'With this ring I thee wed, this gold and silver I give thee, and with all my worldly goods I thee endow.'

After this the priest says, V. Confirm, O God, this which thou hast wrought in us. A. From thy holy temple which is in Jerusalem. Lord have mercy on us. Christ have mercy on us. Lord have mercy on us. Our Father, &c. And lead us not into temptation. A. But deliver us from evil. V. Save thy servants. A Trusting in thee, O my God. V. Send them help, O Lord, from thy sanctuary. A. And defend them from Sion. V. Be to them, O Lord, a tower of strength.

A. Against the face of the enemy. **V.** O Lord hear my prayer. **A.** And let my cry come to thee. **V** The Lord be with you. **A.** And with thy spirit.

Let us pray.

Look down, O Lord, we beseech thee, upon those thy servants, and afford thy favourable assistance to thy own institution, by which thou hast ordained the propagation of mankind; that they who are joined together by thy authority, may be preserved by thy aid. Through Christ our Lord. Amen.

5thly, After this, if the nuptial benediction is to be given, the priest says the Mass appointed in the Missal, for the bridegroom and the bride; and having said the *Pater Noster*, turning about to the new married couple, he says over them the following prayers.

Let us pray.

Mercifully give ear, O Lord, to our prayers, and let thy grace accompany this thy institution, by which thou hast ordained the propagation of mankind; that this tie, which is made by thy authority, may be preserved by thy grace. Through our Lord Jesus Christ, &c.

Let us pray.

O God, who by thy omnipotent hand didst create all things of nothing! who at the first forming of the world having made man to the likeness of God, didst out of his flesh make the woman, and give her to him for his help, and by this didst inform us that what in its beginning was one, ought never be separated: O God, who by so excellent a mystery hast consecrated this union of both sexes, that thou wouldst have it be a type of that great sacrament which is betwixt Christ and his Church: O God, by whom this contract and mutual commerce has been ordained, and privileged with a blessing, which alone has not been recalled, either in punishment of original sin, or by the sentence of the flood, mercifully look on this thy servant the bride, who being now to be given in marriage, earnestly desires to be received under thy protection. May love and peace abound in her; may she marry in Christ faithful and chaste; may she ever imitate those holy women of former times; may she be as acceptable to her husband as Rachel, as discreet as Rebecca; may she in her years and fidelity be like Sarah, and may the author of evil at no time have any share in her actions; may she be steady in faith and the commandments; may she be true to her engagements, and flee all unlawful addresses; may she fortify her infirmity by thy discipline; may she be gravely bashful, venerably modest, and well-learned in the doctrine of heaven; may she be fruitful in her offspring; may she be approved and innocent; and may her happy lot be to arrive at length to the rest of the blessed in the kingdom of heaven; may they both see their children's children to the third and fourth generation, and live to a happy old age. Through the same Lord Jesus Christ, &c.

After the priest's communion, they both receive the blessed sacrament, and in the end of the Mass, before the usual blessing of the people, the priest turns to the bridegroom and bride, and says,

The God of Abraham, the God of Isaac, and the God of Jacob be with you, and may he fulfil his blessing in you, that you may see your children's children to the third and fourth generation, and afterwards enter into the possession of everlasting life, by the help of our Lord Jesus Christ; who, with the Father and the Holy Ghost, liveth and reigneth God for ever and ever. Amen.

Then the priest admonishes them to be faithful to one another, to love one another, and to live in the fear of God, and exhorts them to be continent, by mutual consent, at the times of devotion, and especially at the times of fasting, and of great solemnities, and so he finishes the Mass in the usual manner.

Q. Is there any obligation of receiving this nuptial benediction when persons are married?

A. The Church wishes that it were never omitted in the first marriage, when it may be had, because of the blessing it draws down from heaven, and it would certainly be a fault for persons to marry without it, when and where it may be had.

Q. Why does not the Church allow of this nuptial benediction, when the man or woman has been once married before?

A. Because the second marriage does not so perfectly represent the union of Christ and his Church, which is an eternal tie of one to one.

Q. Why does not the Church allow of the solemnity of marriages from the first Sunday of Advent till after Twelfth-day, and from Ash-Wednesday till after Low-Sunday?

A. Because the times of Advent and Lent are times of penance, as the times of Christmas and Easter are times of extraordinary devotion, and therefore are not proper for marriage feasts, or such like solemnities.

Q. What are the duties of married people to one another?

A. You shall hear them from Scripture.

Ephes. v. 22, 'Let women be subject to their husbands, as to the Lord.' Ver. 23, 'Because the man is the head of the woman, as Christ is the head of the Church: he is the Saviour of his body.' Ver. 24, 'Therefore, as the Church is subject to Christ, so also let women be to their husbands in all things.' Ver. 25, 'Husbands, love your wives, as Christ also loved the Church, and delivered himself for it.' Ver. 28, 'So ought also husbands to love their wives as their own bodies: he that loveth his wife, loveth himself.' Ver. 29, 'For no one ever hated his own flesh, but nourisheth it, and cherisheth it, as Christ also doth the Church.' Ver. 30, 'Because we are members of his body, of his flesh, and of his bones.' Ver. 31, 'For this cause shall a man leave his father and his mother, and shall adhere to his wife, and they shall be two in one flesh.' (Gen. ii.) Ver. 32, 'This sacrament is great, but I say in Christ and in the Church.' Ver. 33,

However, let every one of you in particular love his wife as himself; and let the wife reverence the husband.' See to the same effect, Colos. iii. 18, 19.

1 St. Peter iii. 1, 'Let women be subject to their husbands, to the end, that if any believe not the word, they may be gained without the word by the conversation of the women.' Ver. 2, 'Beholding your chaste conversation in fear.' Ver. 3, 'Whose adorning let it not be in the outward plaiting of the hair, or laying on gold round about, or putting on apparel.' Ver. 4, 'But the hidden man of the heart, in the incorruptibility of a quiet and modest spirit, which is rich in the sight of God.' Ver. 5, 'For in this manner heretofore also holy women, hoping in God, adorned themselves, being subject to their husbands.' Ver. 6, 'As Sarah obeyed Abraham, calling him Lord, whose daughters you are,' &c. Ver. 7, 'Husbands, in like manner dwelling with them according to knowledge, give honour to the women as to the weaker vessel, as to the joint heirs of the grace of life, that your prayers may not be hindered.'

1 Cor. vii. 3, 'Let the husband render the (marriage) debt to the wife ; and in like manner the wife to her husband.' Ver. 4, 'The wife hath not power of her own body, but the husband ; and in like manner the husband hath not power of his own body, but the wife.' Ver. 5, 'Defraud not one another unless perhaps by consent for a time, that you may give yourselves to prayer, and return again together to the same, lest Satan tempt you on account of your incontinency.' Ver. 6, 'Yet this I speak according to indulgence, not according to command.' Ver. 7, 'For I would have you all to be as myself, &c.' Ver. 10, 'But as to them who are joined in wedlock, it is not I but the Lord commands that the wife depart not from the husband. Ver. 11, 'But if she shall depart, that she remain unmarried, or be reconciled to her husband: and let not the husband put away his wife.'

Titus ii. 4. 'They may teach the young women prudence, that they love their husbands, be tender of their children.   Ver. 5, 'Discreet, chaste, sober, having care of the house, gentle, obedient to their husbands, that the word of God be not blasphemed.

There are also excellent documents for married people in the book of Tobias, ch. vi. 16. 'Then the angel Raphael said to him, hear me, and I will show thee who they are over whom the devil can prevail.' Ver. 17. 'For they who in such manner receive matrimony as to shut out God from themselves to their lust, as the horse and the mule, which have not understanding; over them the devil hath power.' Ver. 22. 'Thou shalt take the virgin with the fear of the Lord, moved rather for the love of children than for lust, that in the seed of Abraham thou mayst obtain blessing in children.' And ch. iii. 16. 'Thou knowest, Lord, that I never coveted a husband, and have kept my soul clean from all concupiscence.' Ver. 16. 'I never kept company with them that play, nor with them that walk in lightness did I make myself a partner.' Ver. 17. 'But a husband I consented to take, with thy fear, not with my lust.'

And chap. iii. 8. 'Thou madest Adam of the slime of the earth, and gavest him Eve for his helpmate.' Ver. 9 'And, now, Lord, thou knowest that not for fleshly lust do I take my sister to wife, but only for the love of posterity, in which thy name may be blessed for ever.'

Q. What are the duties of married people with regard to the education of their children?

A. They are obliged to train them up from their very infancy in the fear of God, and to give them early impressions of piety; to see that they be instructed in the Christian doctrine, and that they be kept to their prayers and other religious duties; in fine, to give them good example, and to remove from them the occasions of sin especially bad company and idleness.

Q. Does the Catholic Church allow her children to marry with those that are not of her communion?

A. She has often prohibited such marriages, as may be seen in the sixteenth canon of the Council of Illiberis, the 10th canon of the Council of Laodicea, the 14th canon of the Council of Chalcedon, the 67th canon of the Council of Agde, &c. Though sometimes, and in some places, pastors of the Church, for weighty reasons, have been forced to dispense with this law, and to celebrate such marriages.

Q. Why is the Church so averse to these kind of marriages?

A. 1st, Because she would not have her children communicate in sacred things, such as matrimony is, with those that are out of her communion. 2dly, Because such marriages are apt to give occasion to dissensions in families, whilst one of the parties draw one way, the other another. 3dly, Because there is a danger of the Catholic party being perverted, or at least of not being allowed the free exercise of religion. 4thly, Because there is a danger of the children being brought up in error, of which we have seen some sad instances. Where note, that those bargains are by no means to be allowed of by which the contracting parties agree to have the boys brought up in the religion of the father, and the girls to follow the mother. God and his Church will have no such division, nor give up thus their right to any one.

CHAPTER XX.

Of the Churching of Women after Childbearing.

Q. What is the meaning of the churching of women after childbearing? Is it that you look upon them to be under any uncleanness, as formerly in the old law, or to be any ways out of the Church by childbearing?

A. No, by no means; but what we call the churching of women, is nothing else but their coming to the Church to give thanks to God for their safe delivery, and to receive the blessing of the priest upon that occasion.

Q. What is the form and manner of churching of women?

A. The woman that desires to be churched, kneels
17

down at the door or entry of the Church, holding a lighted candle in her hand; and the priest, vested with his surplice and stole, sprinkles her first with Holy water, and then says:

V. Our help is in the name of the Lord.

R. Who made heaven and earth.

Anthem. This woman shall receive a blessing from the Lord.

Psalm 23.

The earth is the Lord's, and the fulness thereof; the compass of the world, and all that dwell therein.

Because he has founded it upon the seas, and prepared it upon the rivers.

Who shall go up into the mountain of the Lord, or who shall stand in his holy place?

The innocent of hands, and clean of heart, that hath not taken his soul in vain, nor sworn to his neighbour in guile.

He shall receive blessing of the Lord, and mercy of God and his Saviour.

This is the generation of them that seek him, of them that seek the face of the God of Jacob.

Lift up your gates, ye princes, and be ye lifted up, O eternal gates, and the King of Glory shall enter in.

Who is the King of Glory? The Lord, strong and mighty; the Lord, mighty in battle.

Lift up your gates, ye princes, and be ye lifted up, O eternal gates, and the King of Glory shall enter in.

Who is the King of Glory? The Lord of power he is the King of Glory.

Glory be to the Father, &c.

As it was in the beginning, &c.

Anthem. The woman shall receive a blessing from the Lord, and mercy from God her Saviour: for this is the generation of them that seek the Lord.

After this the priest stretches out to her hand the end of his stole, and so introduces her into the Church, saying, Come into the temple of God, adore the Son of the blessed Virgin Mary, who has given to thee to be fruitful in thy offspring.

Then she kneels before the altar, giving thanks to God for his benefits bestowed on her, whilst the priest prays as follows:

Lord have mercy on us. Christ have mercy on us. Lord have mercy on us. Our Father, &c. V. And lead us not into temptation. A. But deliver us from evil. V. Save thy handmaid, O Lord. A. Trusting in thee, O my God. V. Send her help, O Lord, from thy sanctuary. A. And defend her from Sion. V. Let not the enemy have any power over her. V. Nor the Son of iniquity presume to hurt her. V O Lord hear my prayer. A. And let my cry come to thee. V. The Lord be with you. A. And with thy spirit.

Let us pray.

Almighty everlasting God, who, by the blessed Virgin Mary's happy bringing forth, hast changed into joy the pains of the faithful in their childbearing; mercifully look down on this thy servant, who comes with joy to thy holy temple to return thee thanks; and grant that after this life she may, by the merits and intercession of the same blessed Mary, deserve to be received with her child into the joys of everlasting happiness. Through Christ our Lord. Amen.

Then the priest sprinkles her again with Holy water, in the form of the cross, saying, May the peace and blessing of Almighty God the Father, ✠ and the Son, and the Holy Ghost, come down upon thee, and remain with thee for ever. Amen

---

CHAPTER XXI.

Of the Fasts of the Catholic Church.

SECTION I. Of Fasting and Abstinence in general.

Q HAVE you any reason to think that fasting and abstinence is agreeable to God.

A. Yes, certainly: John the Baptist's abstinence is

commended, St. Luke i. 15, and St. Matt. iii. 4. And Anna the prophetess is praised, St. Luke ii. 37, for serving God with fastings and prayers night and day. The Ninivites by fasting obtained mercy, Jonas iii. 5 Daniel joined fasting with prayer, Dan. ix. 3, and by fasting was disposed for heavenly visions, Dan. x. 3, 7 12. The royal prophet humbled his soul in fasting, Psalm xxxiv. (alias xxxv.) Ezra and Nehemiah sought and found seasonable aid from God by fasting, Ezra viii. 23, and Nehemiah i. 4. And God, by the prophet Joel, calls upon his people (Joel ii. 12) 'to turn to him with all their hearts in fasting, weeping, and mourning.'

Q. But did our Lord Jesus Christ design that his followers should fast?

A. Yes, he not only gave them an example by fasting forty days, St. Matt. iv. 2, and prescribed to them lessons concerning fasting, St. Matt. vi. 16, &c., but also expressly affirmed, that after the bridegroom should be taken from them, that is, after his passion, resurrection and ascension, all his children, that is, all good Christians, should fast, St. Matt. ix. 15. St. Mark ii. 20. St. Luke v. 35. Hence we find the Christians at Antioch fasting, Acts xiii. 2; and Paul and Barnabas ordained with prayer and fasting, ver. 3, and priests ordained by them in every Church with prayer and fasting, Acts xiv. 23, and the Apostles 'approving themselves as the ministers of God—in fasting,' 2 Cor. vi. 4, 5, &c.

Q. Has fasting any particular efficacy against the devil?

A. Yes: 'This kind (of devils) can come forth by nothing but by prayer and fasting,' saith our Lord, St. Mark ix. 29.

Q. What are the ends for which Christians are to fast, and for which the Church prescribes days of fasting and abstinence?

A. 1st, To chastise ourselves, and to do penance for our sins, that so, like the Ninivites, we may obtain mercy of God. 2dly, To curb and restrain our passions and concupiscences, and to bring the flesh under subjection to the spirit. 3dly, To be enabled by fasting to raise our souls the easier to God, and to offer him purer prayer.

Q. What are the rules prescribed by the Catholic Church with regard to eating on fasting days?

A. 1st, The Church prohibits all flesh meats on fasting days, and in Lent, eggs also, and cheese formerly wine was prohibited; but this prohibition, by a contrary custom, has been long since laid aside. 2dly, The Church allows her children but one meal on fasting days; besides which, custom has introduced a small collation at night. 3dly, The meal which the Church allows on fasting days must not be taken till towards noon: formerly, for the first twelve hundred years of the Church, the meal was not to be taken in Lent before the evening; and on the other fasting days not till three o'clock in the afternoon. These rules regard the days of fasting; but as to those that are only days of abstinence, such as the Sundays in Lent, the three Rogation days, and the Fridays and Saturdays throughout the year, were only obliged to abstain from flesh on those days, but no ways confined to one meal.

Q. But why does the Church prohibit flesh on days of fasting and abstinence?

A. Not that she looks upon any meats unclean by the new law, but she does it that her children may better comply with the ends of fasting, viz. mortification and penance, by abstaining on those days from that kind of food which is most nourishing and agreeable.

Q. But is not this condemned by the Apostle, 1 Tim. iv. 3, where he calls it 'the doctrine of devils to command to abstain from meats which God hath created to be received with thanksgiving?'

A. The Apostle speaks of the doctrine of those, who, with the Marcionites, Manichæans, and other heretics, forbid the use of meat, not as the Church does, by way of mortification and penance, on days of fasting and humiliation, but as a thing absolutely unclean, and unlawful to be used at any time, as coming from an evil principle. All that know any thing of Church history, know that it was the system of many

17 *

heretics, who also upon the same account absolutely condemned marriage, as tending to the propagation of the flesh. Now they that know these things are guilty of the highest injustice, pretending that those words of the Apostle were levelled at the Catholic Church, when their own conscience must tell them that they were designed for another set of people. The Catholic Church is far from condemning the use of God's creatures in proper times and seasons; but she neither does, nor ever did, think all kind of diet proper for days of fasting, and in this particular the modern Church is so far from going beyond the primitive Christians, that on the contrary, all kind of monuments of antiquity make it evident, that our forefathers, in the first ages of the Church, were more severe in their abstinence than we now are.

Q. But does not the Apostle say, 1 Cor. x. 25, 'Whatsoever is sold in the shambles, that eat, asking no questions for conscience sake?'

A. He speaks not this with relation to the days of fasting, as if any sorts of meat might be eaten on fasting days; but he speaks, as it is visible from the context, with regard to the meats offered to idols; which some weak brethren were so much afraid of eating, that upon this account they durst not eat the meat sold in the shambles, lest it might have been offered to idols. Upon the same principle the Apostle adds, ver. 27, 'If any of them that believe not, invite you to a feast, and ye be disposed to go, whatsoever is set before you eat, asking no question for conscience sake.' Ver. 28, 'But if any man say unto you, This is offered in sacrifice unto idols, eat not for his sake that showed it, and for conscience sake,' &c.

Q. Do you take it then to be a sin to eat meat on fasting days, or otherwise to break the Church-fasts without necessity?

A. Yes, certainly; because it is a sin to disobey our lawful superiors, and more particularly to disobey the Church of God. 'If he neglect to hear the Church, let him be to thee as a heathen and a publican,' St Matt. xviii. 17.

Q. Does not Christ say, St. Matt. xv. 11, 'That which goeth into the mouth doth not defile a man?'

A. True: it is not any uncleanness in the meat, as many heretics have imagined, or any dirt or dust which may stick to it by eating, without first washing the hands (of which case our Lord is speaking in the text you quote) which can defile the soul; for every creature of God is good, and whatsoever corporal filth enters in at the mouth is cast forth into the draught; but that which defiles the soul, when a person transgresses the Church-fast, is the disobedience of the heart, in breaking the precept of the Church, which God has commanded us to bear and to obey. And thus an Israelite would have been defiled in the time of the old law, by eating of blood or swine's flesh; and thus our first parents were defiled by eating the forbidden fruit, not by the uncleanness of the food, but by the disobedience of the heart to the law of God.

Q. What are the conditions that ought to accompany a Christian faith, to make it such a fast as God has chosen?

A. The great and general fast of a Christian is to abstain from sin; and God would not accept of the fasts of the Jews, Isaiah lviii., because on the days of their fasting they were found doing their own will and oppressing their neighbours. So that the first condition that ought to go along with our fasts is to renounce our sins; the second is to let our fasts be accompanied with alms-deeds and prayer, Tob. xii. viii.; the third, to endeavour to perform them in a penitential spirit.

Q. What persons are excused from the strictness of the church fast?

A. Children under age, sick people, women that are with child, or that give suck; likewise those that upon fasting days are obliged to hard labour; and, in a word, all such who, through weakness, infirmity, or other hinderance, cannot fast without great prejudice or danger: where note 1st, That if the cause be not evident, a person must have recourse to his pastor for dispensation. 2dly, That in some of the above mentioned cases a person may be excused from one part of the fast, and not from another; or may be excused from fasting, and yet not from abstinence. 3dly, That such as for some just cause are dispensed with from fasting, ought to endeavour, as far as their condition and circumstances will allow, to be so much the more diligent in their devotions, more liberal in their alms, more patient in their sufferings, and to make up the interior spirit of penance what is wanting to the out ward fast.

SECTION II.

Of the Fast of Lent.

Q. WHEN did the Church first begin to observe the fast of Lent?

A. We know no beginning of it; for it is a fast that has been observed by the Church from the time of the Apostles, and stands upon the same foundation as the observation of the Lord's day, that is, upon apostolical tradition.

Q. Have the ancient fathers often mentioned the solemn fast of forty days, which we call Lent?

A. Yes: it is mentioned by the holy fathers in innumerable places; who also inform us, that they had received it by tradition from the Apostles, see St Jerome, epist. 54, ad Marcellum, and St. Leo the Great, serm. 43, and 46. And the transgressors of this solemn fast are severely punished by the 68th Canon of the Apostles.

Q. Have you any thing else to offer to prove that the fast of Lent comes from an ordinance of the Apostles?

A. Yes: it is proved by that rule of St. Augustine epist. 118, to Januarius, viz. That what is found not to have had its institution from any Council, but to have been ever observed by the universal Church, that same must needs have come from the first fathers, the founders of the Church, that is. from the Apostles. But the fast of Lent is not found to have had its institution from any Council, but to have been observed in all ages, from the very beginning, amongst all Christian people from East to West:–therefore the fast of Lent is an apostolical ordinance and tradition.

Q. For what ends was the fast of Lent instituted?

A. 1st, That by this yearly fast of forty days, we might imitate the fast of our Lord, St. Matt. iv. 2. 2dly, That by this institution we might set aside the tithe, or tenth part of the year, to be more particularly consecrated to God by prayer and fasting; as it was commanded in the law, to give God the tithes of all things. 3lly, That by this forty days' fast, joined with prayers and alms-deeds, we might do penance for the sins of the whole year. 4thly, That we might at this time enter into a kind of spiritual exercises, and a retreat from the world; to look more narrowly into the state of our souls, to repair our decayed strength, and to provide effectual remedies against our usual failings for the time to come. 5thly, That by this solemn fast we might celebrate in a more becoming manner the passion of Christ, which we particularly commemorate in the Lent. In fine, that this fast might be a preparation for the great solemnity of Easter, and for the Paschal communion.

Q. In what spirit would the Church have her children undertake and go through the fast of Lent?

A. In a penitential spirit, that is, with a deep sense of repentance for having offended God; an earnest desire and resolution of a new life, and of mortifying and chastising themselves for their sins. These lessons she inculcates every day in her Office and Liturgy; witness the hymns prescribed for this holy time, the responsories, the collects, tracts, &c. I shall give you a specimen of the spirit of the Church in this regard, by setting down some passages of the scripture, which she orders to be read in the canonical hours of prayer every day during this time.

1. At Lauds, Isaiah lviii. 'Cry out, cease not, raise thy voice like a trumpet, and declare to my people their wickedness, and to the house of Jacob their sins.'

2. At Prime, or the first hour, Isaiah lv. 'Seek the Lord whilst he may be found, call upon him whilst he is near.'

3. At Terce, or the third hour, Joel ii. ' Be converted to me with your whole heart, in fasting, and weeping, and mourning; and rend your hearts, and not your garments, saith the Lord Almigsty.'

4. At Sext, or the sixth hour, Isaiah lv. ' Let the wicked man forsake his ways, and the unjust man his thoughts; and let him return to the Lord, and he will have mercy on him; and to our God, for his mercy is great.'

5. At None, or the ninth hour, Isaiah liii. ' Break thy bread to the hungry, and bring in the needy and the harbourless into thy house: when thou shalt see the naked, clothe him, and despise not thy own flesh.'

6. Ad Vesperas, or Evening-song, Joel ii. ' Between the porch and the altar, the priests, the ministers of the Lord shall mourn, and they shall say, Spare, O Lord, spare thy people; and let not thy inheritance fall into reproach, for the nations to domineer over them.'

To the same effect she often repeats in her Office the following exhortation: ' Let us repent and amend the sins which we have ignorantly committed, lest, being suddenly overtaken by the day of our death, we seek for time of penance; and be not able to find it.'

And again: ' Behold now is an acceptable time, behold now are the days of salvation; let us recommend ourselves in much patience,' &c.

Q. Why do you call the first day of Lent, Ash-Wednesday?

A. From the ceremony of blessing ashes upon that day, and putting them on the foreheads of the faithful, to remind them that they must very quickly return to dust; and therefore must not neglect to lay hold of this present time of mercy, and like the Ninivites and other ancient penitents, do penance for their sins in sackcloth and ashes. The prayers which are said by the Church, for the blessing of the ashes, are directed for the obtaining of God the spirit of compunction, and the remission of sins for all those who receive those ashes; and the priest, in making the sign of the cross, with the ashes on the forehead of each one of the faithful, says these words: ' Remember, man, that thou art dust, and into dust thou shalt return.'

Q. Was it ever the custom of the Catholic Church to meet on that day to curse sinners?

A. No; but to pray to God to obtain mercy for sinners.

Q. What benefit is it to the faithful to have regular times of fasting appointed by the Church, rather than to be left to their own discretion to fast when they please?

A. 1st, It is to be feared, that many would not fast at all, were they not called upon by these regular fasts of the Church. 2dly, It is not to be doubted, but that sinners may more easily and readily find mercy, when they join thus all in a body with the whole Church of God, in suing for mercy.

Q. But is this mercy to be expected, if sinners only mortify themselves in point of eating, and in all other things indulge themselves in their accustomed liberties?

A. It is certain, that the true spirit of penance, which is the spirit of Lent, requires that they should be mortified, not only in their eating, but also by retrenching all superfluities in other things, as in drinking, sleeping, idle visits, and unnecessary divertisements, according to that of the Church Hymn for Lent.

Utamur ergo parcius
Verbis, cibis et potibus,
Somno, jocis, et arctius
Perstemus in custodia.

Q. What do you think of preparing for Lent by a carnival of debauchery and excess?

A. I think it is a relic of heathenism, infinitely opposite to the spirit of the Church. The very name of Shrove-tide, in the language of our forefathers, signifies the season or time of confession; because our ancestors were accustomed, according to the true spirit of the Church, to go to confession at that time, that so they might enter on the solemn fast of Lent, in a manner suitable to this penitential fast.

Q. Why is the Evening Office, or Vespers, said before dinner, on all days in Lent excepting Sundays?

A. It is a relic of the anc ent custom of fasting in Lent till the evening.

Q. Why is the Alleluia laid aside during the time of Lent?

A. Because it is a canticle of joy, and therefore is omitted in this time of penance: but instead of it, the Church, at the beginning of all the canonical hours of her daily Office, repeats those words; 'Praise be to thee, O Lord, King of everlasting Glory.'

Q. Why is the fifth Sunday in Lent called Passion Sunday?

A. Because, from that day till Easter, the Church, in a particular manner, commemorates the passion of Christ.

Q. Why are the crucifixes and altar-pieces covered during this time, in which we celebrate Christ's passion?

A. Because the Church is then in mourning for her Spouse, who in his passion was truly a hidden God, by concealing his divinity, and becoming for us 'as a worm, and no man, the reproach of men, and the outcast of the people,' Psalm xxi.

SECTION III.

Of othe Days of Fasting and Abstinence in the Catholic Church.

Q. DOES the Church observe any other days of fasting and abstinence, besides the forty days of Lent?

A. Yes; she fasts upon the Wednesdays, Fridays, and Saturdays, in the four Ember-weeks; and upon the vigils or eves of some of her festivals; as also upon Wednesdays and Fridays in Advent; and she abstains from flesh on the three Rogation days, on St. Mark's day, and on the Fridays and Saturdays throughout the year..

Q. Which do you call the four Ember-weeks?

A. The four Ember-weeks, are the weeks in which the Church gives Holy Orders, at the four seasons of

the year, viz. the first week in Lent, Whitsun-week the third week in September, and the third week in Advent; and they are called Ember-weeks, from the custom of our forefathers, of fasting at that time in sackcloth and ashes, or from eating nothing but cakes baked under the embers, and from thence called Emberbread.

Q. Why has the Church appointed these fasts of the Ember-days at the four seasons of the year?

A. 1st, That no part of the year might pass without offering to God the tribute of a penitential fast. 2dly, That we might beg his blessing on the fruits of the earth, and give him thanks for those which we have already received. 3dly, That all the faithful might join at these times in prayer and fasting to obtain of God worthy pastors; these being the times of their ordination. Thus the primitive Christians fasted at the times of the ordination of their ministers, Acts xiii. 2 and 3, and chap. xiv. 22.

Q. Why does the Church fast upon the eve or vigils of some holidays?

A. To prepare her children, by mortification and penance, for the worthily celebrating those days.

Q. Why do we abstain upon Fridays?

A. Because our Lord suffered for us upon a Friday. From this rule of abstaining upon Fridays, we except, if Christmas day occur upon a Friday or Saturday, we do not abstain on that day.

Q. What is the meaning of the three Rogation days?

A. The Monday, Tuesday, and Wednesday, before Ascension-day, are called the three Rogation days, or days of solemn supplication and prayer. On these days we keep abstinence, and in every parish we go in procession, singing the Litanies, to beg God's blessing upon the fruits of the earth, and to be preserved from pestilence, famine, &c. Upon the same account we keep abstinence on the day of St. Mark, April 25, with the like solemn supplications and Litanies.

Q. And what is the meaning of keeping abstinence upon Saturday?

A. Because Saturday was the day that our Lord lay

18

dead in the monument, and a day of mourning to his disciples. This abstinence is also a proper preparation for the solemnity of the Lord's Day.

N. B. That in the East, instead of the Saturday, they fast upon the Wednesday, as being the day on which the Jews held their council against Christ, and on which he was sold by Judas.

CHAPTER XXII

Of the Church Office, or the Canonical Hours of Prayer in the Catholic Church.

Q. WHAT do you mean by the Church Office?

A. It is a form of prayer, consisting of Psalms, Lessons, Hymns, &c. used by all the clergy, and by the religious of both sexes in the Catholic Church. This office is divided into seven parts, commonly called the Seven Canonical Hours, according to the different stages or stations of Christ's passion, viz. the Matins or Midnight Office, to which are annexed the Lauds, or Morning Praises of God; the first, third, sixth, and ninth hours of prayer, commonly called prime, terce, sext, and none; the Vespers, or Even-song; and the Complin. All these are duly performed by the clergy and religious every day, according to that of the Royal Prophet, Psalm cxviii. 'Seven times in the day I gave praise to thee.'

Q. Have you any warrant in scripture for these different hours of prayer?

A. Yes; as to the Midnight Office, King David tells us, Psalm cxviii. that 'he arose at midnight to confess to God;' and we find that St. Paul and Silas, even in prison, 'prayed at midnight and sung praises to God,' Acts xvi. 25.

As for the Lauds, or praises of God at break of day, they are also recommended to us by the example of the Psalmist, Psalm lxii. 'O God, my God, to thee do I watch from the morning light;' and by the admonition of the Wise man, Wisd. vi. 22, 'That we ought to get up before the sun to bless God, and at the rising of the light to adore him.'

Of Prime, or the first hour of prayer at sunrising, we may understand that of the Royal Prophet, Psalm v. 'In the morning thou shalt hear my voice,' &c. At Terce, or the third hour of prayer, it was, that the Apostles received the Holy Ghost, Acts ii. 15. At Sext, or the Sixth hour, St. Peter was prayng when he was called by a vision to open the Church to the Gentiles, Acts x. 9. And we read also of St. Peter, with St. John, going up to the temple to the 'ninth hour of prayer,' Acts iii. I. For Vespers, or even-song, and Complin, which are evening prayers, we have the example of the Royal Prophet, Psalm liv. 'In the evening, and the morning, and at noonday, I will speak and declare, and he will hear my voice.' Hence we find, that the night Office, the morning praises, the third, sixth, and ninth hours of prayer, and the even-song, were, among the primitive Christians, regularly observed, not only by the clergy, but also by the rest of the faithful; to which the religious afterwards added the Prime and Complin.

Q. Can you give me a short scheme of the canonical hours of prayer, according to the Roman Breviary?

A. Matins begin with the Lord's Prayer, the Hail Mary, and the Apostles' Creed: then, after a Versicle or two, to call for God's assistance, and the Gloria Patri, &c. follows the 94th Psalm, (alias 95,) by which we invite one another to praise and adore God. Then comes a hymn, which is followed by the Psalms, with their proper anthems, and the lessons of the day, with their responsories. In the Matins, for Sunday, we read eighteen Psalms, and nine lessons: on festivals, and saints' days, we read nine psalms and nine lessons, divided into three Nocturns: on Ferial, or common days, we read twelve psalms and three lessons. The psalms are so distributed, that in the week we go through the whole Psalter: the lessons are partly taken out of the scriptures of the Old and New Testament, partly out of the acts of the saints, and the

writings and homilies of t e holy fathers. Upon fast,
ing days, and during the whole Paschal time, and upon
all Sundays from Easter to Advent, and from Christmas till Septuagesima, we· close the Matins with the
Te Deum.

In the Lauds we recite seven psalms, and one of the
scripture canticles, with their respective anthems, and
a hymn, then the canticle Benedictus, with the prayer
or prayers of the day : and in the end an anthem and
prayer of the blessed Virgin Mary.

The Prime begins with the Pater, Ave, and Creed,
Deus in adjutorium, &c. Gloria Patri, &c. After which
there follows a morning hymn, the 53d Psalm, (alias 54,)
with a part of the 118th, (alias 119,) to which, on Sundays, is prefixed the 117th Psalm, and subjoined the
Athanasian Creed. Then follows an anthem, a capitu-
lum, or short lesson, with its responsory, and divers
prayers to beg God's grace for the following day.

Terce, Sext, and None, begin with Pater, Ave, &c.
and consist each of them of a proper hymn, and six
divisions of the 118th Psalm: which excellent psalm
the Church would have her clergy daily recite, because
every verse of it contains the praises of God's holy law
and commandments, or excites the soul to the love and
esteem thereof, or in fine, prays for the grace to fulfil
the same. After the psalm follows an anthem ; then a
short lesson, responsory and prayer: and each hour is
concluded with a Pater Noster.

Vespers, or even-song, are begun also with Pater,
Ave, &c. and consist of five psalms, with their anthems,
a short chapter or lesson, a hymn, and the Magnificat,
or canticle of the blessed Virgin Mary, with its proper
anthem, and a collect or prayer, to which are usually
joined three or four commemorations, consisting of anthems, verses and prayers.

Complin consists of the Lord's Prayer, the Confiteor,
&c. four psalms, an anthem, hymn, lesson, responsory,
the canticle Nunc dimittis, with its anthem, and some
short prayers, which are closed with an anthem and
prayer of the blessed Virgin, and the Pater, Ave. and
Creed

CHAPTER XXIII.

Of the Festivals of the Catholic Church: We re also of the Holy Week, and the Ceremonies ther of.

Q. WHAT are the days which the Church commands to be kept holy?

A. 1st, The Sundays, or the Lord's day, which we observe by apostolical tradition, instead of the Sabbr.h. 2dly. The feasts of our Lord's Nativity, or Christmas-day; his Circumcision, or New-Year's day; the Epiphany, or Twelfth-day, Easter day, or the day of our Lord's Resurrection, with the Monday following, the day of our Lord's Ascension; Whit-sunday, or the day of the coming of the Holy Ghost, with the Monday following; Trinity Sunday; Corpus Christi, or the feast of the blessed Sacrament. 3dly, We keep the days of the Annunciation, and Assumption of the blessed Virgin Mary. 4thly, We observe the feast of All-saints; of St. John Baptist; of the holy Apostles, St. Peter and St. Paul. 5thly, In this kingdom we keep the feast of St. Patrick our principal patron.

Q. What warrant have you for keeping the Sunday, preferable to the ancient Sabbath, which was the Saturday?

A. We have for it the authority of the Catholic Church, and apostolical tradition.

Q. Does the scripture any where command the Sunday to be kept for the Sabbath?

A. The scripture commands us to hear the Church, St. Matt. xviii. 17. St. Luke x. 16, and to hold fast the traditions of the Apostles, 2 Thess. ii. 15, but the scripture does not in particular mention this change of the Sabbath. St. John speaks of the Lord's day, Kev. i. 10, but he does not tell us what day of the week this was, much less does he tell us that this day was to take place of the Sabbath ordained in the commandments: St. Luke also speaks of the disciples meeting together to break bread on the first day of the week, Acts xx. 7. And St. Paul, 1 Cor. xvi. 2, orders that on the first day of the week the Corinthians should

18 *

lay by in store what they designed to bestow in charity on the faithful in Judea: but neither one nor the other tells us, that this first day of the week was to be henceforward the day of worship, and the Christian Sabbath: so that truly, the best authority we have for this is the testimony and ordinance of the Church. And therefore, those who pretend to be so religious observers of the Sunday, whilst they take no notice of other festivals ordained by the same Church authority, show tha they act by humour, and not by reason and religion; since Sundays and holydays all stand upon the same foundation, viz. the ordinance of the Church.

Q. But ought it not to be enough to keep one day in the week, according as it was prescribed in the commandments, without enjoining any other festivals or holydays; especially since it is expressly said in the commandment, 'Six days shalt thou labour and do all thy work,' Exod. xx. 9?

A. God did not, in the Old Testament, only appoint the weekly Sabbath, which was the Saturday, but moreover ordained several other festivals, commanding them to be kept holy, and forbidding all servile work on them. As the feast of the Pasch or Passover; the feast of Pentecost; the feast of the Sound of Trumpets, on the first day of the tenth month; the feast of Atonement, on the tenth day of the same month, the feast of Tabernacles, on the fifteenth day of the same month, &c. See the 23d chapter of Leviticus. So that when it is said in the law, 'Six days shalt thou labour,' &c. this must needs be understood, in case no holyday came in the week; otherwise the law would contradict itself.

Q. But does not St. Paul reprehend the Galatians, Gal. iv. 10, 11, for observing days, and months, and times, and years?

A. This is to be understood either of the superstitious observation of lucky or unlucky days, &c. or, as it is far more probable from the whole context of the observation of the Jewish festivals; which, with the old law, were now abolished, but were taken up by the Galatians, together with circumcision, upon the recommendation of certain false teachers: but far was it from the design of the Apostle to reprehend their observation of Christian solemnities, either of the Lord's day, or of other festivals observed by apostolical tradition, or recommended by the authori y of the Church of Christ. For these come to us recommended by Christ himself, who says to the pastors of his Church, ' He that heareth you, heareth me : and he that despiseth you, despiseth me,' St. Luke x. 16.

Q. What was the reason why the weekly Sabbath was changed from the Saturday to the Sunday ?

A. Because our Lord fully accomplished the work of our redemption by rising from the dead on a Sunday, and by s nding down the Holy Ghost on a Sunday : as therefore the work of our redemption was a greater work than that of our creation, the primitive Church thought the day, in which this work was completely finished, was more worthy her religious observation than that in which God rested from the creation, and should be properly called the Lord's day.

Q. But has the Church a power to make any alterations in the commandments of God ?

A. The commandments of God, as far as they contain his eternal law, are unalterable and indispensable ; but as to whatever was only ceremonial, they cease to oblige, since the Mosaic law was abrogated by Christ's death. Hence, as far as the commandment obliges us to set aside some part of our time for the worship and service of our Creator, it is an unalterable and unchangeable precept of the eternal law, in which the Church cannot dispense : but forasmuch as it prescribes the seventh day in particular for this purpose, it is no more than a ceremonial precept of the old law, which obligeth not Christians. And therefore, instead of the seventh day, and other festivals appointed by the old law, the Church has prescribed the Sundays and holydays to be set apart for God's worship ; and these we are now obliged to keep in consequence of God's commandment, instead of the ancient Sabbath.

Q. What was the reason of the institution of other festivals besides the Lord's day ?

A. That we might celebrate the memory of the chief mysteries of our redemption ; that we might give God thanks for his mercies, and glorify him in his saints.

Q. In what manner ought a Christian to spend the Sundays and holydays?

A. In religious duties; such as assisting at the great sacrifice of the Church, and other public prayers, reading good books, and hearing of the word of God, &c.

Q. Why does the Church prohibit all servile works upon Sundays or holydays?

A. That the faithful may have nothing to take them off from attending to God's service, and the sanctification of their souls upon these days. And certainly, a Christian that has any religious thoughts, can never think much of devoting now and then a day, to that great business, for which alone he came into this world.

Q. What is the meaning of the institution of Christmas?

A. To celebrate the birth of Christ; to give God thanks for sending his Son into the world for our redemption; and that we may, upon this occasion, endeavour to study and to learn those great lessons of poverty of spirit, of humility, and of self-denial, which the Son of God teaches us from the crib of Bethlehem.

Q. What is the reason that on Christmas-day Mass is said at midnight?

A. Because Christ was born at midnight.

Q. Why are three Masses said by every priest upon Christmas-day?

A. This ancient observance may be understood to denote three different births of Christ; his eternal birth from his Father, his temporal birth from his mother, and his spiritual birth in the hearts of good Christians.

Q. Are all the faithful obliged to hear three Masses on Christmas-day?

A. No, they are not: though it would be very commendable so to do.

Q. What is the meaning of the time of Advent before Christmas?

A. It is a time appointed by the Church for devotion and penance, and is called Advent or coming, because in it we prepare ourselves for the worthy celebrating the mercies of our Lord's first coming, that so we may escape the rigour of his justice at his second coming.

Q. What is the meaning of New-Year's day?

A. It is the octave of Christmas, and the day of our Lord's circumcision, when he first began to shed his innocent blood for us: and on this day we ought to study how we may imitate him by a spiritual circumcision of our hearts.

Q. What is the meaning of the Epiphany, or Twelfth-day?

A. It is a day kept in memory of the coming of the Wise men of the East, to adore our Saviour in his infancy: and it is called Epiphany, or Manifestation, because our Lord then began to manifest himself to the Gentiles. The devotion of this day is to give God thanks for our vocation to the true faith, and like the wise men to make our offerings of gold, frankincense, and myrrh, that is, of charity, prayer, and mortification to our new-born Saviour. On this day the Church also celebrates the memory of the baptism of Christ, and of his first miracle of changing water into wine in Cana of Galilee.

Q. What is the meaning of Candlemas-day?

A. It is the day of the Purification of the Blessed Virgin after childbearing, and of the presentation of our Lord in the temple; when the just man Simeon, who had a promise from the Holy Ghost of seeing the Saviour of the world before his death, received him into his arms, and proclaimed him to be the light of the Gentiles. Upon this account, the Church upon this day make a solemn procession with lighted candles, which are blessed by the priest before Mass, and carried in the hands of the faithful, as an emblem of Christ, who is the true light of the world. And from this ceremony this day is called Candlemas, or the Mass of candles.

Q. What is the meaning of the Annunciation, or Lady-day, the 25th of March?

A. It is the day of our Lord's Incarnation, when he was first conceived by the Holy Ghost in the womb of the blessed Virgin Mary: and it is called the Annunciation, from the message brought from heaven on this day to the Virgin by the angel Gabriel

Q. What is the meaning of the Holy Week before Easter ?

A. It is a week of more than ordinary devotion in honour of the passion of Christ.

Q. What is the meaning of Palm Sunday ?

A. It is the day in which our Lord, being about to suffer for us, entered into Jerusalem, sitting upon an ass, as had been foretold by the prophet Zacharaih, chap. ix. ver. 9, and was received with hosannas of joy, accompanied by a great multitude bearing branches of palms in their hands. In memory of which we go in procession round the Church on this day, bearing also branches of palms in our hands, to celebrate the triumphs of our victorious king.

Q. What is the meaning of the Tenebræ Office in holy week ?

A. The Matins of Christ's passion, which formerly used to be said in the night, and are now said in the evening, on Wednesday, Thursday, and Friday, in holy week, are called the Tenebræ Office, from the Latin word, which signifies darkness ; because towards the latter end of the Office, all the lights are extinguished in memory of the darkness which covered all the earth, whilst Christ was hanging upon the cross: and at the end of the Office, a noise is made to represent the earthquake and splitting of the rocks, which happened at the time of our Lord's death.

Q. What is the meaning of Maunday-Thursday ?

A. It is the day on which Christ first instituted the blessed sacrament ; and began his passion by his bitter agony and bloody sweat. From the *Gloria in excelsis* of the Mass of this day, till the Mass of Easter Eve, our bells are silent throughout the Catholic Church, because we are now mourning for the passion of Christ. Our altars are also uncovered and stripped of all their ornaments, because Christ, our true altar, hung naked upon the cross. On this day also, prelates and superiors wash in the Church the feet of their subjects, after the example of our Lord, St. John xiii.

Q. What is the meaning of visiting the sepulchres upon Maunday-Thursday ?

A. The place where the blessed sacrament is reserved in the Church, in order for the Office of Good Friday, (on which day there is no consecration,) is by the people called the sepulchre, as representing by anticipation the burial of Christ. And where there are many Churches, the faithful make their stations to visit our Lord in these sepulchres, and meditate on the different stages of his passion.

Q. What is the meaning of Good Friday?

A. It is the day on which Christ died for us upon the cross. The devotion proper for this day, and for the whole time in which we celebrate Christ's passion, is to meditate upon the suffering of our Redeemer, to study the excellent lessons of virtue, which he teaches us, by his example, in the whole course of his passion; especially his humility, meekness, patience, obedience, resignation, &c., and above all, to learn his hatred of sin and his love for us; that we may also learn to hate sin, which nailed him to the cross; and to love him that has loved us even unto death.

Q. What is the meaning of kneeling to the cross and kissing it on Good Friday?

A. It is to express, by this reverence outwardly exhibited to the cross, our veneration and love for him, who upon this day died for us on the cross.

Q. What is the meaning of Holy Saturday?

A. It is Easter Eve, and therefore in the Mass of this day the Church resumes the Alleluias of joy, which she had intermitted during the penitential time of Septuagesima and Lent. On this day is blessed the Paschal candle, as an emblem of Christ, and his light and glory; which burns during the Mass from Easter until Ascension, that is, during the whole time that Christ remained upon earth after his resurrection. This day and Whitsun-eve were anciently the days deputed by the Church for solemn baptism, and therefore on this day the fonts are solemnly blessed.

Q. What is the meaning of Easter?

A. It is the chief feast of the whole year, as being the solemnity of our Lord's resurrection. The devotion of this time is to rejoice in Christ's victory over death and hell; and to labour to imitate his resurrec tion, by arising from the death of sin to the life of grace.

Q. What is the meaning of Ascension day?

A. It is the yearly memory of Christ's ascending into heaven, forty days after his rising again from the dead, and therefore it is a festival of joy, as well by reason of the triumphs of our Saviour on this day, and the exaltation of our human nature, by him now exalted above the angels : as likewise, because our Saviour has taken possession of that kingdom in our name, and is preparing a place for us ; and, in the mean time, he there discharges the Office of our High Priest and our Advocate, by constantly representing his death and passion to his Father in our behalf. It is also a part of the devotion of this day, to labour to disengage our hearts from this earth, and earthly things, to remember that we are but strangers and pilgrims here, and to aspire after our heavenly country, where Christ our treasure is gone before us, in order to draw our hearts thither after him.

Q. What is the most proper devotion for the time between Ascension and Whitsunday ?

A. To prepare ourselves for the Holy Ghost, as the Apostles did by retirement and prayer, and to purify our souls from sin, especially from all rancour and impurity.

Q. What is the meaning of the solemnity of Whitsunday or Pentecost?

A. It was a festival observed in the old law, in memory of the law having been given on that day in thunder and lightning; and it is observed by us now in memory of the new law, having been promulgated on this day by the Holy Ghost's descent upon the Apostles in the shape of tongues of fire. The proper devotion of this time is to invite the Holy Ghost into our souls by fervent prayer, and to give ourselves to his divine influences.

Q. What is the meaning of Trinity Sunday?

A. The first Sunday after Pentecost is called Trinity Sunday, because on that day we particularly commemorate that great mystery of Three Persons in one God, and glorify the blessed Trinity for the whole work of our redemption, which we have celebrated in the foregoing festivals.

Q. What is the meaning of the solemnity of Corpus Christi?

A. It is a festival observed by the Church, to give God thanks for his goodness and mercy in the institution of the blessed Sacrament; and t, tnis end are ordained the processions and benedictions of this octave.

Q. What is the meaning of the feast of the Invention, or finding of the cross, May the 3d?

A. It is a day of devotion in memory of the miraculous finding of the cross of Christ, by the empress Helen, mother to Constantine the Great; and the chief devotion of the Church upon this day, as well as upon that of the Exaltation of the Cross, Sept. 14, is to celebrate the victorious death and passion of our Redeemer

Q. What are the days observed by the Church in honour of our Lady, the blessed Virgin Mary?

A. Besides her Purification and the Annunciation, of which we have already spoken, we observe the day of her Conception, Dec. 8, the day of her birth, or Nativity, Sept. 8, and the day of her happy passage to eternity, Aug. 15, which we call her Assumption, it being a pious tradition, that she was taken up to heaven both in body and soul, though not till after she had paid the common debt by death. We also keep the day of her Presentation or consecration to God in the temple, Nov. 21, and of her Visitation, July 2, but only the Annunciation and Assumption are now holydays of obligation.

Q. What is the meaning of keeping the festivals of the blessed Virgin Mary, and of other saints?

A. 1st, To glorify God in his saints, and to give him thanks for the graces and glory bestowed upon them. 2dly, To communicate with these citizens of heaven, and to procure their prayers for us. 3dly, To encourage ourselves to imitate their examples.

Q. Does not the Church also observe some days of devotion in honour of the Angels?

A. We observe Michaelmas day in honour of St.
19

Michael the Archangel, and of all the heavenly legions. We also commemorate an illustrious apparition of St. Michael, May 8, and we keep the day of our Angel guardians, Oct. 2, to give God thanks for giving his angels a charge over us; though these are not days of obligation.

Q. How do you prove that we have angels for our guardians?

A. From St. Matt. xviii. 10, 'Take heed that ye despise not one of these little ones; for I say unto you, that in heaven their angels do always behold the face of my Father who is in heaven.' Heb. i. 4, 'Are they not all ministering spirits, sent forth to minister for them who shall be heirs of their salvation?'

CHAPTER XXIV.

Of the Invocation of Angels and Saints.

Q. WHAT is the doctrine and practice of the Catholic Church, with regard to the invocation of angels and saints?

A. We hold it to be pious and profitable to apply ourselves to them, in the way of desiring them to pray to God for us; but not so as to address ourselves to them, as if they were the authors or dispensers of pardon, grace, or salvation; or as if they had any power to help us independently of God's good will and pleasure.

Q. But in some of the addresses made to the saints or angels, I find petitions for mercy, aid, or defence, what say you to that?

A. The meaning of those addresses, as far as they are authorized by the Church, is no other than to beg mercy of the saints in this sense, that they would pity and compassionate our misery, and would pray for us. In like manner, when we beg their aid and defence, we mean to beg the aid and defence of their prayers; and that the angels, to whom God has given charge over us, would assist us and defend us against the angels of darkness. And this is no more than what

the Protestant Church asks in the collect for Michael
mas day, praying, that as the holy angels always serve
God in heaven, so by his appointment they may succour
and defend us upon earth.

Q. Have you any reason to believe that it is pious
and profitable to beg the prayers of the saints and
angels?

A. We have the same reason to desire the saints
and angels to pray for us, and to believe it profitable so
to do, as we have to desire the prayers of God's servants
here upon earth ; or as St. Paul had to desire so often
the prayers of the faithful, to whom he wrote his epis-
'.es. See Rom. xv. 30. Ephes. vi. 18, 19. 1 Thess.
v. 25. Heb. xiii. 13. For if it be pious and profitable
to desire the prayers of sinners here upon earth, (for
all men here upon earth must acknowledge themselves
sinners,) how can it be otherwise than pious and profitable to desire the prayers of saints and angels in heaven?
Is it that the saints and angels in heaven have less
charity for us than the faithful upon earth? This cannot be, since charity never faileth, 2 Cor. xviii. 8, and
instead of being diminished, is increased in heaven
Or is it that the saints and angels of heaven have less
interest with God than the faithful upon earth? Nei
ther can this be said, for as they are far more holy an-
pure, and more closely united to his divine Majesty than
the faithful upon earth, so must their interest in heaven
be proportionally greater. Or is it, in fine, that the
saints and angels have no knowledge of what passes
upon earth, and therefore are not to be addressed for
their prayers? Neither is this true, since our Lord
assures, ' that there is joy in the presence of the angels
of God over one sinner that repenteth,' St. Luke xv. 10.
Which could not be, if the citizens of heaven knew
nothing of what passes here upon earth.

Q. Have you any instances in scripture of the angels
or saints praying for us, or offering up our prayers to
God?

A. Yes: Zachar. i. 12, ' The angel of the Lord
answered and said, O Lord of hosts, how long wilt thou
not have mercy on Jerusalem, and on the cities of
Judah, against which thou hast had indignation these

threescore and ten years?' Rev. v. 8, 'The four and twenty elders fell down before the lamb, having every one of them harps and golden vials full of odours, which are the prayers of the saints.' Rev. viii. 3, 4, 'And another angel came and stood at the altar, having a golden censer; and there was given unto him much ..icense, that he should offer it with the prayers of all saints upon the golden altar which was before the throne. And the smoke of the incense, with the prayers of the saints, ascended up before God out of the angel's hands.'

Q. Have you any instances in scripture of asking the blessing or prayers of angels or saints?

A. Gen. xlviii. 15, 16, 'God, before whom my fathers Abraham and Isaac did walk, the God which fed me all my life long until this day, the angel which redeemed me from all evil, bless these boys.' Rev. i. 4, 'Grace be unto you, and peace from him who is, and who was, and who is to come, and from the seven spirits which are before his throne.' But if there had been no instances in scripture, both reason and religion must inform us, that there cannot possibly be any harm in desiring the prayers of God's servants, whether they be in heaven or upon earth.

Q. At least there is no command in scripture for desiring the prayers of the angels or saints; what say you to this?

A. The scripture did not command St. Paul to desire the prayers of the Romans, nor does it command a child to ask his father's blessing, nor the faithful to kneel at their prayers, or pull off their hats when they go to Church, yet these things are no less commendable, as being agreeable to the principles of piety and religion, and so it is with regard to the invocation of the saints and angels. In the mean time, we are sure that there is no law nor command in scripture against any of these things, and consequently that they are guilty of a crying injustice, who accuse us of a crime for begging the prayers of the saints, for 'where there is no law there is no transgression,' Rom. iv. 15.

Q. Does not God say, Isaiah xlii. 8, 'I will not give my glory to another?'

A. Yes: but that makes nothing against desiring the saints to pray to God for us; for this is no more robbing God of his honour, than when we desire the prayers of the faithful here below.

Q. But does it not argue a want of confidence in God's mercy, to have recourse to the prayers of the saints?

A. No, by no means; no more than it argues a want of confidence in God's mercy, to have recourse to the prayers of our brethren upon earth. The truth is, though God be infinitely merciful, and ready to hear our prayers, yet it is our duty, and his will, that we should neglect no means by which we may be forwarded in our progress to a happy eternity: and therefore it is agreeable to his divine Majesty, that we should both pray ourselves without ceasing, and that we should also procure the prayers of our brethren, whether in heaven or on earth, that he may have the honour, and we the profit of so many more prayers.

Q. Have you any proof or instances in scripture that God will more readily hear his servants when they intercede for us, than if we alone were to address ourselves to him?

A. Yes: Job xlii. 7, 8, 'The Lord said to Eliphaz the Temanite, My wrath is kindled against thee, and against thy two friends; for ye have not spoken of me the thing that is right, as my servant Job hath. Therefore take unto you now seven bullocks and seven rams, and go to my servant Job, and offer up for yourselves a burnt offering, and my servant Job shall pray for you, for him will I accept: lest I deal with you after your folly, in that ye have not spoken of me the thing that is right, like my servant Job.'

Q. But is it not an injury to the mediatorship of Christ to desire the intercession of the angels and saints?

A. No more than when we desire the intercession of God's servants here; because we desire no more of the saints than we do of our brethren upon earth, that is, we only desire of them to pray for us, and with us, to him that is both our Lord, and their Lord, by the merits of his Son, Jesus Christ, who is both our Mediator, and their Mediator.

Q. Does not St. Paul say, 1 Tim. ii. 5, 'There is one God, and one Mediator between God and man, the man Jesus Christ;' and does not this exclude the inter·cession of the saints?

A. The words immediate.y following are, 'Who gave himself a ransom for all;' so that the plain meaning of the text is, that Christ alone is our Mediator of redemption. But as for intercession and prayer, as nothing hinders us from seeking the mediation of the faithful upon earth to pray for us, so nothing ought to hinder us from seeking the like from the saints and angels, though neither the one nor the other can obtain any thing for us any other way than through Jesus Christ, who is the only Mediator, who stands in need of no other to recommend his petitions.

Q. Have you any thing else to add in favour of· the Catholic doctrine and practice of the invocation of saints?

A. Yes: 1st, That it is agreeable to the 'communion of saints,' which we profess in the Creed, and of which the Apostle speaks, Heb. xii. 22, 23, 24, 'Ye are come unto Mount Sion, and unto the city of the living God, the heavenly Jerusalem, and to an innu·merable company of angels; to the general assembly and Church of the first-born, which are written in heaven, and to God the judge of all, and to the spirits of just men made perfect, and to Jesus the Mediator of the new covenant,' &c.

2dly, That it is agreeable to the doctrine and prac·tice of the ancient fathers, saints, and doctors of the Church, and this by the confession even of our adver·saries. 'I confess,' says Mr. Fulk, in his Rejoinder to Bristow, p. 5, 'that Ambrose, Augustine, and Hierome, held invocation of the saints to be lawful;' and upon 2 Pet. i. § 3, fol. 443, that in Nazianzen, Basil, and Chrysostom, is mention of invocation of saints, and that Theodoret also speaks of prayers to the martyrs: and the Centuriators of Magdeburg, in their fourth century col. 295, allege several examples of prayers to saints in St. Athanasius, St. Basil, St. Gregory Nazianzen, St. Ambrose. Prudentius, St. Epiphanius, and St. Ephrem. All which fathers, together with St. Augustine, St.

Jerome, &c. are also charged by Mr. Brightman (in Apocalypse, c 14, p. 382,) of establishing idolatry by invocation of saints, worshipping of relics, and such like wicked superstitions. And Mr. Thorndyke, in Epilog. par. 3. p. 358, writes thus: 'It is confessed, that the lights both of the Greek and Latin Church, St Basil, St. Gregory Nazianzen, St. Gregory Nyssene, St. Ambrose, St. Jerome, St. Augustine, St. Chrysostom, St. Cyril of Jerusalem, St. Cyril of Alexandria, Theodoret, St. Fulgentius, St. Gregory the Great, St. Leo, and more, or rather all after that time, have spoken to the saints, and desired their assistance.' See Melancthon, quartâ Parte Operum, p. 218; Kemnitius, exam. par. 3, p. 200; Beza in Præf. Nov. Test.; Archbishop Whitgift's Defence against Cartwright, p. 473; and Dailie, Advers. Lat. Tradit. p. 53.

3dly, That it stands upon the same bottom as all other Christian truths, viz. upon the authority of the Church of Christ, which the scripture commands us to hear, with which both Christ and his holy Spirit will remain for ever, and against which the gates of hell shall not prevail. See St. Matt. xvi. 18. xviii. 17 xxviii. 20; St. Luke x. 16; St. John xiv. 16, 17, 26, and xvi. 13.

4thly, That it has been authorized by God himself, by innumerable miracles in every age, wrought in favour of those that have desired the prayers and intercession of the saints. See St. Augustine's City of God, l. 22, c. 8.

Q. But what do you say to Coloss. ii. 18, where St. Paul condemns the religion or worship of angels: and to Rev. xix. 10, where the angel refused to be worshipped by St. John?

A. I say, that neither one nor the other makes any thing against desiring the angels or saints to pray to God for us, for this is not giving them any adoration or divine worship, no more than when we desire the prayers of one another. Now it was adoration, or divine worship, which the angel refused to receive from St. John, Rev. xix. 'I fell at his feet to worship him,' says the Apostle; and it was a superstitious worship, and not the desiring of the prayers of the angels, which is condemned by St. Paul, Coloss. ii. 'A superstitious worship,' I say, either of bad angels, of whom the Apostle speaks, ver. 15, or of good angels, in such a manner as to leave 'Christ not holding the head,' says the Apostle, ver. 19, such was the worship which many of the philosophers (against whom St. Paul warns the Colossians, ver. 8) paid to angels or demons to whom they offered sacrifices, as to the necessary carriers of intelligence between the gods and men. Such also was the worship which Simon Magus, and many of the Gnostics paid to the angels, whom they held to be the creators of the world. See Theodoret, l. 5, Hær. Fab. c. 9.

Q. What do you think of making addresses to the angels or saints upon your knees? Is not this giving them divine worship?

A. No more than when we desire the blessing of our fathers or mothers upon our knees; which is indeed the very case, since that we ask of our parents, when we desire their blessing, is that they would pray to God for us; and this same we ask of the angels and saints.

Q. But is it not giving to the angels and saints the attributes of God, viz. omniscience and omnipresence, that is, knowing all things, and being every where, if you suppose that they can hear or know all our addresses made to them?

A. No: we neither believe the angels and saints to be every where, nor yet to have the knowledge of all things, though we make no question but they know our prayers, since the scripture assures us that they offer them up to God, Rev. v. 8, and viii. 3, 4.

If you ask me, how they can know our prayers without being every where, and knowing all things? I answer, that there are many ways by which they may know them. 1st, The angels may know them by being amongst us in quality of our guardians; and the saints may know them by the angels, whose conversation they enjoy.

2dly, Both angels and saints may see them and know them in God, whom they continually see and enjoy, or by revelation from God, as in God they see the repentance of sinners. St. Luke xv. 10. For they that see God face to face, by the light of glory, discern all his divine attributes, and in them innumerable secrets impenetrable to nature. And therefore, though they themselves are not every where, yet, by contemplating him that sees and knows all things, they have a vast extent of knowledge of things that pass here below. 'In thy light shall we see light,' says the royal prophet, Psalm xxxv. (alias xxxvi. 9.) And we shall be like to him,' says St. John, 1 John iii 2, 'for we shall see him as he is.' For 'now we see,' says St. Paul, 1 Cor. xiii. 12, 'through a glass darkly, but then face to face: now I know in part: but then shall I know, even as also I am known.'

3dly, Both angels and saints may know our petitions addressed to them, by the ordinary way by which spirits speak to one another, and hear one another, and that is, by our directing our thoughts to them with a desire of opening our minds to them; for we can no otherwise understand or explain the speech and conversation of spirits, who having neither tongues nor ears, must converse together by the directing of their thoughts to one another. Now this kind of conversation by the thoughts may extend to ever so great a distance, as being independent on sound and all other corporal qualities, and consequently independent on distance.

Besides all this, the saints, while they were here upon earth, knew very well the miseries we labour under in this vale of tears; they also know that good Christians earnestly desire to be helped by the prayers of God's saints; and as they knew this whilst they were here upon earth, so they know it still. Consequently, as their charity prompts them to pray for the faithful in general, so it is not to be doubted, but they pray more particularly for those who stand most in necessity of their prayers, or most earnestly desire their prayers; it being the property of charity, which is perfect in heaven, to act in this manner. Hence it follows, that though we are even to suppose that the saints did not know in particular our addresses, yet it would still be profitable to desire their prayers, because they certainly pray for Christians in general, and for those more particularly who desire the help of their prayers.

In fine, the experience of seventeen hundred years, and the innumerable favors that have been granted in every age to those that have desired the prayers of the angels and saints, has convinced the Church of God, that this devotion is both pleasing to God and profitable to us; and therefore we may dispense with ourselves from a curious inquiry into the manner of their knowing our requests, since we find by experience so great benefit from them.

Q. Does not the prophet Isaiah say, chap. lxiii. 16, that 'Abraham is ignorant of us?'

A His meaning is plain, that the fatherly care and providence of God over his people was infinitely beyond that of Abraham and Israel, who were their parents according to the flesh. 'Doubtless thou art our Father,' says the prophet, 'though Abraham be ignorant of us, and Israel acknowledge us not: thou, O Lord, art our Father, our Redeemer,' &c. In the mean time, that Abraham was not ignorant of what passed amongst his children (though before Christ had opened heaven by his death, the patriarchs did not as yet enjoy the beatific vision) is clear from what we read, St. Luke xvi. 25, 26.

And here I cannot but take notice, how strangely unreasonable the notions of some people are, who make a scruple of allowing any knowledge to the saints and angels of God, whilst they are ready enough to grant that the devils both know our works and hear the addresses of their impious invokers; as if these wretched spirits of darkness, by nature alone, could know more than the saints, who, besides the light of nature, enjoy the light of grace and glory; or, as if those rebels had acquired any greater degree of perfection and knowledge by their fall, than they would have had if they had remained angels.

Q. But can you prove from scripture, that the saints enjoy God in heaven before the general resurrection?

A. Yes; this is visibly the doctrine of St. Paul, 2 Cor. v. 1 For we know, that if our earthly house of this tabernacle were dissolved, we have a building of God, a house not made with hands, eternal in the heavens.' Ver. 6 and 7, 'Therefore we are always confident, knowing that whilst we are at home in the body, we are absent from the Lord; (for we walk by faith, and not by sight;) we are confident, I say, and willing rather to be absent from the body, and to be present with the Lord.' Where he visibly supposes, that the souls of the saints, when let loose from their bodies by death, enter into the eternal tabernacles, are present with the Lord, and enjoy his sight. The same thing he supposes, Philip. i. 23, 24, 'I am in a strait betwixt two, having a desire to depart, and to be with Christ; which is far better. Nevertheless to abide in the flesh is more needful for you.'

CHAPTER XXV.

Of the Devotion of Catholics to the blessed Virgin Mary; of her perpetual Virginity; of the Beads, Rosary, and Angelus Domini.

Q. WHAT is the meaning of the great respect and devotion of Catholics to the blessed Virgin Mary?

A. It is grounded, 1st, upon her great dignity of Mother of God, and the close relation which she has thereby to Jesus Christ her son; for how is it possible to love and honour Christ with our whole heart, and not value and love his blessed Mother?

2dly, It is grounded upon that supereminent grace which was bestowed upon her to prepare her for that dignity; upon account of which she was saluted by the angel Gabriel, St. Luke i. 28, 'full of grace,' (which the Protestants, who are no great friends to this ever-blessed Virgin, have chosen rather to translate highly favoured;) and both by the angel and by St. Elizabeth, St. Luke i. 42, she is styled, 'Blessed among women.'

3dly, It is grounded upon her extraordinary sanctity for if she was full of grace before she conceived in her womb the fountain of all grace, to what a degree of

sanctity. of grace must she have arrived during so
many years as she lived afterwards? especially since
she bore nine months in her womb the author of all
sanctity, and had him thirty years under the roof, ever
contemplating him and his heavenly mysteries, St.
Luke ii. 19 and 51; and on her part never making any
resistance to the affluence of his graces ever flowing
in upon her happy soul.

4thly, It is grounded upon that supereminent degree
of heavenly glory, with which God has now honoured
her, in proportion to her grace and sanctity here upon
earth, and the great interest she has with her blessed
Son, and through him with his heavenly Father.

Q. Is there any thing in scripture that insinuates
this great devotion, that should be in all ages to this
blessed Virgin?

A. Yes, it was foretold by herself in her Canticle,
St. Luke i. 48, 'Behold from henceforth all generations
shall call me blessed.'

Q. Do you then allow divine honour or worship to
the blessed Virgin Mary?

A. No, certainly; the Church in this, as in all other
things, keeps the golden mean between the two ex
tremes : she condemns those that refuse to honour this
blessed Mother of God; but those much more that
would give her divine worship. She thinks no honour
that can be given to any pure creature too great for
this blessed Virgin : but as she knows that there is an
infinite distance still between her and God, she is far
from offering sacrifice to her, or paying her any worship that belongs to God alone. And whatever honour
she gives the Mother, she refers it to the glory of the
Son, as the chief motive and end of all her devotions.

Q. But why do you call the blessed Virgin the
Mother of God?

A. Because she is truly the Mother of Jesus Christ,
who is true God and true man, and consequently she is
truly the Mother of God; not by being Mother of the
Divinity, but by being Mother of him, who in one and
the same Person, is both God and man. Hence she is
called by St. Elizabeth, Luke i. 'the Mother of my
Lord.'

Q. Why does the Church in her hymns and anthems style the blessed Virgin, Mother of grace, and Mother of mercy?

A. Because she is the Mother of him who is the fountain of all grace and mercy; and is both most willing by reason of her supereminent charity, and most able by her great interest with her Son to obtain grace and mercy for us.

Q. And why is she styled the queen of heaven, or the queen of angels and saints?

A. Because she is the Mother of the King of Hea-ven, and the greatest of all the saints.

Q. What then do you think of those that presume to say she was no more than any other woman; nor ought to have any regard or honour paid to her?

A. Such as these have very little regard to Jesus Christ, whose Mother they treat with such contempt.

Q. And what do you think of the opinion of those that say, she had children by St. Joseph, after the birth of our Saviour?

A. This was a heresy condemned by the Church near fourteen hundred years ago, as contrary to apos-tolical tradition, and to the very Creed of the Apostles, which styles her Virgin. And that indeed she had determined by vow never to know man, the holy fathers gather from her words to the angel, St. Luke i. 34, 'How shall this be, for I know not man?'

Q. Who then were they that are called in the scrip-ture the brethren of our Saviour?

A. They are named by St. Mark vi. 3, James and Joses or Joseph, and Jude, and Simon or Simeon: these were the sons of Mary, the wife of Cleophas, whom the gospel calls the sister, that is, the near kins-woman of the blessed Virgin, and therefore her sons are called our Saviour's brethren, according to the usual scripture phrase, by which those that are near akin are called brothers and sisters.

If you ask me how I prove that Mary the wife of Cleophas was mother to James and Joses, &c., I prove it evidently by comparing the gospels together: St. Matthew, chap. xxvii. ver. 56, acquaints us, that amongst

20

the women who had followed our Saviour from Galilee ministering to him, and who were present at his death, were Mary Magdalene, and Mary the mother of James and Joses, &c. which same thing is attested by St. Mark, chap. xv. ver. 40. Now St. John, xix. 25, expressly informs us, that this Mary, who stood by the cross, was sister to the blessed Virgin, and wife of Cleophas : so that James, Joses, &c. as it is manifest from the gospel, were not children of our Lady, but of our kinswoman Mary, the wife of Cleophas.

Q. But why then is our Saviour called her first-born, St. Matt. i. 25, and St. Luke ii. 7 ?

A. It is a Hebrew phrase, not signifying that any were born after him, but that no one was born before him.

Q. And why is it said of St. Joseph, St. Matt. i. 25, 'that he knew her not till she had brought forth,' &c.

A. This also was said according to a propriety of speech amongst the Hebrews, to signify what was not done before without meddling with the question what was done after : this latter being foreign to the great point which the Evangelist had then in view, which was to assure us that Christ was born of a virgin. We have examples of the like expressions in the Old Testament; as when, Psalm cix. (alias cx.) it is said, 'The Lord said to my Lord, sit thou on my right hand till I make my enemies thy footstool.' Will he therefore cease to sit at the right hand of his Father, after his enemies are made his footstool ? No certainly.

Q. What is the common address which the Church makes to the blessed Virgin Mary ?

A. The angelical salutation of the Hail Mary : a great part of which is taken out of the gospel, St. Luke i. 26, and 42 ; and the other part is added by the Church to beg the prayers of the blessed Virgin for us sinners.

Q. Why do Catholics so often repeat the Hail Mary ?

A. To commemorate the Incarnation of the Son of God ; to honour his blessed Mother, and to desire her prayers.

Q. What is the meaning of the Beads ?

A. It is a devotion consisting of a certain number of Our Fathers, and Hail Marys, directed for the obtaining of blessings from God, through the prayers and intercessions of our Lady.

Q. But is it not highly absurd, that according to the common way of saying the Beads, there are repeated ten Hail Marys for one Our Father?

A. It would be absurd indeed, and blasphemous too, if the meaning of this were to signify that the blessed Virgin is either more powerful or more merciful than her Son; or that we have a greater confidence in her than in him: but we are far from any such notions.

Q. Why then is the Hail Mary repeated so much oftener in the Beads than the Lord's Prayer?

A. Because the Beads, being a devotion particularly instituted to commemorate the Incarnation of Christ, and to honour him in his blessed Mother, it was thought proper to repeat so much the oftener that prayer which is particularly adapted to these ends. In the mean time it may be proper to take notice, 1st, That if in the Beads there be ten Hail Marys said for one Our Father; in the Mass and Office of the Church almost all the prayers are directed to God alone. 2dly, That every Hail Mary, both by the nature of the prayer, and the intention of the Church, is directed more to the honour of the Son than of the Mother; as well because the Church, in honouring the Mother, has principally in view the honour of the Son; as also because this prayer particularly relates to the Incarnation of Christ; and if withal it begs the prayers of the blessed Virgin, it is plain that he is more honoured to whom we desire she should address her prayers, than she, whom we only desire to pray for us.

To which, if we add, that her prayers are ten times better and more acceptable to God than ours, it will appear no ways absurd that we should frequently desire her prayers. For as to the repetition of the same prayer, it is what is recommended to us by the example of our Lord, St. Matt. xxvi. 42, 44, &c., and has nothing of absurdity in it.

Q. What is the meaning of the Rosary?

A. The Rosary is a method of saying the Beads,

so as to meditate upon the Incarnation, Passion and Resurrection of Christ. And it is divided into three parts, each part consisting of five Mysteries, to be contemplated during the repeating of five decads or tens upon the Beads. The first five are called the five joyful Mysteries: viz. the Annunciation, when our Lord was first conceived in his Mother's womb; the Visitation, when the blessed Virgin visited her kinswoman St. Elizabeth, and by her was declared blessed among Women, &c.; the Nativity of our Lord; his Presentation in the Temple, together with the Purification of the blessed Virgin; and his being found in the Temple in the midst of the Doctors, &c. The five next are called the dolorous or sorrowful Mysteries, as having relation to the Passion of Christ; and are his Prayer and Agony in the garden; his being scourged at the Pillar; his Crowning with Thorns; his Carriage of the Cross; and his Crucifixion and Death. The five last are called the five glorious Mysteries, viz. the Resurrection of our Lord; his Ascension into Heaven; the Coming of the Holy Ghost; the Assumption of the blessed Virgin; and her Coronation; together with the eternal Glory of the Saints in the Kingdom of Heaven.

Q. What is the meaning of giving three tolls with the bells every morning, noon, and night, in all Catholic countries?

A. This is to remind the faithful of the great mystery of the Incarnation of the Son of God; and it is the practice of all good Christians, when they hear these bells, to perform the devotion which we call the *Angelus Domini.*

Q. What is this devotion, and in what manner is it performed?

A. The bell tolls three times, with a short space between each time. At the first toll we say, 'The Angel of the Lord declared to Mary, and she conceived of the Holy Ghost;' then we say the Hail Mary, &c. At the second toll we say, 'Behold the handmaid of the Lord, be it done to me according to thy word,' Hail Mary, &c. At the third toll we say, 'And the Word was made flesh, and dwelt amongst us;' Hail Mary, &c. Then we conclude with the following prayer.

Pour forth, we beseech thee, O Lord, thy grace into

our hearts, that we, to whom the Incarnation of Christ thy Son was made known by the message of an angel, may, by his passion and cross, be brought to the glory of his resurrection.   Through the same Christ our Lord, Amen.

This devotion is used in all Catholic countries, and is called the *Angelus Domini*, from the first words, the Angel of the Lord, &c.

CHAPTER XXVI.

Of the Use and Veneration of Relics in the Catholic Church.

Q. WHAT do you mean by Relics?

A. The dead bodies or bones of the saints we call Relics; as also whatever other things have belonged to them in their mortal life.

Q. And what is the doctrine and practice of the Church with regard to these things?

A. We keep such things as these with a religious respect and veneration for the sake of those to whom they have belonged, but principally for the sake of him to whom the saints themselves belonged; that is, for the greater glory of God, who is glorious in his saints, and to whom is referred all the honour that is given to his saints.

Q. What reasons has the Church for showing this respect to the dead bodies or bones of the saints?

A. 1st, Because they have been the victims and the living temples of God, in which his divine Majesty has, in a particular manner inhabited, and which he has sanctified by his presence and grace: and therefore, if God required of Moses, Exod. iii. 5, and of Joshua, Josh. v. 15, to loose their shoes from off their feet, in respect to the ground on which they stood, as being rendered holy by his presence, or that of his angels, we must conclude, that it is agreeable to his divine Majesty that we should testify the like honour to that venerable earth of the bodies of his saints, which he in such an extraordinary manner has sanctified, by abiding in them as in his temples.

20 *

2dly, We know that the bodies of the saints are preordained to a happy resurrection and eternal glory, and upon this account also deserve our respect.

3dly, The bodies and other relics of the saints have been, and are daily the instruments of the power of God, for the working of innumerable miracles, which God, who is truth and sanctity itself, would never have effected, if it had not been agreeable to him that we should honour and respect these precious remnants of his servants.

4thly, The relics and shrines of the martyrs and other saints serve very much to encourage the faithful to an imitation of their virtues, and to help to raise their souls from the love of things present, to the love of things eternal.

Q. Did the primitive Christians show this respect to the relics of the saints?

A. Yes: nothing is more evident from all kind of monuments of antiquity, than that the veneration of the relics of the saints is one of the most ancient things in Christianity. The learned Church Historian, Eusebius, l. 7, c. 19, relates that St. James' chair was kept with great veneration by the Christians of Jerusalem, from the Apostles' time, till the days in which the historian wrote, that is, till the beginning of the fourth century. The acts of the martyrdom of St. Ignatius, bishop of Antioch, disciple of the Apostles, who suffered at Rome, anno 107, written by the Christians who accompanied him to Rome, bear record, that his holy relics were carried to Antioch by the Christians, and left to that Church as an inestimable treasure. The Christians of Smyrna, in the account that they give of the martyrdom of their holy bishop St. Polycarp, disciple of the Apostles, inform us, that the faithful carried away his relics, which they valued more than gold and precious stones, Euseb. Hist. l. 4, c. 15. And that this veneration of relics was approved by all the most holy and most learned bishops and doctors of the Church, and condemned by none but infidels and heretics, such as Julian the Apostate, Eunomius, and Vigilantius, may be seen in the writings of the holy fathers. See St. Basil, in Ps. 115, t. 1, p. 274. Homil. 5, in Martyrem Julittam, p. 217. Hom. 20 in 40. Martyres, p. 479. St. Gregory Nyssen, Orat. de S. Theodoro Martyre, t. 3. St. Gregory

Nazianzen, Orat. 3, in Julianum, t. 1, p. 76, 77. St. Cyril of Jerusalem, Catech. 18. St. John Chrysostom, ad Pap. Ant. Hom. 40, 47, 59, l. contra Gentiles, Hom. 26, in 2 Cor. 2, &c. St. Ambrose, Epist. 22. St. Hierome, l. adversus Vigilantium. St. Augustine, l. 9. Confess. c. 7. Serm. 92, de Diversis, l. 22, of the City of God, c. 8. Epist. 103. Theodoret, l. 8, contra Græcos, &c. To pass over many others, who all agree in approving this practice: and all or most of them bear record, that God also has approved it by innumerable miracles.

Q. But have you any instance in scripture of miracles wrought by the bones of God's saints, or other things belonging to them?

A. Yes; we read 2 (alias 4) Kings xiii. 21, of a dead man raised to life by the touch of the bones of the prophet Elisha; and Acts xix. 12, 'that from the body of Paul, were brought unto the sick, handkerchiefs or aprons, and the diseases departed from them, and the evil spirits went out of them.'

Q. But does not Christ reprehend the Scribes and Pharisees for building up and adorning the sepulches of the prophets, St. Matt. xxiii. 29, 30, 31?

A. He does not reprehend them for the action, which 1 itself was good, but for their wicked dispositions; inasmuch as, whilst they should seem to honour the prophets, and thereby obtain the favour of the people, they sought all the while to fill up the measure of their fathers, by persecuting unto the death the Lord of prophets.

Q. What kind of honour does the Catholic Church allow to relics?

A. An inferior and relative honour, as to things belonging to God's saints; but by no means divine honour.

Q. But are not candles allowed to burn before them? and are they not sometimes fumed with incense?

A. These are honours indeed, but such as we may give to one another; as in effect we incense in the Church both clergy and people, and burn candles to our princes upon occasions of joy: for since these honours are no ways appropriated to God either by the nature of the things in themselves, or by any divine ordinance, why may not the Church of God allow them to the relics of the saints? not as divine honours, but as tokens of our love and respect to them; of our joy for the triumphs of Christ in his saints, and as emblems of their eternal life, light, and glory.

Q. Does not this practice of the veneration of relics expose the faithful to the danger of idolatry and superstition, by honouring false relics?

A. No. 1st, Because the Church of God, by her public canons, and her zealous pastors, takes what care she can to prevent such impostures. 2dly, Because, if by the wickedness of men it should sometimes happen that the faithful should be imposed upon in this regard, so far as to honour a false relic for a true one, there would be neither any idolatry nor superstition in the case, but a mistake, on their part, innocent, as when a charitable Christian relieves an impostor or a hypocrite, innocently believing him to be a real object of charity.

Q. But if the Church has so much zeal against false relics, how comes she to tolerate them in so many cases, as when divers Churches pretend to possess the body of the same saint, for some or other of these must be false relics?

A. You are too hasty in concluding that these must needs be false relics, 1st, Because it often happens that some part of the body of a saint is in one place, and some part in another, in which case both places claim the body of such a saint, and though they really possess only a part of it; and yet neither the one nor the other is therefore to be charged with honouring false relics. 2dly, Many of the saints and martyrs have borne the same names, and hence it easily happens, that relics, which indeed belong to one saint, are attributed to another of the same name. 3dly, There have been many ancient martyrs, whose names at present are not known, whose relics nevertheless have been all along honoured by the Church: now it was easy that the ignorance of some, or the vanity of others, might attribute to them the names of other saints: so that these may be true relics, notwithstanding they do not all belong to the saints to whom they are attributed.

Q. What is the meaning of making pilgrimages to the shrines or other memorials of the saints?

A. To honour God in his saints, to excite devotion by the sight of those places sanctified by these heavenly pledges, and to obtain graces and blessings of God, by the prayers of the saints: for though God be every where, and his bounty and mercy be not confined to any particular place, yet the experience of all past ages convinces us, that it is his holy will and pleasure to bestow his favours more plentifully, and to show more frequent and miraculous effects of his power and goodness in some places than in others, see St. Augustine, epist. 137.

Q. Have not Catholics a more than ordinary veneration for the wood of the cross, the nails, thorns, and other instruments of Christ's passion?

A. Yes, they have, because these things have so close a relation to the passion of Christ, by which we were redeemed, and have been sanctified by the blood of our Redeemer.

CHAPTER XXVII.

Of the Use of Pictures and Images in the Catholic Church.

Q. WHAT is the doctrine of the church with regard to pictures or images of Christ and his saints?

A. 1st, That it is good to keep them and retain them, and to have them in churches, not only for ornament, and for the instruction of the ignorant, but for the honour and remembrance of Christ and his saints, and for to help to raise our thoughts and hearts to heavenly things. 2dly, That there is a relative honour due to them, by reason of the persons whom they represent. See the second council of Nice, Act. 7, and the council of Trent, Sess. 25.

Q. Does the catholic church give divine worship to the pictures or images of Christ or his saints?

A. No, by no means: the second council of Nice, in the 7th Action or Sessions, has expressly declared, that divine worship is not to be given them; to which the council of Trent, in the 25th Session, has added, that we 'are not to believe that there is any divinity or power in them for which they are to be worshipped: and that we are not to pray to them, nor put our trust or confidence in them.'

Q. But does not the first (or second) command-

ment absolutely forbid the making of any image, or the likeness of any thing in heaven, earth, or sea?

A. No: it only forbids the making of idols, that is, of such images as are made for gods, and are worshipped as such; or in which a divinity or divine virtue and power is believed to reside. Hence the ancient version of the Septuagint (which is venerable by having been made use of by the apostles themselves) renders the words of the commandment thus, 'thou shalt not make to thyself an idol,' &c. And that God does not absolutely forbid the making of the likeness of any thing, is not only the general belief of all Christians, who carry about with them without scruple the likeness of their kings in the current coin of their respective countries, but is visible from scripture, wherein God commanded the making of two cherubims of beaten gold, to be placed over the ark of the covenant in the very sanctuary, Exod. xxv. 18, 19, 20, 21, and in like manner commanded the making of the brazen serpent, for the healing of those who were bit by the fiery serpents, Numb. xxi. 8, 9, which serpent was an emblem of Christ, St. John iii. 14, 15.

Q. But at least does not God forbid by this commandment all honour or reverence to pictures or images?

A. He forbids all honour or reverence to idols or image gods, but not the relative honour which catholics show to the pictures of Christ and his saints, for the sake of the persons represented by them, for it is visible, that the same images which, by this commandment are forbid to be honoured, are also by the express words of the commandment forbid to be made. Now, few or no Christians suppose that the pictures of Christ, or his saints are forbid to be made; therefore they cannot infer from this commandment, that they are forbid to be honoured, since this commandment does not speak of them at all, but only of idols or images set up to be worshipped for gods.

Q. What then do you mean by this relative honour, which you allow to the pictures of Christ and his saints?

A. By a relative honour, I mean an honour which is given to a thing, not for any intrinsic excellence or dignity in the thing itself, but only for the relation which it has to something else, which it represents or brings to our remembrance ; as when Christians bow to the name of Jesus, which is an image of remembrance of our Saviour to the ear as the crucifix is to the eye.

Q. Have you any instances of this kind of relative honour allowed by protestants?

A. Yes: in the honour they give to the name of Jesus, to their churches, to the altar, to the bible, to the symbols of bread and wine in the sacrament, to the king's chair, &c. Such also was the honour which the Jews gave to the ark and cherubims, to the sanctuary, &c. and which Moses and Joshua gave to the land on which they stood, as being holy ground, Exod. iii. 5. Josh. v. 15.

Q. How do you prove that there is a relative honour due to the images or pictures of Christ and his saints?

A. Because it is evidently agreeable, as well to nature and reason, as to piety and religion, to express our esteem and affection for those whom we honour and love, by setting a value upon all things that belong to them, or have any relation to them. Thus good Christians, that love God with their whole hearts, honour all things that are dedicated to his service, or that are memorials of him, or have a relation to him; as his temples, his altars, his name, his word, his sacraments, the sacred vessels, &c. And thus it is that we honour the effigies of Christ, of his blessed Mother, and of the saints, as memorials and representations of them, and as helps to raise our thoughts to them. And is it not thus that a loyal subject, a dutiful child, a loving friend, value the pictures of their kings, father, or friend? And would not these very men that make no scruple of abusing the image of Christ, severely punish such as would abuse the image of the king?

Q. Do you then allow of worshipping God by an image?

A. If you mean by worshipping God by an image, the raising up our hearts to God, by or upon occasion of the sight of the picture or image; or referring to Jesus Christ and to his worship whatever honour or respect we show to his picture or image; there can be no reason to disallow the worshipping of God by a picture or image,

But if worshipping God by an image be so understood, as if the divinity in some particular manner resided in the image ; or some virtue or power, for which it should be worshipped or trusted in ; or as if our worship or prayers were believed to be more acceptable to God and to have more influence upon him, when offered or presented by or through any such image, such kind of worshipping God by an image is not only not allowed but condemned by the Catholic Church.   See the Council of Trent, Sess. 25.

Q. What means then the blessing of crucifixes or other images, if no virtue or power be believed to reside in them after they are blessed ?

A. The Church blesses all things that are used about the altar ; not by way of imparting to them any intrinsic power or virtue, but by way of dedicating them to the divine service, and begging God's blessing for those that make use of them ; so that whatever advantage may be supposed in the use of them, after they are blessed more than before, is wholly to be attributed to the prayers of the Church.

Q. But are there not certain images to which great miracles are attributed ; therefore Catholics must believe that in these, at least, there is some divinity, virtue, or power ?

A. There have been many instances of undoubted miracles wrought by God, in the Churches of the blessed Virgin and other saints, in favour of those that have sought their prayers and intercession before the pictures of images.   But these miracles are not to be attributed to any divinity or power in the image, but to the Almighty power of God, moved to work these wonders by the prayers of the saints, and bearing testimony thereby to the faith of his Church, and showing his approbation of her religious practices.

Q. What do you think of the images or pictures of God the Father, or of the blessed Trinity ?

A. I think that no corporeal image can bear a resemblance with the Divinity : and consequently that it would be unlawful to pretend to make any such likeness or resemblance.   But where no such resemblance is pretended, I do not take it to be more unlawful to paint God the Father, under the figure of a venerable man, because he was so represented in the vision of Daniel, chap. vii. ver. 9, than it is to paint the Holy Ghost under the figure of a dove, because he appeared so when Christ was baptized, St. Matt. iii. 16.

Q. What do you think of the charge of idolatry laid to the Church by some of her adversaries, upon account of the use and veneration of images?

A. I think that nothing could be more visibly unjust than such a charge. Since idolatry is giving divine honour and service to an idol, or false God: which is far from being the case of the Catholic Church. We acknowledge one only true and living God, in three persons, Father, and Son, and Holy Ghost: to him alone do we offer sacrifice or any other divine honours. Him alone do we adore in spirit and truth. Whatever else in heaven or on earth we religiously honour, we honour for his sake, and for the relation it has to him. And as for the worship of idols or false gods, it has been banished out of the world by the labours and preaching of our Church alone: so far are we from abetting idolatry.

Q. What then do you think of the parallel which some would make between the heathen and Catholic worship?

A. I think that it is infinitely unjust and unreasonable, as must appear to any unprejudiced mind by the following remarks.

1st, Catholics adore and offer sacrifice to one only true and living God: the Heathens adored and offered sacrifices to many false gods.

2dly, The supreme object of Catholic worship is the sacred Trinity blessed for evermore: the supreme object of the Heathen worship was the sun, or some other part of God's creation; or else some wicked man, or more wicked devil. For Heathen idolatry, according to the Apostle, Rom. i. 25, 'changed the truth of God into a lie, and worshipping and serving the creature more than the Creator, who is blessed for ever.' The sun and his symbol, the fire, was of old the sovereign god of the Persians; as he was of late of the inhabitants of Peru: the same was worshipped as their chief god by the Phœnicians under the name of Baal; by the Ammonites under the name of Moloch; by the Moabites under the name of Chamos; by the Accaronites

21

under the name of Beelzebub; by those of Gaza, under the name of Marnas, &c. according to Vossius, Selden, and the whole nation of the critics, alleged by the Protestant doctor Parker, test. p. 97. Him they called the king of heaven; as they called the moon or Astarte the queen of heaven. Of like nature was the sovereign object of the worship of the Egyptians, viz. Ammon the ram, and Osyris the bull, which are the two first signs of the Zodiac, and were worshipped as symbols of the sun, according to doctor Parker, *Ibidem.* The chief god of the Grecians and Heathen Romans, was Jupiter, who was originally a king that reigned in Crete; as the wiser Heathens have acknowledged. He was not esteemed eternal by any of them; but the son of Saturn, that is, of time; and by much posterior to heaven and earth. As for his idols and oracles, he who gave answers thereby was no God, but an arch devil, as Christians have ever believed.

3dly, Catholics honour, though not with any part of divine worship, the angels and saints of God, as belonging to him, and as truly worthy of honour, upon account of the excellent gifts of grace and glory received from him: but they ask nothing of them but what they know must come from God's hands; and therefore, their usual address to them is, Pray for us. The Heathens not only give the sovereign worship of adoration and sacrifice to their inferior deities, but looked upon them in many respects independent of their chief god (whilst they made him, himself independent upon fate) and accordingly they addressed themselves to them not as intercessors, (for in the whole Heathen theology we shall scarce find an *Ora pro nobis*) but as distributers of blessings and gifts to men, according to their different offices and powers.

4thly, Those whom the Catholics honour with an inferior veneration for God's sake, are indeed the ministers and servants of the one true God. The inferior deities of the Heathens were wicked wretches, such as Mars, Bacchus, Hercules, Venus, &c. or rather devils, as we learn from many texts of scripture. See Levit. xvii. 7. Deuter. xxxi. 17. Ps. cvi. 37. 1 Cor. x. 20.

5thly, As to images; not to speak of the immense distance between the objects represented by Catholics and by Heathens, it is certain that the Heathens, at least the generality of them, believed the very idols to be gods; for which see Gen. xxii. 30, 32. Exod. xx. 23. Levit. xix. 4. Judges xviii. 24. 2 Kings xvii. 29, and xix. 18. Isai. xliv. 17. Jerem. ii. 26, 27. Acts xix. 26. And as for those who would seem to be more refined in their notion and worship, they believed at least that the idols by consecration became the bodies of their gods, the places of their peculiar residence, the symbols of their presence, and the seats of their power. And accordingly these, as well as the others, offered prayers and sacrifice to the idols, and gave them the names of the deities which they worshipped in them. Now we neither believe our images to be gods, nor to be the bodies of God, nor the peculiar places of his residence, nor symbols of his presence, nor to have any power or virtue in them; nor do we put our trust in them, or pray to them, or offer sacrifice or other divine honours to them. Therefore there is no similitude between the Heathen worship and ours.

As for the Jewish worship of the golden calf in the wilderness, and afterwards of the calves of Jeroboam at Bethel and Dan, which some are willing to extenuate, as if they did not take these images to be gods, but thereby only meant to worship the God of Israel, the Scripture gives us a quite different account; witness these texts, Exod. xxxii. 8, 'They have made them a molten calf, and have worshipped it, and have sacrificed thereunto, and said, These be thy gods, O Israel, which have brought thee up out of the land of Egypt.' Ver. 31. 'They have made them gods of gold.' Psalm cvi. (alias cv.) 19, 20 21, 'They made a calf in Horeb, and worshipped the molten image: they changed their glory (their God) into the similitude of an ox that eateth grass: they forgot God their Saviour, which had done great things in Egypt.' Acts vii. 39, 40, 41, 'To whom our fathers would not obey, but thrust him from them, and in their hearts turned back again into Egypt, saying to Aaron, Make us gods to go before us.——And they made a calf in those days, and offered sacrifice to the idol, and rejoiced in the works of their own hands. Then God turned and gave them up to worship the host of heaven.' And of the calves of Jeroboam, 1 Kings xii. 28, 'He made two calves of gold, and said unto them, Behold thy gods, O Israel, who brought thee up out of the land of Egypt;' and ver. 32, 'He sacrificed to the calves that he had made;' and 1 Kings xiv. 9, 'He is accused by the prophet Abijah, to have gone and made him other gods and molten images,' and 'to have cast the Lord behind his back.' 2 Chron. xi. 15, 'He ordained him priest for the high places, and for the devils, and for the calves which he had made.' 2 Chron. xiii. 8, 'There are with you golden calves, which Jeroboam made unto you for gods. Ver. 9, 'Have ye not cast out the priest, &c. and made you priests after the manner of the nations——of them that be no gods.' Ver. 10, 'But as for us, the Lord is our God.'

But if any one will be contentious and maintain that these idolatrous Israelites intended to worship in these calves, not the Egyptian Osiris, nor any other false divinity, but the God of Israel, because Aaron (who made the calf against his will by compulsion of the people) seems to give it the proper name of the God of Israel, Exod. xxxiii. 5, 'To-morrow is a feast to the Lord.' Supposing this to be true, their worship would still have been idolatrous, and these calves properly idols; because they believed (as is manifest from the texts above quoted) these very calves to be gods; or, if you will have it so, to be the Lord of Israel; or, at least, that the divinity had upon their dedication insinuated itself into them; and accordingly they gave divine praises and offered sacrifice to them. Now to believe any image to be God, or to imagine any divinity, power, or virtue in it, for which it is to be worshipped, or to offer sacrifice to an image, is an idolatrous worship, and cannot be excused, however the image be pretended by its worshippers to represent the true God.

Q. Is there not in one of the Church hymns, and in one of the anthems of the Roman Breviary, a prayer to the cross? How then do you maintain that the Catholic Church does not attribute any power to images, nor prays to them?

A. The prayer you speak of is not directed to the wood of the cross, but Christ crucified, by a figure of speech, as when St. Paul says Gal. vi. 14, that he glories in the cross of Jesus Christ.

CHAPTER XXVIII.

Of Exorcisms, and Benedictions, or Blessings of Creatures in the Catholic Church, and of the Use of Holy Water.

Q. WHAT do you mean by Exorcism?

A. The rites and prayers instituted by the Church for the casting out devils, or restraining them from hurting persons, disquieting places, or abusing any of God's creatures to our harm.

Q. Has Christ given his Church any such power over the devils?

A. Yes, he has: see St. Matt. x. 1; St. Mark iii. 13; St. Luke ix. 1; where this power was given to the Apostles; and to the seventy-two disciples, St. Luke x. 19; 'and two other believers, St. Mark xvi. 17. And that this power was not to die with the Apostles, nor to cease after the Apostolic age, we learn from the perpetual practice of the Church and the experience of all ages.

Q. What is the meaning of blessing so many things in the Catholic Church?

A. We bless Churches, and other places set aside for divine service; altars, chalices, vestments, &c. by way of devoting them to holy uses. We bless our meats and other inanimate things which God has given us for our use, that we may use them in moderation, in a manner agreeable to God's institution; that they may be serviceable to us, and that the devil may have no power to abuse them to our prejudice. We bless candles, salt, water, &c. by way of begging of God that such as religiously use them may obtain his blessing, &c.

Q. But does it not savour of superstition to attribute any virtue to such inanimate things as blessed candles, Holy Water, *Agnus Dei's*, &c.?

A. It is no superstition to look for a good effect from the prayers of the Church of God; and it is in virtue of these prayers that we hope for benefit from these things when used with faith, and daily experience shows that our hopes are not vain.

Q. What do you mean by *Agnus Dei's?*

21 *

A. Wax stamped with the image of the Lamb of God, blessed by the Pope with solemn prayers, and anointed with the holy chrism.

Q. What warrant have you in scripture for blessing inanimate things?

A. 1 Tim. iv. 4, 5, 'Every creature of God is good, and nothing to be refused, if it be received with thanksgiving, for it is sanctified by the word of God in prayer.'

Q. Why does the Church make use of the sign of the cross in all her blessings and consecrations?

A. To signify that all our good must come through Christ crucified.

Q. What do you mean by Holy Water?

A. Water sanctified by the word of God and prayer.

Q. What is the use of Holy Water?

A. It is blessed by the Church in solemn prayers, to beg God's protection and blessing upon those that use it, and in particular that they may be defended from all the powers of darkness.

Q. Is the use of Holy Water very ancient in the Church of God?

A. It is very ancient, since it is mentioned in the Apostolical Constitutions, l. 8, c. 29. And as for the English nation in particular, it is visible from the epistles of St. Gregory the Great, l. 9, epist. 71, 'that we received it together with our Christianity.'

Q. Have the holy fathers and ancient Church Writers left upon record any miracles done by Holy Water?

A. Yes, they have; more particularly upon those occasions when it has been used against magical enchantments and the power of the devil. See instances in St. Epiphanius, Hær. 30; in St. Hierome, in the Life of St. Hilarion; in Theodoret, l. 5, Histor. Eccl. c. 21; in Palladius Histor. Laus. c. 6, &c.

Q. What is the order and manner of blessing Holy Water?

A. 1st, The priest signs himself with the sign of the cross, saying, 'Our help is in the name of the Lord.' Ans. 'Who made heaven and earth.' Then he proceeds to the blessing of the salt which is to be mingled with the water, saying,

The Exorcism of the Salt.

I exorcise thee, O creature of salt, by the living +
God, by the true + God, by the holy + God; by that
God, who by the prophet Elisha commanded thee to be
cast into the water to cure its barrenness, that thou
mayest by this exorcism be made beneficial to the faithful, and become to all them that make use of thee health-
ful both to soul and body, and that in what place soever
thou wilt be sprinkled, all illusions and wickedness and
crafty wiles of Satan may be chased away and depart
from that place; and every unclean spirit commanded in
his name, who is to come to judge the living and the dead,
and the world by fire. Amen.

Let us pray.

O Almighty and everlasting God, we most humbly
implore thy infinite mercy that thou wouldst vouchsafe
by thy piety to bless + and to sanctify + this thy creature of salt, which thou hast given for the use of man
kind: that it may be to all that take it for the health of
mind and body; and that whatever shall be touched or
sprinkled with it, may be free from all uncleanness, and
from all assaults of wicked spirits, through our Lord
Jesus Christ, &c.

After this the Priest proceeds to the blessing of the water, as follows.

I exorcise thee, O creature of water, in the name of
God + the Father Almighty, and in the name of Jesus
Christ + his Son our Lord, and in the virtue of the Holy
+ Ghost; that thou mayest by this exorcism have power
to chase away all the power of the enemy; that thou
mayest be enabled to cast him out and put him to flight
with all his apostate angels, by the virtue of the same
Jesus Christ our Lord, who is to come to judge the
living and the dead, and the world by fire. Amen.

Let us pray.

O God, who for the benefit of mankind hast made use of the element of water in the greatest sacraments, mercifully hear our prayers and impart the virtue of thy blessing + to this element, prepared by many kinds of purifications; that this thy creature made use of in thy mysteries may receive the effect of thy divine grace for the chasing away devils and curing diseases; and that whosoever shall be sprinkled with this water in the houses or the places of the faithful, may be free from all uncleanness, and delivered from evil; let no pestilential spirit reside there, no infectious air; let all the snares of the hidden enemy fly away; and may whatever envies the safety or repose of the inhabitants of that place be put to flight by the sprinkling of this water, that the welfare which we seek by the invocation of thy holy name may be defended from all sorts of assaults. Through our Lord Jesus Christ, &c.

Then the Priest mingles the salt with the water, saying,

May this salt and water be mixed together in the name of the Father, + and of the Son, + and of the Holy + Ghost.   Amen.

V.   Lord be with you.
R.   And with thy spirit.

Let us pray.

O God, the author of invincible power, King of an empire that cannot be overcome, and for ever magnificently triumphant; who restrainest the forces of the adversary, who defeatest the fury of the roaring enemy, who mightily conquerest his malicious wiles; we pray and beseech thee, O Lord, with dread and humility, to regard with a favourable countenance this creature of salt and water, to enlighten it with thy bounty, and to sanctify it with the dew of thy fatherly goodness, that wheresoever it shall be sprinkled all annoyance of the unclean spirit may depart, and all fear of the venomous serpent may be chased away, through the invocation of thy holy name; and that the presence of the Holy Ghost may be every where with us, who seek thy mercy. Through our Lord Jesus Christ, who with thee and the same Holy Ghost liveth and reigneth one God, for ever and ever. Amen.

The Blessing being ended, the Priest sprinkles himself and the people with the water, saying,

Anthem. Thou shalt sprinkle me, O Lord, with hyssop, and I shall be cleansed; thou shalt wash me, and I shall be made whiter than snow.

Psalm. Have mercy on me, O God, according to thy great mercy, &c.

Glory be to the Father.

After which he repeats the Anthem, 'Thou shalt sprinkle,' &c. *Then returning to the altar, he says,*

V. O Lord, show us thy mercy.
R. And give us thy salvation.
V. O Lord, hear my prayer.
R. And let my cry come to thee.
V. The Lord be with you.
R. And with thy spirit.

Let us pray.

Hear us, O holy Lord, Almighty Father, everlasting God, and vouchsafe to send thy holy angel from heaven to guard, cherish, protect, visit, and defend, all that dwell in this habitation. Through Christ our Lord. Amen.

CONTENTS.

The Genius of Christianity; *or, the Spirit and Beauty of the Christian Religion.* By V. De Chateaubriand. With a Biographical Notice, and Critical and Explanatory Notes, by Rev. C. I. White, D. D.............cloth, $2.50; cloth gilt, $3 00

Hughes and Breckenridge's Oral Discussion of the Question, Is the Roman Catholic Religion, in any or in all its Principles or Doctrines, inimical to Civil or Religious Liberty? And of the Question, Is the Presbyterian Religion, in any or in all its Principles or Doctrines, inimical to Civil or Religious Liberty? By Rev. J. Hughes, of the Roman Catholic, and Rev. J. Breckenridge, of Presbyterian Church. cl. 2.50; lib. style, 3 00

The Primacy of the Apostolic See Vindicated. By the Most Rev. F. P. Kenrick, *Archbishop of Baltimore.*
7th Revised and Enlarged Edtion.   8o. cloth, 3 00

An Abridged Library Edition of

Lingard's History of England, *with a Continuation, from 1688 to 1854.* By James Burke, Esq., A. B. And an *Appendix to 1874.* The whole preceded by a *Memoir,* with a fine Steel Portrait of Dr. Lingard, and *Marginal Notes Just Published,* in 1 volume of 700 pp. 8o. cloth bev., $3.50; cloth gilt, $4 00

Dr. Lingard's History of England is so well known, and its reputation so universally established, that it is deemed superfluous to dwell on its merits. The *ipsissima verba* of the great Historian, has been preserved in the abridgment.

Catholic Sermons.—*The Catholic Pulpit.* Containing a Sermon for every Sunday and Holyday in the year, and for Good Friday. With several occasional Discourses.
762 pp. 8o. $3.50; library style, $4

History of the Society of Jesus, *from its Foundation to the Present Time.* From the French of Daurignac, with an Appendix from 1862 to 1877. Second Revised and Enlarged Edition, with Portrait of St. Ignatius and the first nine. 2 vols. in one. 12o. cloth bev., $2 50; cloth gilt, $3.00.

☞The very best collection of sermons in the English language.

One Hundred Short Sermons, being a plain and familiar Exposition of the Apostles' Creed, The Lord's Prayer, The Angelical Salutation, The Commandments of God, The Precepts of the Church—The Seven Sacraments, &c. With an Introduction, by Archbishop Spalding..................8o. cloth, 3 00

Every priest and Every Catholic family should possess a copy of a work so very valuable in itself, and so strongly recommended by the highest authorities.

The New Glories of the Catholic Church. With a Preface, by Cardinal Wiseman.......... 12o. cloth, $1 50; cloth gilt, 2 00

Milner's End of Religious Controversy. In a friendly correspondence between a Religious Society of Protestants and a Catholic Divine. New edition................8o. cloth, 1 00

Cheap Edition for General Circulation. Paper, 75 cts; 12 copies, $6; 20 copies, $9; 50 copies, $20; 100 copies, $37.50.

Murphy & Co., *Publishers & Catholic Booksellers, Baltimore.*

Cobbett's History of the Reformation *in England and Ireland.*
12o. cloth, 75 cts.

Order and Chaos. A Lecture, by T. W. M. MARSHALL. 25

An Essay on the Harmonious Relations *between Divine Faith and Natural Reason.* By Hon. A. C. BAINE. 12o. cloth, 1 50

The Bible Question Fairly Tested. Containing the use of the Bible, by FENELON, with Fletcher's Illustrations, &c. 18o. cl. 75

Bishop Ulathorne on the *Immaculate Conception*.......cloth, 60

The Studies and Teachings of the Society of Jesus at the Time of its Suppression, 1750-1775. By MAYNARD. cloth, 1 00

Moore's Travels of an Irish Gentleman in Search of a Religion. By THOMAS MOORE.................12o. cloth, 1 50

The Happiness of Heaven. By a Father of the Society of Jesus. 6th Revised Edition. cloth bev, $1; cloth gilt, 1 50

God Our Father. By the Author of Happiness of Heaven. Third Revised Edition. cloth bev., $1; cloth gilt, 1 50

The Paradise of God; *or, the Virtues of the Heart of Jesus.* By a Father of the Society of Jesus...........cloth, $1; gilt, 1 50
This Work is the result of deep meditation on the Gospels, and shows the Sacred Heart in its life and action as a perfect model of our hearts.

Sister Eugenie. *The Life and Letters of a Sister of Charity.*
cloth bevelled, $1; cloth gilt, 1 50

Memoirs of a Guardian Angel. With the Approbation of Abp. SPALDING. 2d edition. cloth bev. $1; cloth gilt, 1 50

The Holy Communion: *It is my Life, &c.*
2d Revised Edition. cloth bev. $1; cloth gilt, 1 50

Devotion to the Sacred Heart of Jesus. From the Italian of SECONDO FRANCO, S. J..............cloth, $1; cloth bev. gilt, 1 50

The Paradise of the Earth; or, the True Means of Finding Happiness in the Religious State, according to the Rules of the Masters of Spiritual Life. cloth, $1.50; cloth bev. gilt, 2 00

The Love of Religious Perfection; or, how to Awaken, Increase, and Preserve it in the Religious Soul. 18o. cloth, 75

The Choice of a State of Life. By Father ROSSIGNOLI, S. J. Dedicated under the auspices of the Blessed Virgin Mary, to Catholic youth.................................18o. cloth, 90

Short Meditations for Every Day in the Year; on the Gospels of the Sundays and Festivals; together with Exercises for a Three Days' Retreat. Translated from the German, by Rev. T. NORTHEN. With an *Introduction*, by Abp. SPALDING.
12o. cloth, 2.00

MURPHY & Co., *Publishers & Catholic Booksellers, Baltimore.*

The Love of Jesus; *or, Visits to the Blessed Sacrament for every Day in the Month.* To which is added the Devotion of the Forty Hours, with an Introduction, by an American Clergyman............32o. cloth, 50 cts.; cloth bev., red or gilt edges, 75

Manual of the Sodality *of the Blessed Virgin Mary.* 80th Revised and Enlarged Edition; with appropriate Hymns, set to Music, etc.......................32o. cloth, 45 cts.; cloth gilt edges, 60

This excellent Manual of Devotional Exercises contains the various Offices composed by the Church to honor the Virgin Mary, with appropriate Litanies, and Hymns set to Music. It will be found useful in our colleges, and in fact, wherever the children of Mary congregate.

Manual of the Sodality of the Sacred Heart of Jesus.
A complete Manual of Devotion to the Sacred Heart.
Fourth Enlarged Edition. 32o. cloth, 50 cts.; cloth gilt, 75

To render the Second Edition more worthy of the Sacred Heart, whether members of the Sodality or not, it has been made a COMPLETE MANUAL OF DEVOTION TO THE SACRED HEART, so that all may find in it the mental or vocal prayers which they may desire, either for daily use or for the occasions of special devotions to the Sacred Heart which occur during the year.

Olier's Christian Catechism *of Interior Life*.......cloth gilt, 75

Spiritual Combat. To which is added, the *Peace of the Soul, Happiness of the Heart*, etc.......................32o. cloth, 56

Think Well On't; *or, Reflections on the Great Truths of the Christian Religion.* 32o. Various bindings, from 30 to 60 cts.

The Garden of Roses and Valley of Lilies. By A'KEMPIS.
32o. various bindings, from 50 cts. to $2 00

The Following of Christ. By A'KEMPIS. With Practical Reflections, and a Prayer at the end of each Chapter.
48o. various bindings, from 50 cts. to $2 50

Liguori's Preparation for Death; *or, Considerations on the Eternal Maxims.* 12o. cloth, reduced to 75 cts.. cl. gilt, 1 25

Bishop David's Spiritual Retreat of Eight Days. Edited with additions and an introduction, by Abp. SPALDING.
cloth bevelled, $1 25; cloth bev., gilt, 1 50

Practical Piety. By ST. FRANCIS DE SALES.
cloth bevelled, $1; cloth bevelled, gilt, 1 50

A Treatise on General Confessions...................cloth, 45

The Means of Acquiring Perfection. By LIGUORI........25

The Apostleship of Prayer. By Rev. J. RAMIERE, S. J.
Second edition........................12o. cloth, 1 50

Manual of the Apostleship of Prayer. By. Rev. H. RAMIERE, S. J. Second edition.......................cloth, 35

Catechism of the Devotion *to the Sacred Heart of Jesus.*
cloth, 40.........paper, 25 cts.; per 100, $15 net.

MURPHY & Co., *Publishers & Catholic Booksellers, Baltimore.*

Catechism of the Apostleship of Prayer.
cloth, 40.........paper, 25 cts.; per 100, $15 net.
These two little Books are admirable for the clearness of their explanations and fulness of details on the subjects they treat.

The Apostleship of Prayer Association. Explanation and Practical Instruction......Price 5 cts.; *net* per 100, $3.00.

Rosary of the Apostleship, changed Monthly.
Price per doz. 45 cts.; per 100, $3.00 *net.*

Tickets of Admission to the Apostleship of Prayer.
per 100, 50 cts.; 500, $1.50; 1,000, $2.50 *net.*

The same in German. Same prices.

Scapular Prints of the Sacred Heart. per 100, 30 cts. *net.*

A Novena in Honor of St. Joseph, from the Italian. To which is added the *Litany of St. Joseph, &c.*, pap. 20; flex. cl. 25

Novena and Prayers to Our Lady of Lourdes. *For the Sick and Afflicted*......................paper, 25 cts.; flexible cloth, 40

Holy Way of the Cross. Illustrated. paper 10; cloth, 15

Circles of the Living Rosary, (Illustrated.) An entirely new translation.........per doz. sheets, 50 cts.; per 100, $3 *net.*

Patron Saints. By ELIZA ALLEN STARR. With 12 fine full page Illustrations on wood. cloth, $2.50; cloth gilt, 3 00
This is a book about the Saints, embellished with 12 fine Engravings, written expressly for American children, and the author evidently thinks that Saints belong as much to America as to the oldest Catholic country in the world.

Collet's Life of St. Vincent de Paul. cloth, $1.25; gilt, 1 50

Manual of the Lives of the Popes, from St. Peter to Pius IX. By J. C. EARLE, B. A.........120. cloth, $1.50; gilt, 2 00

Life of Christ. By ST. BONAVENTURE. To which are added, the *Devotion* to the *Three Hours, Agony of our Lord on the Cross,* and the *Life of the Glorious St. Joseph.* cl. 1 00

Life of St. Francis Xavier. With a Preface, by the Rev. Father FABER..............120. cloth, $2; cloth gilt edges, 2 50

Life of St. Patrick, *Apostle of Ireland.* To which are added the *Lives of St. Bridget,* Virgin and Abbess, and *St. Columba,* Abbot and Apostle of the Northern Picts........12mo. cloth, 75

Jesuits! (*Paul Féval's celebrated work.*) From the Tenth French Edition. By T. F. Galwey. A complete Translation of the entire Work, 348 pages; 12o. fine cloth, $1; paper, 50 cts.
It is undoubtedly the best popular historical sketch of the Jesuits ever published and contains not one dull page.

Library of the Sacred Heart. 6 vols. 18o. cloth bev. *Black and Gold,* in Boxes, $6; cloth gilt, $9. Comprising the following Popular Works: *Devotion to the Sacred Heart of Jesus— The Paradise of God—The Holy Communion: It is my Life. &c.—God Our Father.* By Author of Happiness of Heaven—*Practical Piety.* By SAINT FRANCIS DE SALES.—*The Happiness of Heaven.*

MURPHY & Co. *Publishers & Catholic Booksellers, Baltimore.*

Metropolitan Edition of Butler's Lives of the Saints.

With the Recommendation of the Most Rev. Archbishop KENRICK.

☞ New and Improved Edition, with Fine Engravings. Seven different styles of bindings, from $7 to $22 per copy.

This edition is printed on fine paper, from a good, clear and bold type, and is justly be considered the *most complete*, as it is unquestionably *the cheapest editi*

Catholic Tales, etc.

Pauline Seward. A Tale of Real Life. BRYANT. cloth, $2; cl. gilt, 2 50
The Truce of God. A Tale of the 11th Century. cloth, $1; cl. gilt, 1 50
LADY FULLERTON'S TALES. 3 *vols. 12o. cloth, $1.50; cloth gilt, $2 per vol.*

1. Lady Bird.——2. Grantley Manor.——3. Ellen Middleton.

Father Oswald. A genuine Catholic Story. cloth, $1.00; cloth gilt, 1.25
Student of Blenheim Forest; or, Trials of a Convert. cl. $1.25; cl. gt. 1 75
The Catholic Youth's Magazine. Complete in 4 volumes, small 4to.
150 fine Illustrations. cloth, $1.25; gilt edges, 1 50

Moral Tales, etc. Uniform Series. Square 16o.

The Queens and Princesses of France.................cloth, 60	gilt, 80
Tales of the Angels. By FATHER FABER.............cloth, 60	gilt, 80
Father Laval; or, the Jesuit Missionary.............cloth, 60	gilt, 80
The Oriental Pearl. A Catholic Tale...................cloth, 60	gilt, 80
The Catholic Bride. From Italian of Dr. PISE.......cloth, 60	gilt, 80
Lorenzo; or, the Empire of Religion.................cloth, 60	gilt, 80
Fenelon on the Education of a Daughter.............cloth, 60	gilt, 80

Uniform Series of Hendrik Conscience's Short Tales.

12 volumes, cloth, $12; cloth gilt, $15, in boxes.

The Young Doctor — Ludovic and Gertrude — The Amulet — The Fisherman's Daughter — The Poor Gentleman — Happiness of Being Rich — The Miser — The Conscript and Blind Rosa — Ricketicketack and Wooden Clara. Count Hugo of Craenhove — The Curse of the Village — Village Innkeeper.

Pontmartin, the acute French Critic and Reviewer, has likened the Stories of Conscience to "pearls set in Flemish gold," and in point of delicacy of treatment and high moral value, they richly justify the comparison.

50,000 COPIES SOLD!

THE MOST POPULAR CATHOLIC BOOK EVER PUBLISHED IN THE U. S.

The Sale of upwards of 50,000 Copies of

ARCHBISHOP GIBBONS'

FAITH OF OUR FATHERS,

and the Constantly Increasing Demand, is a Gratifying Evidence of its Real Merits and Popularity. The object of this volume is to present, in a Plain and Practical Form, an Exposition and Vindication of the Principal Tenets of the Catholic Church. Now Ready, the 11th Enlarged and Revised Edition, 55th *Thousand*, price $1; cloth gilt, $1.50. Cheap Edition for General Circulation, price in paper, 50 cts. In lots of 25 copies, $7.50. 50 copies, $14. 100 copies, $25 *net.*

☞ M. & Co.'s PUBLICATIONS *sent by Mail prepaid, on receipt of price.*
☞ *Complete Catalogues of* MURPHY & CO.'S PUBLICATIONS *can be had on application.* ☞ *Experienced Canvassers wanted in all parts of the U. S. and Canada, to sell the Faith of our Fathers and other Popular Works. For terms, &c., Address*

MURPHY & CO., *Publishers & Catholic Booksellers, Baltimore.*

Popular Standard Prayer Books.

Published with the Approbation of the Abp. of Baltimore.

They are universally considered the most accurate, the *Best* and *Cheapest* Prayer Books published. All the principal Prayers a e in *large type*. They contain all the Prayers and Devotions necessary for all occasions and circumstances that may arise in the life of a Christian, and only such Prayers and Devotions as are approved and sanctioned by the Church.

St. Vincent's Manual. The Visitation Manual. Manual of the Sisters of Charity; A New Manual of Catholic Devotions. Large Type. *Just Published.* Gems of Devotion. The Key of Heaven. Christian's Guide to Heaven. The Child's Prayer and Hymn Book. The Catholic Manual for Children, &c. They comprise in various bindings, upwards of 100 different styles, at prices varying from 20 cts. to $15 per copy.

☞ *The Catholic Child's Prayer Book, Embellished with 36 Fine Engravings, Illustrating the Holy Sacrifice of the Mass.* Various Bindings, from 25 cts. to $1. *Just Published.*

BOOKS FOR THE CLERGY, Published by Order of the Councils.

The Authorized Laws of the Catholic Church in the U. S.
Revised Edition.

Acta et Decreta Concilii Plenarii Baltimorensis Secundi.
8o. cl., bev., $3.50; cl., extra, bev. gilt, 4.00; turkey ant.. 6.00

The Decrees, with Documents, etc.
For the use of Theological Seminaries; one of the Decrees of the Council requiring that its Legislation should be taught in all Theological Institutions 8o., 1 50

Sta'uta Balt. Diœces., Synodus Diœcesana Balt. Octava
Quœ antecedentium etiam complectitur Constitutiones, 1875. 12o. cloth, 1 25

Ritus et Preces, ad Missam Celebrandum in usum Præcipue corum, qui sacris initiantur ....32o. 50 cts. to 2 00

Manual of Piety, for the use of Seminaries 32o. cloth, 60; roan, 75; arab., gilt, 1.00 ....super extra, 1 50
☞ The Decrees of the Second Plenary Council of Baltimore have been introduced into this edition.

The Rituale Romanum;
with the *Appendix approved* by *Sacred Congregation of Rites*, and other *Additions* suited to the *wants* and *convenience* of the *Clergy* of the *U. S* Ordered by the Xth Provincial Council of Baltimore. It is comprised in one vol. of nearly 600 pages demi octavo. Printed in *Red* and *Black*, from New Type, on super sized and calendered paper, and bound in the very best manner. Cloth bev., $3 50 morocco cloth bev., gilt, $4 00; morocco antique......... 6 00

☞ CATALOGUES OF MURPHY's & Co's PUBLICATIONS, comprising a Large and Varied List of *Standard Catholic Works of Devotion* and *Instruction, Historical, Controversial, Theological, Biographical* and *Musical Works, School Books. Tales, Novels, &c.,* together with a great variety of STANDARD PRAYER BOOKS, in various Bindings, can be had on application.

MURPHY & Co. *Publishers & Catholic Booksellers, Baltimore.*

7

Noethen's History of the Catholic Church. *New Revised*
Enlarged Ed. demi 8o. cl. various bindings, from $2 to $3 50

Shadows of the Rood; *or, Types of our Suffering Redeemer.*
Jesus Christ, occurring in the BOOK OF GENESIS. 18o. cloth, 75

Our Lady of Litanies. By MACLEOD........12o. cloth, 1 00

Legends of Holy Mary. By MACLEOD. 12o. cloth,   60

Eliza Despres; *or, the Fatal Effects of Reading Bad Books.*
152 pages, square 16o. cloth, 60

The Pearl Among the Virtues; *or, Words of Advice to*
Christian Youth. From the German of De Doss, by a Catholic Priest. In a very neat vol. cloth, 75 cts.; cl. gilt, 1 00

The Catholic Keepsake. *A Gift Book Suitable for all*
Seasons. Tinted paper, very neat, 12o. cl. $1.25; cl. gilt, 1 50

Challoner's Catholic Christian Instructed. MURPHY'S
Cheap Large Type Edition. paper 25 cts.........per 100, $15 00

Ward's Tree of Life; *or, the Church of Christ Illustrated.*

This Ecclesiastical and Historical Chart presents at a glance a complete History
of the Church, from its first establishment to the present period, rendering it
valuable for reference, and an appropriate ornament to the church, parlor or
library. It is printed from a fine Line Engraving, on a sheet 25 x 40 inches, hand-
somely colored, varnished and mounted on rollers, and sold at the low price of
$4. ☞ It should have a conspicuous place in the house of every Catholic.

MUSIC BOOKS, with Gregorian Chant.

☞ In ordering, Round or Square Notes should be specified. ☜

Holy Week. Containing the Offices of the Holy Week,
from the Roman Breviary and Missal, with the Chants in
Modern Notation..... .... 1 25

Holy Week. Uniform with the above in style and price,
in Gregorian or Square Notation.......... .... 1 25

The Roman Vesperal. Containing the complete Vespers
for the whole year, with Gregorian Chants in Modern Notation......... ....cloth, 1 50

Kyriale; or, Ordinary of Mass. A complete Liturgical
Manual of Gregorian Chants for the use of Catholic Choirs
and Congregations, containing the *Kyrie, Gloria, Credo, Sanc-*
tus, Agnus Dei, etc., according to the different Feasts and
Sundays of the year. *Fifth Edition.* With an *Appendix,* in-
cluding the *Hymns, Psalms, Anthems, Litanies,* and *Prayers*
for the *Exposition,* during the *Exposition,* and at the *Benedic-*
tion of the Most Blessed Sacrament, and enlarged by the addi-
tion of *Masses* and *Obsequies* for the *Dead* ....cloth, 1 00

Kyriale; or, Ordinary of Mass. Same as above, with Gregorian Chants in Modern Notation. 12th ed.........cloth, 1 00

MURPHY & Co. *Publishers & Catholic Booksellers, Baltimore.*

MX 002 243 788

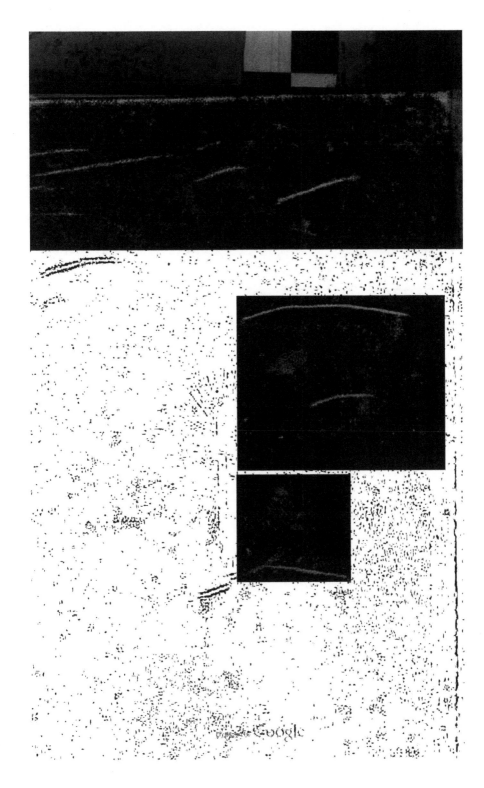

Lightning Source UK Ltd.
Milton Keynes UK
UKHW020923150822
407319UK00007B/1381